A

Philip E. Lilienthal

■   ■   ■

B O O K

The Philip E. Lilienthal imprint
honors special books
in commemoration of a man whose work
at the University of California Press from 1954 to 1979
was marked by dedication to young authors
and to high standards in the field of Asian Studies.
Friends, family, authors, and foundations have together
endowed the Lilienthal Fund, which enables the Press
to publish under this imprint selected books
in a way that reflects the taste and judgment
of a great and beloved author.

On the Cultural Revolution in Tibet

On the Cultural Revolution in Tibet

in Tibet

The Nyemo Incident of 1969

Melvyn C. Goldstein
Ben Jiao
Tanzen Lhundrup

UNIVERSITY OF CALIFORNIA PRESS
Berkeley · Los Angeles · London

University of California Press, one of the most
distinguished university presses in the United States,
enriches lives around the world by advancing scholar-
ship in the humanities, social sciences, and natural
sciences. Its activities are supported by the UC Press
Foundation and by philanthropic contributions from
individuals and institutions. For more information,
visit www.ucpress.edu.

University of California Press
Berkeley and Los Angeles, California

University of California Press, Ltd.
London, England

Library of Congress Cataloging-in-Publication Data

Goldstein, Melvyn C.
    On the Cultural Revolution in Tibet : the Nyemo
Incident of 1969 / Melvyn C. Goldstein, Ben Jiao, and
Tanzen Lhundrup.
        p.   cm.   (The Philip E. Lilienthal Asian
Studies Imprint)
    Includes bibliographical references and index.
    ISBN 978-0-520-25682-8 (cloth : alk. paper)
    1. Tibet (China)—History—Nyemo Incident, 1969.
2. China—History—Cultural Revolution, 1966–1976.
I. Jiao, Ben. II. Tanzen Lhundrup. III. Title.
IV. Title: Nyemo Incident of 1969.
DS786.G6356   2009
951'.5056—dc22   2008025403

Manufactured in the United States of America

17 16 15 14 13 12 11 10 09
10 9 8 7 6 5 4 3 2 1

This book is printed on Natures Book, which contains
50% postconsumer waste and meets the minimum
requirements of ANSI/NISO Z39.48–1992 (R 1997)
(Permanence of Paper).

*To the Tibetans in China and in exile who
have helped me over the years but who have
preferred to remain anonymous*

Melvyn C. Goldstein

We investigate the past not to deduce practical political lessons, but to find out what really happened.

T. F. Tout

Contents

List of Illustrations   xi

Acknowledgments   xiii

Explanation of Romanization, Brackets,
and Abbreviations   xv

Introduction   1
1. The Cultural Revolution in Tibet   11
2. Gyenlo and Nyamdre in Nyemo County   59
3. Gyenlo on the Attack   86
4. Destroying the Demons and Ghosts   107
5. The Attacks on Bagor District and Nyemo County   122
6. The Capture of the Nun   137
7. Conclusions   162
8. Epilogue   172

Appendix 1. The Nun's Manifesto   183

Appendix 2. Leaflet Publishing the Text of a Speech
Criticizing the Regional Party Committee   185

Appendix 3. The Truth about the Struggle to Seize
the Power of the *Tibet Daily Newspaper* Office   191

Notes   197

Selected Glossary of Correct Tibetan Spellings   213

References   223

Index   229

Illustrations

MAPS

1. Tibet Autonomous Region   *xvii*
2. Prefectures in Tibet, showing Lhasa Municipality   *xviii*
3. Nyemo County   *xix*

FIGURES

1. Nyemo woman whose hands were cut off by the nun's followers   2
2. Axe and "cutting board" used in mutilations   *115*
3. Lama Chamba Tenzin just before his execution   *150*
4. Struggle session in Nyemo   *155*
5. Rebels about to be executed in Nyemo   *156*
6. Rebels after their execution   *159*

Acknowledgments

We want to thank the many individuals in the Tibet Autonomous Region and inland China* who graciously agreed to share their life experiences with us, as well as the excellent Tibetan researchers such as Sonam Gyatso, who helped collect the interviews used in this book. Goldstein also wishes to thank the Tibet Academy of Social Sciences (Lhasa), whose researchers have offered him outstanding advice, assistance, and collaboration since 1985. We also thank Professor Toni Huber for beginning the process leading to this book by inviting Goldstein to give a paper on the Cultural Revolution at a conference he organized in Berlin in 2006 on conflict in Tibetan society.

Thanks are also in order to the many students at Case Western Reserve University who have worked at the Center for Research on Tibet, such as Oleh Holowatyj, Steven Pieragastini, Allyson Kruper, Stacey McKenna, Lily Stanley, Cierra Chiwanga, Stephanie Siryj, Ilya Malinskiy, and Joe Galenek. Several colleagues such as Professors Uradyn Bulag and Robbie Barnett offered very helpful comments regarding this history, and Professor Atwood Gaines graciously shared his knowledge and insights regarding shamans/oracles and mental illness with us. We also want

*Because it is politically incorrect for Tibetans in China to refer to the non-Tibetan parts of the People's Republic of China as "China," since that implies to some that Tibet and China are separate entities, the Chinese term *neidi,* meaning "inner" or "inland" (tib. *nangsa*), is normally used. We will translate the term as "inland China."

to thank sincerely the Henry Luce Foundation, which funded the Tibetan Oral History Project, and the National Endowment for the Humanities, which funded the research project on the Cultural Revolution in Tibet (Grant # RZ-20585-00). Without their support this study would not have been possible. And last, but certainly not least, we deeply appreciate the support and assistance provided by our editor Reed Malcolm and his excellent staff at the University of California Press.

Explanation of Romanization, Brackets, and Abbreviations

Tibetan written and spoken forms diverge considerably in that the written form contains consonant clusters that are not pronounced. For example, the written Tibetan word *bsgrubs* is actually pronounced "drub," and *rtsis dpon* is pronounced "tsipön." Throughout the text of this book, the spoken (phonetic) pronunciation is given for Tibetan terms. The proper Tibetan spellings (romanization) are cited in the "Selected Glossary of Correct Tibetan Spellings" at the end of the book according to the system of T. V. Wylie (1959).

The phonetic rendering of Tibetan names, however, has no universally accepted standard, so sometimes Tibetan names and terms cited in quotations will vary considerably from those we use in the narrative; for example, Dzongpön is spelled in some quotations as Jongpoen, and Lobsang Samden is sometimes written as Lopsang Samten.

Chinese names are cited in the pinyin used in the People's Republic of China with the family name before the personal name, for example, in Zhang Guohua, Zhang is the family name and Guohua is the personal name.

Square brackets are used for something the authors have added to a quotation, whereas parentheses are used either for the phonetics of a Chinese or a Tibetan term or for something that was in parentheses in the original rendering of a quotation translated here.

The following abbreviations are used in the text or in the documents cited in the text:

CCP	Chinese Communist Party
ch.	Chinese language
H	history and political collection of the Tibet Oral History Archive
OR	oral history collection of the Tibet Oral History Archive
PLA	People's Liberation Army
PRC	People's Republic of China
TAR	Tibet Autonomous Region
tib.	Tibetan language
tib.-ch.	Tibetan and Chinese languages mixed

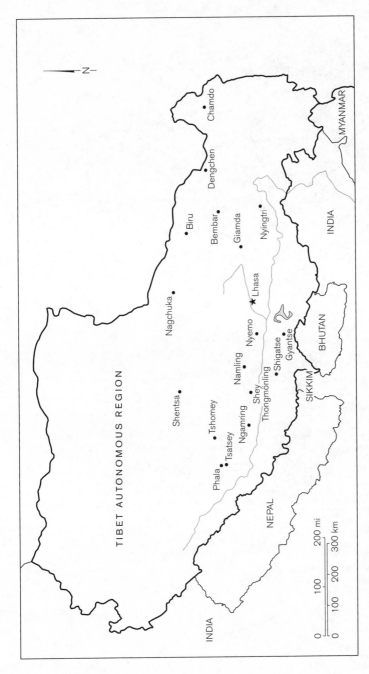

Map 1. Tibet Autonomous Region.

Map 2. Prefectures in Tibet, showing Lhasa Municipality.

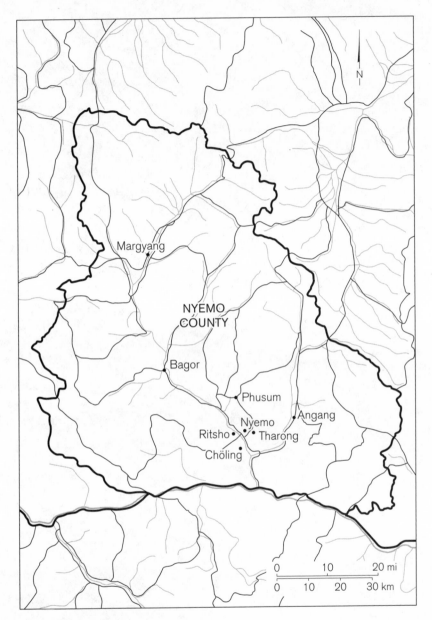

Map 3. Nyemo County.

Introduction

By late 1968, the violent fighting between revolutionary factions that had devastated inland China during the Cultural Revolution was winding down as revolutionary committees and military control commissions were established and order was restored.[1] In the Tibet Autonomous Region (TAR, hereafter called Tibet), however, this conflict continued, and during the summer of 1969, bloody violence erupted in roughly a quarter of the rural counties (tib. *dzong*; ch. *xian*). The most famous of these incidents took place in Nyemo, a county in the southwestern portion of Lhasa Municipality (see maps 1–3), on 13–14 June 1969. Conventional wisdom holds that on those two fateful days, hundreds of Tibetan villagers led by Trinley Chödrön, a young nun who believed gods were possessing and speaking through her, launched a series of bloody attacks against local officials and the troops of the People's Liberation Army (PLA) stationed there. According to Chinese records, this force killed fifteen PLA soldiers, seven cadres, and thirty-two grassroots officials and activists.[2] In addition, during a two-week period before and after the attacks, more than twenty local Tibetans had their arms and legs hacked off by the nun's followers, as the following eyewitness account of one of the surviving victims illustrates.

> I was five months pregnant and working as an official for the local *xiang* [government],[3] but I couldn't stay there [because my father had been attacked and killed, and I had heard the nun's forces also wanted to seize me]. So I took my daughter on my back and fled [with my husband] to a

Figure 1. The Nyemo Village woman whose hands were cut off by the nun's followers in June 1969.

nomad family about four hours from my home on the other side of the mountain. I hid there for about a month and then returned when I heard that PLA troops had arrived at the county seat [because I thought it was safe]. However, on the road back we [ran into the nun's people and] were caught.

They tied my husband's hands behind his back but left me untied because I was carrying my infant in my hands, but still they kicked me and yelled at me, saying, "You female demon (tib. *dümo*), move ahead! You have to go to the 'dharma protector' (tib. *chösung*) [the nun/goddess]." They also yelled [the war cry] '*ki hi hi*' and shot [Tibetan] muskets and hit people with [the back of their] swords. . . . When we arrived near our house, I heard some people there yell [to others], "Come! The demons are arriving." I was so afraid that I don't remember how I got there.

. . . They took me to [the place they called] the slaughtering ground (tib. *sheyra*) [which was about four hundred meters from the nun's small one-story house by the nunnery] to cut off my hand. . . . They brought an axe and a wooden chopping block and put my arm on the chopping block. Their axe was not sharp, so they had to hit it several times, and even then they couldn't sever the hand entirely. My hand was dangling. . . . The pain was extraordinary. . . . After that [a relative of mine came and] tied my arm's stump with a piece of rubber to stop the bleeding.

[However] [a]bout an hour or so later, they came back yelling that I had to come out of my house. My mother told them, "My daughter is dying [so leave her alone]," but they didn't believe her and came inside the house and said, "The nun dharma protector (tib. *ani chösung*) told us not to leave you, and to kill you." . . .

I remember that it was a moonlit night. They said, "That axe isn't sharp; we need a sword." Then they took a long shiny sword that was very sharp and struck my other hand, cutting it off right away. I didn't feel pain. Probably it was because I was too scared. I screamed and thought I would die, and it would have been better if I had died. I couldn't stand it.

. . . That same night they took my husband to the slaughtering ground. After tying his hands and legs to stakes, they cut off one of his legs.[4]

The reaction of a neighbor to this event further illuminates the atmosphere extant at that time: "After they cut off [the husband's] leg, they just left him there [in the slaughtering ground]. My late wife suggested that maybe I should help him back to his house, because otherwise he would die. I told her that we should not do that, because if we were to help we would also be killed. So I said, 'Just leave him there. Maybe someone else will help him home.' [I was afraid] I would be killed."[5]

Despite such brutality, the Nyemo incident has captured the imagination of Tibetans and Westerners alike, because the conventional image of the nun involved is that of an underdog—a young, Joan of Arc–like woman heroically leading a major uprising that threatened China's control over Tibet. For example, a Tibet Justice Center report states, "According to the Tibetan Government in Exile, a nun from Nyemo led a full-scale uprising in 1969 which spread to eighteen counties and threatened to take over Lhasa."[6]

Another Tibet Justice Center report on the role of Tibetan women in the fight against the Chinese government also mentioned this event: "In 1969, when the Cultural Revolution was in progress, another demonstration by women was carried out under the leadership of a nun called Trinley Choedon . . . in her native town of Nyemo. It seems that this movement succeeded in expelling the Chinese and the Tibetans working for the Chinese from Nyemo. It was reported that the movement spread to some 23 counties."[7]

An article on nuns by the anthropologist Hanna Havnevik similarly comments, "It is said that she [the nun] had a network of contacts stretching from Mount Kailash to Kham, and that she organized a guerrilla movement which killed many Chinese."[8]

And the Dalai Lama mentioned this event in his autobiography, "It was not till over a year later that I learned of a large-scale revolt that took place in several different parts of Tibet during 1969. According to some reports, even more people were killed during the reprisals that followed than in 1959 [the 1959 uprising]."⁹

The Chinese side initially considered this an "armed counterrevolutionary revolt" (ch. *wuzhuang fangeming panluan*) paralleling the 1959 uprising. For example, in a park called Martyr's Park, which was built to commemorate those who died in Nyemo, the event is referred to as one of the "Two Nine Revolts" (ch. *liang jiu panluan*)—that is, the two rebellions with the number nine in their dates, 1959 and 1969.¹⁰ However, within the Chinese Communist Party (CCP), this designation was internally disputed from the start, some former revolutionary leaders arguing that this was not about Tibetans opposing Chinese, as was the case in 1959, but was merely the two revolutionary factions engaged in serious conflict.¹¹ Given this dissent, the Chinese government reinvestigated this issue several times, rehabilitating many of those who were initially incarcerated and politically labeled as state enemies, and then finally in 1987 it was downgraded from a counterrevolutionary *revolt* to only a counterrevolutionary *killing event/incident* (ch. *sharen shijian*).¹² In the West and among Tibetan exiles, however, the nun continues to be valorized as a heroic female freedom fighter who fought bravely to defend Tibet and drive out the Chinese.¹³

Academic analysis of the Nyemo incident has been cursory, discussions consisting of, at most, a few pages in chapters, articles, and books. This circumstance is, of course, understandable given the heretofore almost complete absence of primary and secondary data, but it has created the curious situation wherein the fact of the occurrence of a major revolt of sorts in Nyemo is well known, but the cause of the event is at best not well known and at worst misunderstood.

One of the most widely cited academic accounts comes from Warren Smith's monograph, *Tibetan Nation*. Smith's brief discussion of the Nyemo incident states that it was a nationalist conflict arising as a result of the Communist Party's attack on all aspects of Tibetan culture during the Cultural Revolution. Smith contends, that as the Cultural Revolution progressed, Tibet's two revolutionary mass organizations polarized along ethnic lines, the Gyenlo faction (ch. *zaofan*) becoming predominately Tibetan and the Nyamdre faction (ch. *dalianzhi*) becoming mostly Chinese. As a result, the factional conflict in Tibet, he says, "took on a nationalistic content previously absent."¹⁴ Consequently, despite mentioning other factors (such as food shortages, grain requisitions, the introduction of communes, and the onset of factional strife), by asserting that the revolutionary factions were ethnically based, Smith is able to conclude that the Nyemo incident was essentially an expression of Tibetan anger at Chinese oppression—a popular uprising of the oppressed minority ethnic Tibetans against their majority Han tormentors. Smith, therefore, agrees with those who have labeled the events in Nyemo as the "Second Tibetan Revolt," the first being 1959.[15]

A recent article by Robert Barnett on Tibetan women in politics also briefly mentions the nun, arguing that she led a movement to contest the Chinese *state:*

> From the Chinese point of view, the most dangerous revolt in Tibet since 1959, and the most recent major incident preceding the 1987 protests, was the Nyemo uprising of 1969, which had been led by the famous nun Trinley Chodron. As a charismatic rural leader, she had been able to mobilize a large number of armed male followers, who had swept across northern Tibet before being themselves wiped out and executed. Nyemo Ani, as she was known, was not a political activist in the modern, rationalist sense: she was considered by her followers to have been possessed by a powerful deity, a minister of the legendary Tibetan hero King Gesar. She therefore recalled a much older tradition of threats posed to the state by millenarian and similar religious movements, familiar to the Chinese from the Taiping rebellion.[16]

A third well-known scholar of modern Tibet, Tsering Shakya, has also discussed the Nyemo disturbances:

> In 1969 there was widespread rebellion throughout Tibet, eventually crushed by the PLA. The best-documented episode is the revolt led by Trinley Chodron, a young nun from the xian (county) of Nyemo, who marched her followers armed with swords and spears to the local Party headquarters, and slaughtered both the Chinese officials and the Tibetan cadres working for them. At first the Party ignored the massacre, thinking it was a manifestation of the Cultural Revolution [in which] as we know, murders could be exonerated if they fell under the rubric of class struggle.
>
> But the authorities soon realized that these Tibetan peasants were rebelling not in the name of the "newly liberated serfs" but in defense of their faith. What was more, they targeted only Chinese Party officials and those Tibetans seen as colluding with the colonizing power. The revolt spread from Nyemo through eighteen counties of the Tibetan Autonomous Region (TAR), and the Party was forced to send in the PLA to suppress it.[17]

Finally, the well-known Tibetologist Hildegard Diemberger briefly mentions the Nyemo nun's uprising in an article on female mediums in Tibet. She follows Shakya's and Smith's analyses, adding, "What originally looked like a Gyenlog attack on local cadres was reappraised as something threatening Chinese national interests. This shift was probably triggered by the ethnicization of the movement."[18]

A very different interpretation, however, has been presented by Wang Lixiong, a well-known Chinese intellectual who has studied and written on Tibet. He rejects the nationalistic arguments cited above and the idea that this was the Second Tibet Revolt. Instead, he explains the incident as the outgrowth of the introduction of communes in Tibet:

> In 1969, an armed "revolt" broke out against the introduction of People's Communes into Tibet, which had been spared them in the period of the Great Leap Forward; this eventually spread to over forty counties. The Dalai's camp saw this "Second Tibetan Revolt" as a continuation of the resistance of the fifties. In reality, the two were very different. During the earlier uprising, the peasants were fighting, in a sense, for the interests of the aristocracy. In 1969, they fought for their own ends. They did not want the pastures and livestock that had been redistributed among them from the old landowners to be appropriated by the People's Communes. . . . The "nationality question," later the cause of so much trouble, seemed scarcely worth consideration. Tibetans seemed on generally calm terms with the Han and the Dalai Lama almost forgotten, both in Tibet and in the West.[19]

This materialistic interpretation prompted a strong rebuttal from Tsering Shakya, who disagrees sharply with Wang's view:

> His account secularizes the rebellion, explaining it in utilitarian terms—the peasants wanted to protect the gains of the initial land reforms from the extension of People's Communes—while stripping it of the cultural and religious elements that reveal its nationalist content. In doing so, he grossly distorts the historical record. For example: Trinley Chodron told the PLA after her capture that she had been visited by a bird who had come as a messenger from the Dalai Lama, and who had told her to drive out the Chinese. Other rebels claimed to be reincarnations of Ling Gesar, the mythical hero-king of Tibetan epic who fought for the Buddhist religion. There can be no mistaking the symbolism here. Indeed, we can describe the revolt of 1969 as a millenarian uprising, an insurgency characterized by a passionate desire to be rid of the oppressor.[20]

Shakya, Smith, and Diemberger, therefore, explain this incident as fundamentally an ethnic or nationalistic affair—Tibetans versus Chinese; Barnett's brief comment suggests that he also views it mainly as an attack by Tibetans against the Chinese, but against the Chinese-run state, not the Han per se. Wang, on the other hand, sees it primarily in terms of Tibetans' economic self-interest. Wang's dismissal of nationalistic motives has led Shakya to charge that Wang has grossly distorted the historical record, but is this a fair assessment? Alternatively, might not

Shakya and others, inadvertently, have distorted the historical record by downplaying economic and other motives and by presenting this as a Tibetan versus Chinese affair?

In this monograph we address this issue and for the first time present a detailed examination of what actually transpired in Nyemo in 1969. We show that while each of the above-mentioned explanations contains important elements of truth and represents an excellent beginning, new data about the history of the Nyemo conflict reveal a far more convoluted etiology that is inexorably intertwined with the bitter and bloody factional struggles that raged during the height of the Cultural Revolution in Tibet between Tibet's two main revolutionary mass organizations—Gyenlo and Nyamdre—both of which believed they were the true adherents of Mao Zedong's views. We show how the Nyemo incident was primarily not a conflict of Tibetans versus Han Chinese but rather an outgrowth of the decision made by Gyenlo's leadership in Nyemo to seize control of the county from their hated rival, Nyamdre. More specifically, we show how Gyenlo in Nyemo sought to use the presence of widespread rural anger and anxiety to mobilize Tibetan villagers to its side and how it utilized a young nun (and the gods who were possessing her) to energize and activate the masses to fight for it against Nyamdre. The comments of a Gyenlo leader in Nyemo illustrate the way the Gyenlo revolutionaries tactically utilized the nun to motivate rural Tibetans:

> If there is some situation we cannot stop, we will send the crazy one [the nun] to activate them [the villagers] once again to beat them back. The masses believe in superstition [religion], so if the crazy one activates them, they will be fearless. That's good! This is the great invention of Nyemo County. We have to employ her. First we send her to do some religious dances [go into a trance], then we drive the masses to attack. The cadres from the Lhasa headquarters agreed with the method we took and indicated that we should use the religious dances [trances] to activate the masses to attack. Therefore, if we want to attack in the future, we need to prepare for it; the religious dance [trance] of the nun is the weapon to access the masses' mental world.[21]

However, we also show in this study that Gyenlo's decision to utilize the nun in this manner inadvertently created conditions that facilitated her development into a powerful charismatic leader who sought to restore religion and who many villagers believed had supernatural powers. The revolutionary leaders of Gyenlo in Nyemo understood that this was happening but, for reasons we will discuss later, chose to see this as adding to the utility of their "invention" and weapon, so continued to make prominent use of her right up to the end. As a result, the incident in Nyemo took on the feel of three-dimensional chess, with linked events simultaneously occurring on two different planes.

The new data on which this study is based derive from two sources:

1. Taped interviews in Tibet with seventy-five Nyemo inhabitants who were adults during this period

2. A recently discovered set of Chinese documents that were brought to India sometime after the end of the Cultural Revolution

The taped interviews were conducted by Case Western Reserve University's Center for Research on Tibet under the direction of Melvyn Goldstein as part of a larger project with the Tibet Academy of Social Sciences on change in Tibet. One component of this project was the collection of roughly six hundred oral or life histories from Tibetans living in different areas and from all walks of life. These taped interviews (conducted in the privacy of people's homes) elicited narratives on the lives of individual Tibetans since their childhood and therefore cover three broad periods: the traditional, or "old," society, as it is now called (up to 1959); the period of the 1959 uprising and the onset of "Democratic Reforms" (1959–66); and the era of the Cultural Revolution and collectivization (1966 on). Since Nyemo County was one of the field sites for the oral history interviews, it yielded a substantial corpus of firsthand accounts of Nyemo during the Cultural Revolution, including the Nyemo nun incident.

The reliability of oral history accounts of past events is always a concern. Not only is memory faulty, but also speakers always have the potential to color their accounts for self-serving reasons. We tried to control for this by using the large corpus of interviews as a sounding board against which to compare any single account. Our interviews facilitated this process by including Gyenlo and Nyamdre activists, individuals who were just regular members of each faction, and villagers, officials, and soldiers who were allied with neither side. We were also careful to notice the position of interviewees in the historical incident and to give preference to firsthand (eyewitness) accounts. In the end we feel confident that we are able to represent the different attitudes and experiences in Nyemo accurately.

The Nyemo interviews are part of the "common-folk" subcollection of the Tibet Oral History Collection and Archive, which also includes a large collection of interviews with political figures on modern Tibetan history and a collection of almost two hundred taped interviews with Drepung monks on life in their monastery up to 1959. A supplementary collection of common-folk interviews was recorded with Tibetans in India. When completed, the Tibet Oral History Archive will contain about thirty thousand to forty thousand pages of English transcripts (of the interviews), together with the original Tibetan-language interviews and an integrated glossary. The collection is being compiled and edited by Melvyn Goldstein at the Center for Research on Tibet at Case Western Reserve University and will eventually be available in person and online at the Library of Congress.

Excerpts from many of these common-folk interviews are quoted in this study, since they provide a compelling window into how this incident was experienced. However, since the history of the Nyemo incident is still a politically sensitive topic in China, we decided not to use the real names of the interviewees. Instead, we cite the unique interviewee catalog number used in the Tibetan Oral History Archive (e.g., OR.0030.01) instead of the person's name. In this notational system, "OR" refers to the common-folk oral history collection, and "0030.01" refers to tape 01 of interviewee number 30. The abbreviation for the political collection is "H," so the citation "H.0030.01" refers to tape 01 of interviewee 30 in that collection. In the future, when the Tibet Oral History Archive is available to the public, these catalog reference numbers will enable readers to find and listen to the specific interview in the original as well as read an English transcript of the entire interview. For more about the Tibet Oral History Archive, see the Center for Research on Tibet's Web site.[22]

The Chinese documents include several hundred pages of government documents, revolutionary faction pamphlets, wall posters, and so forth on the Cultural Revolution in Tibet. Some of this material was already available in the translations of the *Survey of China Mainland Press Supplement,* but the new materials include an invaluable subset that deals specifically with the regional disturbance in Nyemo.

The new Nyemo data include reports written by teams sent from Lhasa to investigate the incident and the archival data they attached as appendices to the reports. These appendices include selections from the transcripts of the extensive interrogations and confessions (tib. *ngolen yigja;* ch. *jiaodai cailiao*) that villagers and cadres made in 1969–71 following the suppression of the incident. Especially useful were the materials from the euphemistic "study class" (tib. *lobjong dzindra;* ch. *xuexi ban*) held in Lhasa in 1971, in which the top Gyenlo cadres from Nyemo were detained, isolated, and interrogated separately for almost a year regarding what they and the others had done. This resulted in a series of statements by different cadres about the same events, made independently of each other.

As a result of these new data, this important historical event can now be examined in depth for the first time, and in the chapters that follow, we will present a more complete revisionist analysis of the causes of the amazing events that transpired in Nyemo in 1969. At the same time, readers should understand that despite these new data, the historical record regarding Nyemo is still far from complete, and a number of issues that remain unclear may never be fully understood.

Because of the central role of the Gyenlo and Nyamdre revolutionary factions in the Nyemo incident, it is impossible to separate the history of the Nyemo incident from the broader history of the Cultural Revolution in Tibet, particularly the intense conflict that developed between Gyenlo and Nyamdre in Lhasa. Chapter 1, therefore, will provide the reader with a selective introduction to the Cultural Revolution in Tibet, particularly in Lhasa, with an eye to facilitating an understanding of the events in Nyemo.

CHAPTER I

The Cultural Revolution in Tibet

In 1966, Mao unleashed the Cultural Revolution to eliminate his enemies and reshape relations within the party. Unlike the standard Chinese Communist Party purges that took place entirely within the rarified air of the party itself, in the Cultural Revolution, the driving forces of the cleanup—Red Guards and revolutionary workers—were outside the party. Mao sought to mobilize the masses to discover and attack what he called bourgeois and capitalist elements who had insinuated themselves into the party and, in his view, were trying to subvert the revolution.[1]

The Cultural Revolution is generally considered to have begun in 1966 when the Politburo issued Mao's so-called May 16th Notice. Widely called the first official document of the Cultural Revolution, it is described in a chronology of important events in the history of the Communist Party in Tibet:

> The "Notice" . . . [declares] that "the representatives of the bourgeoisie who have sneaked into the party, government, army, and literary and art circles are counterrevolutionary revisionists. Once they obtain the opportunity, they will seize power and transform the proletarian dictatorship into a bourgeois dictatorship." The "Notice" requests people to "hold the red flag of the Great Proletarian Cultural Revolution high and completely expose the reactionary bourgeois position of those so-called academic authorities who oppose the party and socialism. We should completely criticize the reactionary bourgeois thought in academic circles, educational circles, press circles, literary-art circles, and publishing circles and seize the leading power in these areas. To do this, we must simultaneously criticize

the representatives of the bourgeoisie who sneaked into the party, government, army, and all cultural circles."[2]

The first activists were young students called Red Guards, who began attacking their teachers and administrators, searching to uncover those who
were following the capitalist road (ch. *zouzipai*) and had sneaked into
the party. While they were creating chaos in their schools in inland China,
in Lhasa the Party Committee of the Tibet Autonomous Region (ch. *dang
gongwei*) (hereafter called the Regional Party Committee) followed
Mao's lead and launched the Cultural Revolution in Tibet.[3] By the end
of May, the Regional Party Committee had formed the Leading Team of
the Great Proletarian Cultural Revolution in Lhasa, appointing as its director Wang Qimei, a PLA commander who had come to Tibet with the
advance force of the Eighteenth Army Corps in September 1951. The minister of the Propaganda Department, Zhang Zaiwang, was appointed
vice-director.[4] At this time, the most powerful figure in Tibet was Zhang
Guohua, the military commander who had come to Tibet in October 1951
as the head of the main PLA military force, the Eighteenth Army Corps.
He had remained there since then and in 1966 was in control of the three
main organs of power: the Regional Party Committee, the People's Assembly of the TAR, and the Tibet Military Region Headquarters.

Under Zhang Guohua's leadership, the Regional Party Committee held
an enlarged meeting in Nyingtri (in Kongpo) from 15 June to 5 July 1966
to discuss how to implement the Cultural Revolution. From the start,
Zhang Guohua and the Regional Party Committee sought to manipulate
the Cultural Revolution so that they, rather than local Red Guards or
other revolutionary workers and cadres, would be in control of mass
demonstrations and struggle sessions against the "holders of power" in
the party. The Regional Party Committee, therefore, did not issue a call for
the masses to mobilize and take the lead to search out capitalist-roaders.
Rather, its members themselves decided who among the power holders
were reactionaries, that is, whom to sacrifice. For example, at the meeting
in Nyingtri, a few important party members such as Jin Sha (chief editor
of the *Tibet Daily Newspaper* and deputy minister of TAR's Propaganda Department)[5] were accused and singled out to be examined and
criticized by the masses. The meeting also instructed party members not
to encourage large parades and demonstrations and to keep close control over all weapons. It similarly instructed the army to follow the instructions of the Regional Party Committee, not the revolutionary groups
involved in the Cultural Revolution campaigns.[6] Zhang Guohua's idea

was for the Cultural Revolution to be played out under the close scrutiny of the Regional Party Committee according to a carefully scripted score.

Back in Beijing, the incipient chaos in schools in June and July prompted Liu Shaoqi to send work teams (tib. *leydön ruga;* ch. *gongzuo dui*) to "exercise leadership," that is, to try to restrain the students and restore order.[7] In Lhasa, a similar strategy was employed when the Regional Party Committee sent a work team to the *Tibet Daily* on 12 July to "lead" (ch. *lingdao*) the work of the Cultural Revolution there, in other words, to control what was to be written about the Cultural Revolution and the Regional Party Committee.[8]

Mao, however, disapproved of work teams constraining workers and students, that is, controlling the Cultural Revolution, labeling this as an act of "white terror" (ch. *baise kongbu*).[9] Consequently, at the start of August he intervened to clarify the direction of the new campaign by publishing his famous "big-character poster" (ch. *dazi bao*),[10] which said tersely and forcefully, *"Bombard the Headquarters"* (ch. *paoda silingbu*), that is, vigorously attack the party headquarters to uncover and criticize those in power who were taking China down the wrong road to capitalism. A few days later, on 8 August, the Eleventh Plenum of the Eighth Central Committee (over which Mao presided) promulgated its famous "Decision concerning the Great Proletarian Cultural Revolution," in which Mao's thinking was spelled out in more detail:

> Although the bourgeoisie has been overthrown, it is still trying to use the old ideas, culture, customs, and habits of the exploiting classes to corrupt the masses, capture their minds, and endeavor to stage a comeback. The proletariat must do just the opposite: it must meet head-on every challenge of the bourgeoisie in the ideological field and use the new ideas, culture, customs, and habits of the proletariat to change the mental outlook of the whole of society. *At present, our objective is to struggle against and crush those persons in authority who are taking the capitalist road, to criticize and repudiate the reactionary bourgeois academic "authorities" and the ideology of the bourgeoisie and all other exploiting classes and to transform education, literature and art.*[11]

The implementation of the Cultural Revolution was now shifting to the masses in the persons of Red Guards, other young students, and workers operating outside the direct control of the party leadership in schools, factories, and offices. Mao's approval of them carrying the so-called spearhead of the Cultural Revolution was symbolized by his presiding over massive meetings of as many as several million young Red Guards and masses from all over the country in Tiananmen Square. At the first of

these, on 18 August, Lin Biao addressed the gathering and explicitly called
on the Red Guards to "destroy all the old thoughts, culture, customs,
and habits of the exploitative class" and called on the people of the whole
country to support the "proletarian revolutionary spirit of the Red
Guards, who are the ones who dare to act, dare to break, dare to carry
the revolution, and dare to rebel."[12]

The next day, 19 August, Lin Biao, Mao's wife, Jiang Qing, and other
pro-Mao leftists met with Red Guards from the Second Middle School of
Beijing and urged them to put up big-character posters to "wage a war
against the old society." The following day, 20 August, Red Guards in
Beijing and other big cities went to the streets and started to "destroy the
four olds and establish the four news."[13] Three days later, the *People's
Daily* published an editorial approving this, proclaiming in its title, "It
is very good."[14] Mao's Cultural Revolution ideology was now actively
being implemented.

On 12 August, less than a week after the issuance of the Eleventh
Plenum's decision, the Tibet Autonomous Region's Party Committee held
a large meeting, which was attended by about fourteen hundred people
who were active in the Cultural Revolution. At the meeting, Zhang Guohua called on all levels of cadres "to be brave enough to mobilize the
masses, trust them, and depend on them to carry out the Great Cultural
Revolution." He also requested all organizations to establish Cultural
Revolution leading teams and Cultural Revolution committees as soon
as possible.[15] On 18 August, an enlarged meeting of the Regional Party
Committee issued its own decision on how to implement the Central
Committee's 8 August decision. An official chronology of important
events in Tibet said of this:

> Since May of this year, people both inside and outside the party in the
> whole region actively studied the important instructions from the Central
> Committee of the CCP and the decisions from the Southwest Bureau and
> the Regional Committee of the CCP. A new upsurge of the Great Proletar-
> ian Cultural Revolution appeared in the whole region. The "decisions". . .
> suggested that in the future, if the members of the Cultural Revolution
> leading team, the Cultural Revolution Committee, or the Cultural Revo-
> lution Representative's Congress were not well qualified for their posts,
> they should be suspended or transferred. Every piece of work in the whole
> region should be arranged with the Great Cultural Revolution being placed
> at the center. First, put emphasis on the Great Cultural Revolution in the
> party and political organizations of the TAR, in the prefectures, and in the
> education departments. The work at the county level should be combined
> with the "three educations" and "four removes." All the factories, mines,

enterprises, farming and herding areas, towns, and counties with work teams should pay attention to fully mobilizing the masses to carry out the Great Cultural Revolution by themselves. The Cultural Revolution in the propaganda, culture, and school organizations of the army should be arranged by the Regional Party Committee according to the above spirit.[16]

All of this led students and teachers at the Lhasa Middle School and the Tibetan Teacher's College to organize their own Red Guard organizations. One of the Han teachers (who later became a top revolutionary leader in Gyenlo) recalled:

> [I]n August 1966 the Red Guards were everywhere in the whole country, and Lhasa didn't want to be left behind. Therefore we formed our own Red Guard organizations. . . . Most of the students in my school were Tibetans. It was a concern that the Tibetan students might get into trouble, for they didn't know the right [ideological] direction. Therefore, the Party Branch at the Lhasa Middle School decided to select a few young teachers to join the Red Guards, working as leaders. I remember I used to lead students to "destroy the four olds."[17]

However, Zhang Guohua and the Regional Party Committee, despite their activist revolutionary rhetoric, were not enthusiastic about allowing the Red Guards and revolutionary masses to run rampant in Tibet. In Zhang's view, the TAR was just recovering from the uprising of 1959 and the implementation of Democratic Reforms, and a new wave of chaos could destabilize the region. This view, in a real sense, was an extension of the position of Mao and the Central Committee in the 1950s, when they opted to utilize a "gradualist" policy to incorporate Tibet into the PRC, because they felt the circumstances in Tibet were significantly different from those the PLA had encountered in the rest of China.[18] Remnants of this gradualist view, in fact, continued to a degree even after the implementation of a new socialist political system in Tibet following the 1959 uprising. For example, in 1959, the top leaders of China were still concerned that moving forward too fast with socialism in Tibet could be counterproductive, so they decided to eschew starting socialist agriculture (collectives) in 1959 in favor of allowing rural Tibetans to enjoy a period of private farming. Phündra, a senior Tibetan translator at that time, recalled a key 1959 meeting among Zhou Enlai, Mao Zedong, the Panchen Lama, and Ngabö at which this issue came up.

> At this time they were implementing communes in China, and in Tibet some said we should implement them there as well. Mao and Zhou Enlai

met then with Ngabö and the Panchen. I was the translator. Zhou Enlai
spoke first, saying, "Do not implement communes in a hurry. First divide
the land and give it to the peasants. Let them plant the land and get a taste
of the profits of farming. In the past they had no land." Then Mao said,
"Do not start communes too quickly. If you give land to those who had no
land in the past and let them plant it, they will become very revolutionary
in their thinking and production will increase."[19]

Zhang Guohua, of course, had been in charge of Tibet during the 1950s
so not only understood how different Tibet was but also agreed with
the view that it was important for all policies to take account of these
differences. The new campaign in China, the Cultural Revolution, therefore, should also be implemented in keeping with the special situation
in Tibet. There should be, in essence, a special, less volatile, "Cultural
Revolution" in Tibet. Consequently, he supported preventing the more
radical students and workers from bombarding the headquarters in an
unsupervised manner, although he had no problem with their carrying
out the campaign against the "four olds" and struggling violently
against the class enemies of the old society. And within work units, the
masses could accuse one another of having capitalist-roader views but
not the top leadership. Consequently, more work teams were sent to
offices and work units to maintain this control. As it had been in the
1950s, stability in the CCP in Tibet continued to be a priority for Zhang
Guohua.[20]

One of the important aspects of the Cultural Revolution in inland
China was for Red Guards to travel to other parts of the country and
"link up" (ch. *chuanlian*) with activists there to propagate Mao's thinking and exchange experiences. Tibet was not immune from this, so beginning in early September some Red Guards from the Tibetan Nation-
ality Institute in Xianyang (ch. *xianyang xizang minyuan*) and Beijing
began to arrive in Lhasa.[21] Together with local Red Guards, they intensified the campaign against the "four olds" and class enemies, the latter
including progressive former Tibetan officials who had been incorporated
into the new administration after 1959. Not surprisingly, some of the
young revolutionaries in Lhasa also wanted to follow Mao's instructions
and attack the holders of power in their work units. However, such at-
tempts were initially blocked by the leadership. For example, in August,
when students at the Tibet Post and Telecommunications School vocif-
erously targeted their school authorities, the leaders quickly diffused the
situation by graduating the class early (to scatter the students). The following document written by these students a year later, in 1967, conveys

their frustration and anger at the Regional Party Committee, whom they felt was behind their early graduation:

> The May 16th Notice clearly revealed that some work units were controlled by a handful of leaders who held the capitalist line. Those leaders were so afraid of their mistakes being exposed that they used many excuses to suppress the movement of the masses. They attempted to lead the mass movement in the wrong way by changing its aims and confounding right and wrong. When they felt that they were too isolated to carry out their evil plans, they relied on playing tricks and spreading rumors to confuse the concepts of revolution and counterrevolution and to suppress the revolutionary factions.
>
> We graduated in mid-August last year. Why did they let us graduate at that particular time? It was the plot of the Regional Party Committee. Let us tell you the truth about it. At the very beginning of the Great Cultural Revolution, students struggled against one another for more than two months because the Regional Party Committee followed the policy of "discharging lots of arrows at the same time" (ch. *luan jian qi fang*).[22] Many young students under eighteen years of age who were educated in the thought of Chairman Mao were considered to be counterrevolutionaries and were severely criticized.
>
> On 8 August, the Central Committee of the CCP issued the decision of starting the Great Cultural Revolution. Students at our school pointed their spearhead at the school authorities. Our struggle frightened the leaders at the Regional Party Committee and the Party Committee of the Post and Communications Bureau. By kicking us out of school on 15 August, they temporarily realized their plot.
>
> When we started to work at new work units, the Great Cultural Revolution began. We didn't know anything about it. While other people were engaged in the Great Cultural Revolution, we could only watch them and were not able to provide any help.
>
> From this we can see that the Regional Party Committee has always insisted on the reactionary capitalist line. They openly opposed the instructions from the Central Committee and tried to obstruct the Great Cultural Revolution. They tried to split the forces of the masses to reach their sinister goal. Let all the revolutionary proletarian factions be united and let us work together to completely smash the reactionary capitalist line of the Regional Party Committee. . . .
>
> *Lhasa Revolutionary Gyenlo Headquarters*
> *"Driving Out Tigers" (ch. qu hu) United Operational Headquarters*
> *"New Universe" (ch. xin yu) Fighting Team of Tibet Post*
> *and Telecommunications School*
>
> 23 January 1967[23]

Another famous example of such suppression had occurred on 24 August 1966 at the Forestry Company in Kongpo when some young revolutionary workers led by a doctor in the public health clinic put up a big-character poster attacking the company's party committee. The party leaders responded furiously, calling a mass meeting, at which they proclaimed, "This is the limit. Openly writing a large character poster to incite the masses to attack the party is a *counter-revolutionary* incident."[24] This was followed by a purge of 127 workers (about one-quarter of the total), who were labeled as reactionary "monsters and demons" (ch. *niugui sheshen*) and were paraded through the streets wearing paper hats and so forth. These workers also underwent beatings and severe political repression, which for some included placement in the company's own internal "reform through labor" camp. At least one died there.[25]

Consequently, although the Regional Party Committee was able to keep the spearhead turned away from themselves and from the leadership in bureaus and offices and thereby keep the government and party functioning normally, beneath the surface anger was simmering among a segment of the revolutionary masses and Red Guards who felt that the Regional Party Committee was not adhering to Mao's clear instructions to ferret out the capitalist-roaders who had sneaked into the party. They wanted to do more than attack the "four olds," the feudal elite, and the lower-level employees in their work units.

On 19 September, the first crack in the wall the Regional Party Committee had erected around the Cultural Revolution occurred when a big-character poster openly advocated the bombardment of the Regional Party Committee itself. This poster was not only hung on the streets of Lhasa but also mailed to many different counties in Tibet. Written by Yue Zongming of the Cultural Items Preservation Office, the poster openly defied the Regional Party Committee and called for the revolutionary masses to point the spearhead at that committee, saying: "Bombard the party headquarters, set fire to the leadership of the Regional Party Committee, and seize the capitalist-roaders in authority."[26]

Zhang Guohua and the party establishment realized the danger this posed and vigorously attacked the poster and its author, banning the poster from being shown in public or sent by post and labeling the author as a counterrevolutionary. On 25 September, for example, the Regional Party Committee's Propaganda Department wrote an amazing twenty thousand–character handbill titled, "It is not allowed to bombard our proletarian revolutionary headquarters." In this, the Propaganda Department laid out the Regional Party Committee's ideological rationalization for banning the 19 September poster, arguing that since the Regional Party Committee was a proletarian headquarters, anyone who advocated bombarding it was a counterrevolutionary. Yue Zongming, therefore, was subjected to severe criticism at struggle sessions, where he and others involved were forced to recant and make self-confessions.[27]

The following week (on 30 September), at an enlarged meeting of the Regional Party Committee, Zhang Guohua enunciated some of the reasons why he felt that the situation in Tibet required a different operationalization of the Cultural Revolution. The official summary of his comments reported:

> Zhang Guohua talked about how to implement the spirit of the Central Committee's Eleventh Plenum. He said that the upsurge of the Cultural Revolution in Tibet had appeared and the current work was to welcome and promote the Cultural Revolution. [However] [i]n Tibet, individual [in contrast to collective] economy prevailed, and the struggles at the border were sharp and complicated. The problems of nationalities, especially the problems of religion, obviously existed. There are great differences among the organizations in the cities, counties, townships, and farming and herding areas, as well as the interior areas and the border areas. He said that we should firmly support the students in Tibet, *but* we should persuade them not to seize reactionaries among the troops or search the soldiers' quarters and should persuade the troops not to go out into the streets.[28]

Despite the massive government response to the 19 September poster, a month later, on 21 October, a revolutionary group calling itself the Red Guard Combat Team wrote a big-character poster demanding that the Regional Party Committee call a public meeting to vindicate the 19 September poster and rehabilitate its authors.

The following week, on 28 October, the Red Rebels, a faction that later became part of Gyenlo, decided to attack Ngabö, the most important of the former progressive Tibetan aristocrats and a top official in the Tibet Autonomous Region government. They marched to the compound of the Tibet Autonomous Region and demanded that he come out and answer their questions, that is, defend himself before the revolutionary masses. One young activist who was involved in that event recalled:

> One night, we were told to go the courtyard of the Tibet Autonomous Region. People said that Ngabö should come out to meet the masses. He came, and we were going to take away his position. As you know, he was one of the most powerful men in Tibet at that time. After some people took Ngabö to the mass meeting, those people who were standing at the front of the masses did lots of struggling against him. Of course we, the other people, shouted in support of our leaders. Then somebody took Ngabö back into the building. We stood there continuing to shout that Ngabö should be brought to the meeting of the masses.

While we were conducting this struggle session against Ngabö, somebody informed the central government. I think they told the central government that the masses were doing a struggle session against Ngabö and
asked whether they should allow the masses to continue. . . . The next
morning Ngabö was in inland China. He must have been sent from Lhasa
[to Beijing] by the central government.

Q: When the masses were struggling against him, did he say anything?
A: He did. He said he had exploited the masses in the old society and was
very sorry about that. When people were struggling against him, he had
guards stay beside him so that people could not get close to him. I think those
guards were told to take care of him. He had guards, so it was impossible for
us to get to him, but we shouted lots at him. It was a stupid action. Ngabö
recited the experiences of his life at the meeting, and then he left the meeting
of the masses. . . . The next day, when we were going to continue the struggle
session against him, we were told that he had gone to inland China.[29]

The person who intervened on behalf of Ngabö was Zhang Guohua, who,
ironically, had returned to Lhasa that same day from a stay of three weeks
in Beijing. As soon as Ngabö was attacked, Zhang contacted Zhou Enlai,
who arranged for a plane to take Ngabö immediately to safety in Beijing.[30]
This action further inflamed the more radical revolutionary masses, solidi-
fying their belief that the Regional Party Committee was trying to thwart
Mao's call to cleanse the party and government leadership.

At this point, Zhang Guohua felt it was important to try to prevent
more Red Guards, particularly Han Red Guards from Beijing, from coming to Tibet and further radicalizing the Cultural Revolution there, so he
explicitly asked Zhou Enlai to order the various Cultural Revolution
organizations not to allow Han Chinese Red Guards to come to Tibet.[31]
Zhou approved this, but the Red Guard groups from Beijing ignored the
order, and in early November, Metropolitan Red Guards arrived from
Beijing in three groups and set up the Blazing Prairie Combat Regiment
(ch. *liaoyuan zhandou tuan*).

These Beijing Metropolitan Red Guards, who would become one of
the core founding units of Gyenlo, were not as easy for the Regional Party
Committee to manipulate as the Lhasa students and workers had been.
As a result of this, the focus of the spearhead now started shifting in a
serious way toward the party leadership, particularly the Regional Party
Committee itself. The Cultural Revolution as experienced in Beijing was
now about to start in Lhasa.[32]

Between 7 and 11 November, the Blazing Prairie Combat Regiment,
in conjunction with Tibetan Red Guards and other young revolutionaries in Lhasa, put up four hundred to five hundred posters criticizing the

Regional Party Committee and its head, Zhang Guohua. These posters said things such as "Completely criticize the reactionary capitalist line of the Regional Party Committee [in Tibet]." They also accused the Regional Party Committee of "waving a red flag to oppose the red flag," that is, of pretending to adhere to Mao's call to scrutinize the holders of power while actually trying to prevent that.[33]

A week later, a group of ten revolutionary organizations launched a citywide debate on whether the Regional Party Committee had been implementing a bourgeois reactionary line. This was the first open clash between what would become Tibet's two competing revolutionary organizations—Gyenlo and Nyamdre. More than ninety people spoke, the majority supporting the view that the Regional Party Committee was a true proletarian organization. Soon after this, they merged to form the Headquarters of Defending Mao Zedong's Thoughts and then, a few months later, linked up with others such as the One Thousand Serf Fighters (ch. *nong mu zhan*) from the Xianyang Nationalities Institute, who had arrived in Lhasa in early December, forming the even larger revolutionary group called Nyamdre. A minority of the speakers that day attacked the Regional Party Committee and soon afterward formed Gyenlo Headquarters.[34]

A Han revolutionary leader from the Lhasa Middle School recalled what his anti–Zhang Guohua organization was thinking at this time:

> Our group had clear aims. We were trying to "turn the world upside down" [laughs] and "find all the 'capitalist-roaders' and knock them down and step on them" [laughs]. That was the language people used at that time. . . . Those people who were close to the leaders at the Regional Party Committee were later called "royalists."[35] They [the revolutionaries close to the leaders] argued that the leaders were nice people and had been working hard for the local residents. However, we didn't care about that. What we really cared about were the orders from the Central Committee [the Eleventh Plenum] that we knew we were supposed to follow. It was fine with us if none of the leaders were capitalist-roaders, but if there were any, we wanted to go ahead and struggle against them. . . . Actually, we were not sure who those capitalist-roaders were . . . but we thought we should see whether we could find followers of the capitalist road in Tibet.[36]

Meanwhile, back in Beijing on 16 November, the State Council reiterated its instructions banning the exchange of revolutionary experiences in Tibet, but this too was ignored. Then on 4 December, the State Council announced specific new regulations requiring the Red Guards from inland China who were still in Lhasa to leave Tibet and return to their own localities by 20 December. The Regional Party Committee was so eager to see them leave that they actually organized a "farewell meeting" for the departing Red Guards. However, they were thwarted in this, because the Beijing Red Guards in Lhasa had contacted the Central Cultural Revolution Group, headed by Mao's wife, Jiang Qing, pleading to be allowed to remain because, in their view, their presence was critical to eliminating the bourgeois reactionary line that was present there. And their pleas succeeded. To the chagrin of Zhang Guohua, the powerful Central Great Cultural Revolution Group intervened and gave the Beijing Red Guards permission to remain.[37] The Cultural Revolution in Lhasa was now entering a new and much more radical phase.

A Lhasa Red Guard group at the broadcast station in Lhasa commented on this in December 1966:

> Some major leaders of the Regional Party Committee were so afraid of the Red Guards from fighting units such as Blazing Prairie that they tried to obstruct the Red Guards before they came [from Beijing] and then sent people to surveil them after they arrived. After the notice was issued from the Central Committee to temporarily stop the great linking-up, they tried their best to drive the [inland Chinese] Red Guards out. They hurriedly held a "send-off meeting" [to send the Red Guards back] long before the time limit of the 21st, which was the date stipulated by the Central Committee. So why were you so afraid of the Red Guards? Does that mean that you were ashamed of what you have done? You were afraid because the Red Guards have complete revolutionary spirit and will never give up to the reactionary line. Comrades of our three fighting units in the broadcast station have discussed this problem with Comrade Zhang Zaiwang [vice-director of the Leading Team of the Cultural Revolution in Tibet]. However, Comrade Zhang Zaiwang did not accept our opinions and insisted on driving the Red Guards out. What is the result now? The team from the Central Great Cultural Revolution Group [in Beijing] has supported their staying in Tibet and carrying on the revolution with the local revolutionary masses. This was the clearest and loudest reply to those who insisted on driving the Red Guards out. We most strongly support this decision and enthusiastically welcome the Red Guards from fighting units like the Blazing Prairie to carry on the revolution together with us. Those who have abused the Blazing Prairie and tried to drive them out should shut up now.[38]

By mid-December 1966, therefore, the conflict among different revolutionary factions was escalating over the status of the Regional Party Committee as well as other issues, such as whether the labeling of some workers and Red Guards as reactionaries and counterrevolutionaries should be abolished. Red Guards from inland China together with local groups pushed to investigate and struggle against the top members of the Regional Party Committee, in particular Zhang Guohua, whom they derisively called the "indigenous emperor" (ch. *tuhuangdi*). The situation in Lhasa was on the brink of spinning out of control. Liu Shaoming, later the head of the more conservative revolutionary faction called Nyamdre, commented on how he and Zhang Guohua felt about these Red Guards:

> We resented Red Guards from the inland areas at that time. Why do we need you to come to Tibet to fan the fires and tell us what to do with the Cultural Revolution? Why do we need you to be our savior and tell us what to do? Although I don't know much about Tibet, you are from the inland area, so what do you know about Tibet? Tibet is an ethnic region and has its own characteristics. Tibet is an ethnic as well as a border area, so how can it be treated the same way as the inland areas? Doing that will throw it into chaos. There is an ethnic issue in Tibet. What do you students from the inland areas know about it? We were secretaries [heads] in the government departments and not young students, and we worked with the Party Committee. We had different modes of thinking and needed to take these issues into consideration. We couldn't do whatever they wanted us to do. That's how the contradiction came into being.[39]

The more radical revolutionary organizations convened a mass meeting in Lhasa on 19 December, at which Zhang Guohua was induced to make a self-criticizing speech on behalf of the Regional Party Committee in the hope that this would satisfy them and calm the situation. At this meeting, he vaguely admitted mistakes in the Regional Party Committee's political line, but things did not calm down.[40] A few days later, on 23 December, some revolutionary masses entered the compound of the Regional Party Committee, where they remained and carried out debates trying to uncover capitalist-roaders.

At this point, a number of the more radical revolutionary groups felt they could more effectively pressure the power holders if they joined forces, so on 22 December they inaugurated a new large revolutionary group under the leadership of the Beijing Red Guard's Blazing Prairie Combat Regiment. This new organization united thirty-five revolutionary organizations and was called the "general headquarters of the revolutionary rebels (Gyenlo) of Lhasa" (ch. *lasa geming zaofan zongbu*), commonly abbreviated as "Gyenlo Headquarters" (ch. *zaozong*) or just "Gyenlo" (ch. *zaofan*).[41] At this time it had almost a thousand members, including workers, cadres, and students, organized into fifty-one combat regiments.

A Gyenlo leaflet published at the time of its creation spells out vividly its commitment to rebel against the party leadership:

> In the new situation of the Great Proletarian Cultural Revolution, surrounded by war drums repudiating the bourgeois reactionary line, the Lhasa Revolutionary Gyenlo Headquarters is born!
>
> What is this Gyenlo Headquarters of ours doing? It is to hold high the great red banner of Mao Zedong's thought and to rebel by applying Mao Zedong's thought. We will rebel against the handful of persons in authority in the party who are taking the capitalist road! We will rebel against all the monsters and freaks! We will rebel against the bourgeois royalists! We, a group of lawless revolutionary rebels, will wield the iron sweepers and swing the mighty cudgels to sweep the old world into a mess and bash people into complete confusion. We will rebel against persons stubbornly persisting in the bourgeois reactionary line! We don't fear gales or storms or flying sand or moving rocks. We don't care if that handful of people in authority taking the capitalist road and the very few persons stubbornly persisting in the bourgeois reactionary line oppose us or fear us. We also don't care if the bourgeois royalists denounce us or curse us. We will resolutely make revolution and rebel. To rebel, to rebel, and to rebel through to the end in order to create a bright red proletarian new world.[42]

A scathing publication dated 26 December 1966 further illustrates the intensity of those who opposed the more moderate views of the Regional Party Committee (and the other revolutionary organizations that they saw as sympathetic toward the Party Committee). This long statement, published as a leaflet, categorically rejected Zhang Guohua's arguments about the need for calm in Tibet and critically spelled out a number of actions the party leadership had taken to impede and prevent the revolutionary Red Guards from effectively "bombarding" the headquarters. The full text is presented in appendix 2:

1. During the Great Cultural Revolution in our region, the Regional Party Committee did not have just a few minor shortcomings or errors; it mistakenly carried out the reactionary bourgeois line and lost its direction.

2. We do not agree with the opinion of some comrades that "the Regional Party Committee carried out the reactionary bourgeois line *unconsciously*." We think that the Regional Committee of the CCP *completely and consciously* carried out the reactionary bourgeois line in the Great Cultural Revolution. It attempted to suppress the revolutionary masses and to protect a handful of leaders who held the capitalist line. The Regional Party Committee also tried to suppress the Great Cultural Revolution in our region.

3. Besides Guo Xilan, who has already been proved to oppose Mao Zedong, other leaders in our Regional Party Committee are still implementing the reactionary capitalist line. *We are determined to uncover these leaders no matter how much they have contributed to the party and no matter how high their current positions are. No one can protect them.*

4. We cannot treat the comrades in the Regional Party Committee alike. We will criticize those who have formulated and are still implementing the reactionary capitalist line in Tibet. We will overthrow those who stubbornly insist on the reactionary capitalist line and oppose the revolutionary line of Mao Zedong.

5. Some major leaders of the Regional Party Committee have not been truly implementing the instructions of Chairman Mao and the Central Committee and have not been working hard with the masses to criticize the reactionary line. On the contrary, they have been playing tricks and taking new measures to trick the masses as well as insisting on the reactionary capitalist line. There are indications that their following the reactionary line has become a more and more serious problem.

Allied headquarters (ch. lianhe zuozhanbu) of the broadcast
station in Tibet (26 December 1966)[43]

Less than a week later, on 28 December, in response to the establishment of Gyenlo, a number of the mass organizations supportive of the Regional Party Committee, such as the Serf Fighters from the Nationalities Institute, joined together and established the Headquarters of Defending Mao Zedong's Thoughts (ch. *hanwei mao zedong sixiang zhandou zongbu*) (abbreviated as "Headquarters of Defending") (ch. *han zong*).[44] In February 1967, this became the core of Nyamdre.

Mao's instructions to destroy the four olds and attack the bad classes were easy to fathom and operationalize, but his call to root out the revisionists and counterrevolutionaries in high places was more enigmatic and open to widely differing interpretations. Consequently, although all the revolutionary factions believed they were following Mao's instructions, they disagreed about which specific officials were bourgeois capitalist-roaders. Interfactional tension and conflict, therefore, now divided the revolutionary organizations and their followers into two discrete coalitions of factions, Nyamdre and Gyenlo, the former more conservative and latter more radical with regard to how far they should go in "bombarding" the headquarters of the Regional Party Committee—in other words, to what extent they should support Zhang Guohua's contention that, because the situation in Tibet was special, the Cultural Revolution had to be carried out carefully so as to not exacerbate existing tensions.

As this interfactional conflict intensified, intrafaction solidarity also intensified, creating powerful loyalties and allegiances among members of factions. A recollection of a Nyamdre activist about members in his group illustrates this well: "People had deep loyalty to one another. Everyone treated one another as if they were one's relative." And when he was asked what he felt when he met a stranger who claimed he was Nyamdre, he said, "I felt very happy. When I exchanged views on ideology with someone from our faction and talked about the greatness of our faction and the mistakes made by the Gyenlo faction, I was moved. The strength of the faction was really powerful."[45]

Ren Rong, a strong supporter of Zhang Guohua and his emphasis on stability in the party and army in Tibet, spoke of a parallel split within the Regional Party Committee between Zhang Guohua and Deputy Party Secretary Zhou Renshan over how to conduct the Cultural Revolution.

> The general leaders in the Military Region [Headquarters], including Zhang Guohua, Chen Mingyi, and me, had almost the same idea about this. We thought some actions during the Cultural Revolution were right, for example, eliminating superstition and the four olds. We all agreed with these points. I also thought it was right that people should correct their own mistakes, but I did not approve of criticizing and seizing cadres without any genuine evidence. And we all disapproved of seizing power from those people. Things happened like this at the beginning.
>
> In all the offices/organizations (ch. *jiguan*) in the military region, a few people who were ultra-leftists (ch. *jizuo*) took actions frequently and intensely. They seized power, not only the power of offices, but also the power of the military region. During that time, these people did such things frequently. Some local people also did so. The people from both of the two factions supported the Cultural Revolution, but they did it in different ways after the Cultural Revolution began. One group arrested capitalist-roaders and criticized and denounced them, while the other group thought they should do everything after investigation and analysis and could not treat problems in general. At that time, the general orientation for carrying out the Cultural Revolution was to arrest those major leaders. . . . This was Zhou Renshan's point. He thought that no matter whether those people were capitalist-roaders or not, they should be arrested first.[46]

Consequently, as 1966 ended, conflict in Lhasa was taking a major turn for the worse with the escalation and intensification of interfactional conflict and animosity. It would quickly transform Tibet into the chaos and anomie that Zhang Guohua and the party establishment had initially feared would happen if the evolution of the Cultural Revolution was not managed carefully.

On 6 January 1967, the Cultural Revolution's factional activism in inland China moved to a new level when Shanghai rebel factions launched the so-called January Storm (ch. *yiyue fengbao*), during which they seized the authority of the Shanghai Party Committee and the committee of the Shanghai People's Congress. This quickly spurred action in Lhasa, where on the evening of 10 January a group in the *Tibet Daily Newspaper* office called the Revolutionary Rebels of Red News (ch. *hongse xinwen zaofan tuan*) launched their own version of the January Storm, together with Gyenlo activists from other units in Lhasa, and struck at the heart of the Tibetan establishment by taking control of the *Tibet Daily Newspaper.* This was a direct attack on the Regional Party Committee, which had taken control of that office and seized its editor, Jin Sha, in July 1966. Gyenlo, however, felt the newspaper was not publicizing Mao's revolutionary calls to action correctly and was not covering Red Guard activities adequately, so felt it should rectify this by taking over the paper's operation. This meant that Gyenlo now controlled what would be published. This was followed by the seizure, one after another, of the Xinhua News Agency Office, the broadcast station, the Temporary Lhasa City Committee, and many other departments, bureaus, and offices.[47] One of the top leaders of Gyenlo recalled the event:

> If you ask me—and I was there from the very beginning until the end—
> I would say we were closely following the instructions from the Central
> Committee. Whenever we got an order from the Central Committee, we
> acted immediately. That was the way we did it. There might have been mis-
> takes in our understanding of the orders—for example, we didn't quite
> understand the January Storm—but the newspapers said that it was correct
> to take the power. . . . The Central Committee affirmed it. That movement
> had great impact on the entire country. It made us think about what we
> should do, and not long after that we took over the *Tibet Daily* [laughs]. . . .
> At that time we thought that the publishing house should be controlled by
> the proletariat, as ordered by Chairman Mao, and that we, as the represen-
> tatives of the proletariat, should keep the publishing house in our control.[48]

This takeover, however, was attacked by those at the Headquarters of Defending, who were more conservative and supported Zhang Guohua; they charged that the takeover and the first edition of the new *Tibet Daily* were reactionary, not revolutionary. In the ensuing weeks, chaos reigned as each side struggled to seize or keep control of the paper. The revolutionary rivals of Gyenlo saw this as Gyenlo trying to take control of the Cultural Revolution in Tibet. And, of course, they were correct.

In response to such attacks by the anti-Gyenlo factions, the following lengthy document was written by two of the main Beijing Red Guard factions in Gyenlo to justify Gyenlo's takeover. The different views about how to carry out the Cultural Revolution were now making interfaction conflict a top issue. Called "The Truth about the Struggle to Seize the Power of the *Tibet Daily Newspaper* Office," this statement gives an excellent feel for the intellectual and emotional intensity of the escalating conflict:

> .The primary concern of the revolution is political power. All power should belong to the revolutionary left.
>
> The revolutionary left rebel groups of the *Tibet Daily Newspaper* started their fight to rebel and seized power on the night of 10 January. The "Revolutionary Rebels of Red News" were the main force among the leftist groups. However, after the incident, some people said that we had already seized control from Jin Sha, so after that the power was already in the hands of proletarian groups. Consequently, when the struggle to seize power was again carried out, weren't they [Gyenlo] attempting to seize power from the proletariat? Others, however, said that this rebellion was great, because after the struggle, the leading power was returned to the *real* revolutionary rebel groups. What is the truth? Why did a struggle of seizing power happen at the office of a newspaper? What was its process? What were its characteristics? These questions are the concerns of most of the people of Tibet right now. This incident has direct impact on the Great Cultural Revolution in Lhasa and [elsewhere] in Tibet. Therefore, according to the highest instructions, we, the soldiers of the Blazing Prairie Combat Regiment and the Red Flag (ch. *hong qi*) group from the Beijing Academy of Aviation, carried out investigations and found the truth. We believe this incident was a revolutionary one. The revolutionary leftists did a good job.
>
> Without investigation, it is perfunctory to make conclusions. Only after careful examination can we get the points right.
>
> One. Why did they seize power?
>
> Chairman Mao told us that we should never accept wrong leadership, because it will do harm to the revolution. We should suppress those people who dare to attack Chairman Mao. We should not hesitate to reject any work that goes against the instructions of Chairman Mao. We should suppress those who dare to oppose Chairman Mao and also suppress all work that opposes the instructions of Chairman Mao. The leaders of some regions who are carrying out the bourgeois reactionary line that runs counter to the thoughts of Chairman Mao should be dismissed from office until they are able to carry out the line of Chairman Mao. Dismissing those leaders is a revolutionary action. Nobody should say no to it.

After this clear introduction, the document laid out Gyenlo's view that it was imperative to follow the instructions of Mao Zedong and Beijing, not the views of the leaders of the Regional Party Committee of the TAR.

Someone said that actions like this [taking control of the *Tibet Daily*] do not follow the leadership of the Communist Party. That is total nonsense. The leaders of the Central Committee, Chairman Mao, and the thoughts of Chairman Mao are the real leading powers of the Communist Party. As for Tibet, the leaders of the Regional Party Committee of the TAR are just leaders of the local area. They are not equal to the leaders of the Central Committee of the Chinese Communist Party. Those who believe that "the leaders of the Regional Party Committee of the TAR are as powerful as those of the Central Committee" are definitely wrong, and they will fail if they use this wrong idea to suppress the movement of the masses in Tibet.

Our most respected and beloved leader, Chairman Mao, launched this Great Proletarian Cultural Revolution. The Great Cultural Revolution touched everybody to his very soul. We should rebel against all things that run counter to thoughts of Chairman Mao in order to create a new bright red China and a new bright red world. *However, with the coming of the Great Cultural Revolution, some leaders of the Regional Party Committee of the TAR became very frightened. They started to use the publishing house of the* Tibet Daily Newspaper, *which they controlled, to serve the reactionary bourgeois line. They did not allow reports [to be published] about the spirit of rebellion of the revolutionary masses in the Great Cultural Revolution and the success of Chairman Mao's Red Guards. On the contrary, they used the paper to spread the dark side of the Red Guards, exaggerating the Red Guards' mistakes, slandering the Red Guards, creating a white terror, and blocking information about the Great Cultural Revolution in order to destroy it.*

Was it just a minor problem? No, it wasn't. It was a matter of principle. The newspapers and periodicals of the Communist Party are tools of publicity for the proletarian class, and they should be used to publicize the ideas of Chairman Mao. Chairman Mao said, "We must always stick to the truth, and the truth must have a clear-cut stand." Members of the Communist Party consider it wrong to conceal one's own opinions. The publicity work of our Communist Party should be active, clear, and sharp. No hemming and hawing. However, the *Tibet Daily* became the propaganda tool of some leaders of the Regional Party Committee of the TAR in order to implement the reactionary line of the bourgeoisie. Was it all right? No, it should not have been done.

To rebel, we should resist the wrong leadership of some leaders of the Regional Party Committee of the TAR and completely refuse their ideas. The soldiers of the "Revolutionary Rebels of Red News" in the *Tibet Daily* started the rebellion under the instructions of Chairman Mao, who said, "It is justified to rebel." They spread the revolutionary spirit of the *Wenhui Daily* (ch. *wenhui bao*) and the *Liberation Daily* (ch. *jiefang ribao*) [newspapers in Shanghai].

On 10 January, the members of "Revolutionary Rebels of Red News" started the struggle to seize power. On 11 January, they solemnly declared that they firmly support the leadership of the Central Committee of the

Communist Party, which is headed by Chairman Mao, and firmly resist the wrong leadership of some leaders of the Tibet Regional Party Committee. *They also said that from then on, all control of the publicity work would be taken away from some leaders of the Regional Party Committee. The power of control will not be given back to those leaders until the reactionary bourgeois line is completely criticized and those leaders of the Regional Party Committee of the TAR who persisted in the reactionary line are completely overthrown. This rebellion represented justice because it was to protect the revolutionary line of Chairman Mao and the thoughts of Chairman Mao. . . .*

Three. Was it "Very Good" or "Very Bad"?

After the incident of seizing power at the publishing house occurred, different opinions appeared. Some people said it was a very bad way of struggling. Were they correct? Of course not! This struggle to seize power was supported by the workers of the revolutionary rebels at the publishing house. The struggle was against the wrong direction of some leaders of the Regional Party Committee and their reactionary bourgeois line. *Those leaders did not allow us to publicize the spirit of rebellion of the revolutionary rebel masses, but we insisted on doing so. Those leaders wanted to propagate the dark side of Chairman Mao's Red Guards, but we insisted in letting people know how the Red Guards have contributed to the Great Cultural Revolution under the instructions of Chairman Mao. Those leaders wanted to implement the reactionary bourgeois line, but we insisted on criticizing it and guarding the revolutionary line of Chairman Mao. How could someone say it was a very bad struggle? Actually it was extremely good. Someone said this incident was a "counterrevolutionary incident" and it was an "adverse current." These were false rumors. [Slogans omitted.] Now just a few people still insist on holding this wrong opinion. They are separating themselves from the masses, and they are opposing the masses and the ideas of Chairman Mao. In the end they will fail. [Slogans omitted.] We believe "the struggle to seize power" was good, and it was the right direction. Those comrades who are not clearly aware of the facts will agree with us after they know the truth. We insist on supporting the workers of revolutionary rebel groups running the* Tibet Daily Newspaper *as the mouthpiece for the ideas of Chairman Mao. We welcome the new birth of the* Tibet Daily Newspaper. *. . . [See appendix 3 for the full text of this document.]*[49]

Three weeks later, on 5 February, Gyenlo activists marched to the government offices of the TAR to further "seize power" in various offices, in essence paralyzing the party and government organizations.[50] Two days after that, they took control of the Public Security Bureau. At the same time they were also seizing, interrogating, and arresting members of the opposing revolutionaries, such as the Defenders of the Thoughts of Mao Zedong. A draft report favorable to the Regional Party Committee explained these events:

Once the Gyenlo Headquarters was established, especially after seizing power on 3 [*sic, 5*] February, its members pointed their struggle spearhead at the revolutionary organizations such as the Headquarters of Defending and the Headquarters of Nyamdre. . . . They regarded themselves as the natural-born "revolutionary and rebel faction." They slandered whoever did not agree with their opinions and manners as people who are "protecting the emperor." They threatened the members of the Headquarters of Defending, telling them to surrender to the Gyenlo Headquarters within two days or a "dictatorship" would be implemented over them. The members of Gyenlo Headquarters carried out activities that involved beating, smashing, arresting, and looting. At the same time they implemented the white terror.

According to the incomplete statistics compiled by four headquarters, including the Headquarters of Defending, Gyenlo Headquarters arrested 56 members of the masses, put 9 people under house arrest, interrogated 10 people illegally, surrounded and accused 46 people, and beat 116 people. (Among these 116 people, 16 were seriously injured, and 4 who were sent to the hospital were fatally injured.)

Gyenlo Headquarters also smashed [other] headquarters, including the Headquarters of Defending three times. They destroyed broadcast trucks and printing houses and so forth. After the members of Gyenlo Headquarters seized power, they established the so-called Dictatorship Committee (ch. *zhuanzheng weiyuanhui*) to further carry out their counterrevolutionary dictatorship against the revolutionary masses and cadres.[51]

This offensive by Gyenlo led directly to the merging of several opposing mass organizations, including the Headquarters of Defending, into a second, larger, and competing revolutionary coalition organization—Nyamdre.[52] While still leftist and revolutionary in ideology, Nyamdre, like the Headquarters of Defending, was more conservative in supporting the more moderate views of most of the Regional Party Committee and Zhang Guohua regarding Tibet and the Cultural Revolution. Liu Shaoming, one of the top leaders of Nyamdre, explained in an interview (together with his wife) how this emerged out of the Gyenlo attacks on the Regional Party Committee compound on 5 February:

At that time, [the Gyenlo] people wanted to destroy the printing house and the archives of the Regional Party Committee. The combat team (ch. *bing tuan*) of the Regional Party Committee itself did not have enough manpower. So since the surrounding areas in Lhasa were also concerned about the Regional Party Committee, they [these areas] were organized to increase their [the committee's] strength. Ten separate organizations [joined together].

[His wife interrupts.] At that time, the people of the Regional Party Committee were protecting the archives office. A whole row of rooms were used to store archives [records]. In addition, people of the Regional Party Committee protected the printing house. They were very understaffed, so many people from other work units volunteered to come inside and help us out. . . . I was in the courtyard at that time. They [Gyenlo] drove in with many vehicles, trying to take away the archives and destroy the printing press. The people opposing them were not clearly organized yet . . . [but] defended.

In addition, they [Gyenlo] wanted to drive out all the secretaries [leaders] and parade them around. . . . We needed to protect those small buildings, and obviously we didn't have enough hands. Therefore, many people from various organizations, such as workers' and peasants' organizations, volunteered to go to the Regional Party Committee to lend a hand. Later, they came together gradually and thought that they should be united.

[Liu]: Only when we united could we deal with them [Gyenlo].

[Wife]: There were the Headquarters of Defending, the combat team, and some [people from other] headquarters (ch. *silingbu*). A lot of them. The situation was like that. The seizure of power from the Regional Party Committee and the attempt to take away the archives became a catalyst and made them feel that they should unite.[53]

Liu Shaoming commented more specifically about this action:

In the beginning, Gyenlo Headquarters and Red Guards from the inland areas were very powerful. They beat up people [cadres] who therefore had nowhere to stay [safely], not at the newspaper, not at the hospital. They had to leave. [Note: The officials had to move from one place to another to escape from the physical abuse of the Red Guards.] The Red Guards from the interior areas wanted to destroy the printing house of the Regional Party Committee—the printing house of the General Office (ch. *bangong ting*). It printed the publications of the Regional Party Committee at that time. The Red Guards thought the printing house was the black den of Zhang Guohua and wanted to destroy it, so the people of the General Office went in more than a dozen vehicles to protect the printing house. . . . At that time, the staff of the Regional Party Committee established combat teams in order to defend against Gyenlo. They were not organized in the beginning.

While this was happening, some young people of the Classified Documents Department (ch. *jiyao chu*) of the Regional Party Committee joined with Red Guards from the interior area and Gyenlo Headquarters and tried to get me to take files from the General Office so that they could write big-character posters about all the major leaders. I absolutely refused. That was out of the question. I was a secretary and knew the potential impact [of these files]. I heard that they later tried to break into the Archives Office (ch. *dangan shi*) of the Regional Party Committee. . . . At that time, the Archives Office was at the Regional Party Committee [headquarters]. When they tried to destroy the printing house, the cadres of the General Office were organized to defend it and the Archives Office. When [the attackers] went there, some cadres and their family members laid down at the gate and said, "Run over us if you want to get in." They didn't dare to do this.[54]

For Gyenlo, therefore, Nyamdre was not a true representative of the views of Mao and the revolution but rather a pro–Zhang Guohua creature of the Regional Party Committee. A former top leader of Gyenlo conveyed his group's disdain when he sarcastically said of the new Nyamdre alliance, "The two factions were therefore formed. The Central Committee used to say that those people [in Nyamdre] had a deep love toward the Communist Party, so it was natural that they also loved the local Communist Party leaders [laughs]. Therefore, their stance of 'protecting the leaders' was understandable."[55]

In December 1966, the two factions argued and debated under the rubric of the "free airing of views" (tib. *gyeshey gyeleng*; ch. *da ming da fang*), which meant that people should express their views without reservation. This was also referred to as "big debates" (tib. *tsöba chembo*; ch. *da bianlun*). By February 1967, however, putting up posters and debating turned physical, with violent struggles occurring in conjunction (tib. *thragbö thabdzö*), at first with slingshots and stones, then progressively with swords, iron rods, spears, bombs, and eventually guns. Initially, both factions were present in virtually all of the work units and neighborhoods; however, this changed after the physical fighting began between Gyenlo and Nyamdre and the two groups started raiding each other's sites, seizing locations, and beating up (struggling against) members from the other group. Gyenlo units seized places where only a small number of people from Nyamdre lived, and Nyamdre similarly seized places where not many people from Gyenlo lived. Therefore, some localities quickly became all one faction or the other. For example, the Potala-Shöl area was Nyamdre, but the nearby People's Hospital was Gyenlo. And at the "1 July" State Farm (opposite Drepung Monastery), everyone was Nyamdre, since the Gyenlo members who had been there had fled for safety to the Cement Factory, which was now completely Gyenlo. All of Lhasa became fragmented like that.

The army, ostensibly taking a stance of neutrality between the factions, was supposed to try to stop the violent fighting by placing its troops between the fighters to separate them peacefully. One Tibetan PLA soldier recalled this, explaining in an interview how his unit intervened to try to prevent serious outbreaks of interfactional violence:

> They said that as soldiers we could not hold any ideology during the Cultural Revolution, the ideology of neither Nyamdre nor Gyenlo. Wherever fighting arose between the two factions, we were sent to mediate and stop them from fighting. . . . We stayed in the Potala Palace, where we used a

telescope to observe where the fighting was occurring. When we saw a fight, we had to call the Military Region Headquarters and inform them of this, and then they would send us to stop the fighting.

The main fighting in Lhasa was on the western and northern sides of the city, and the worst was at the Second Guest House of the Tibet Autonomous Region (what used to be the Yabshi house). When the fighting was bad, we were sent to stop it. If it wasn't too bad, we stayed in the Potala Palace and watched what was happening through telescopes. This went on for four to five months in 1967–68.

Q: Did you see fighting every day?
A: Not every day. Sometimes there was and sometimes there wasn't. . . .

Q: How many people were with you observing from the Potala?
A: One platoon (ch. *pai*) that consisted of three squads (ch. *ban*). There were ten or eleven people in a squad. We had to watch from the Potala day and night.

Q: Could you see at night?
A: Not too clearly, but they usually threw bombs, and we could see them explode, so would call in and report that they were bombing at such and such.

Q: How many times did you go from the Potala to stop fighting?
A: Many times. More than I can count. We would go down via the road at the back of the Potala. If we went via the front, they would shoot at us from the Second Guest House.

Q: How did you stop the fighting?
A: We stood in the middle of the two factions and mediated, telling them not to fight. There was nothing else we could do.

Q: Did you advise both sides not to fight?
A: Yes. But they would not listen to us.

Q: Did you get hit?
A: Yes. I was hit many times. When we went to stop the fighting, they hit us with sticks saying, "You people are fake soldiers." . . . They beat us severely.

Q: Did you hit them back?
A: We were not allowed to hit back.

Q: Did you people have any ideology (tib. tawa*)?*
A: We had none at this time. Later our officers were Gyenlo, but we common soldiers had none. They told us we were not allowed to adhere to a faction. . . .

Q: When you went to stop the factional fighting, did you carry guns?
A: No, we weren't allowed to. They [the PLA leaders] had collected our weapons.

Q: What were you allowed to do when you went to stop the fighting?
A: Mostly we could only carry Mao's little red book in our hands. If Nyamdre came running to attack Gyenlo, we went into the middle and tried to stop them. And vice versa. So we soldiers got hit the most.

Q: Were the soldiers in the middle mainly Tibetans?
A: No. There were both Tibetans and Chinese.
Q: Were you able to break them up?
A: Yes, but we got hit a lot in the head by stones and sticks.[56]

On 9 February, Gyenlo took another bold step to further secure its position by trying to neutralize the Tibet Military Region Headquarters. Led by the Beijing Metropolitan Red Guards, Gyenlo activists pushed their way into the Tibet Military Region Headquarters in collaboration with pro-Gyenlo PLA troops there who called themselves the Allied Combat Team of the military region (ch. *junqu lianhe bingtuan*). Ostensibly they were demanding that the leaders of Military Region Headquarters support the Gyenlo seizure of power on 5 February, but actually they were hoping to garner large-scale support from the troops and officers.[57]

The following official description of Gyenlo's incursion into the military headquarters compound reveals the very negative view the government and army had of Gyenlo:

> After the incident of 5 February, [when] Gyenlo Headquarters seized political and financial power from the Regional Party Committee of the TAR, they thought their position was still not secure without seizing military power. Therefore . . . they wanted to instigate rebellion within the army to stage a "military coup d'état." They openly instigated the army to "change their aim" and "turn their weapons around to strike." [On 9 February] [t]hey gathered the masses who were unaware of the truth to continuously attack the leading organs of the military region. They also colluded with a few reactionary members inside the military region to attempt to seize the military's power. They spread rumors to foment bad relations between the army and the masses. They abused the leading comrades of the military region for a long period of time and kidnapped and beat our army officials and soldiers many times. They grabbed the soldiers' collar badges, insignia, and their weapons. They openly shouted things such as "Commence a life-or-death fight to the end with the military region" and "Wash the highland city [Lhasa] with blood."[58]

The specter of pro-Gyenlo combat teams within the army acting in concert with Gyenlo combat teams from Lhasa raised the frightening possibility of the army becoming split into two overtly competing revolutionary factions or, worse, becoming entirely loyal to Gyenlo. This prompted a quick and powerful response. The very next day, under instructions from the Central Military Committee in Beijing, the Tibet Military Headquarters moved to restore order by suspending the practice of the Cultural Revolution in the army, that is, by resuming normal operations within the military in Tibet and by declaring martial law in the military headquarters compound.[59] At the same time, the army immediately suppressed the pro-Gyenlo Allied Combat Team, arresting its leaders. The following 13 February document, written by Gyenlo activists, defiantly describes the army's tough response:

> To all the revolutionary comrades in Lhasa and Tibet:
>
> The Great Cultural Revolution has come to a decisive battle to achieve complete success for the entire movement. As in the whole country, the masses in Lhasa and the entire Tibet region have already been fully mobilized. They have also seized power from a few party leaders who hold on to the reactionary capitalist line. The situation now is wonderful and ready for the decisive battle. However, let us take a look at how a few leaders of the Tibet Military Region Headquarters behaved and insisted on the reactionary capitalist line:
>
> 1. Troops representing the Military Region Headquarters had different opinions from those of the Allied Combat Team of the military region [the pro-Gyenlo army group]. . . .
> 3. On the night of 9 February, they used fascist savage ways to treat the Allied Combat Team of the military region. Thirteen revolutionary cadres were illegally detained. (More were detained secretly.) They surrounded about five hundred people of the Allied Combat Team for more than ten hours and did not allow them to study the works of Chairman Mao or use the bathroom. They even attempted to destroy completely the revolutionary rebel corps by taking away their freedom of speech. . . .
> 6. They recently transferred troops from other military regions to Tibet. Why did they do that?
> 7. They ordered troops to collect weapons and ammunition from every big work unit on the afternoon of 9 February. What was the purpose of doing that?
> 8. They suddenly blocked the roads to Lhasa and started to check all the vehicles going in and out of Lhasa. Vehicles were allowed to get into Lhasa but were not allowed to leave.
> 9. They cut communication between our region and the Central Committee. Why?
> 10. The place where the troops are stationed was full of heavily armed soldiers. Why?
>
> Revolutionary comrades, we should rise up to smash all the schemes of the Party Committee of the Military Region Headquarters. [Slogans omitted here.]
>
> *Lhasa Revolutionary Gyenlo Headquarters*
> *Allied Operational Headquarters of the School*
> *of the Department of Transportation*[60]

Despite purging the pro-Gyenlo troops and taking these precautionary moves, the army did not immediately move to take control of the entire city at this moment. Instead, troops first tried peacefully to regain control of the *Tibet Daily,* that is, without having to storm the compound. With approval from the State Council and the Central Military Committee in Beijing, the army began discussions with Gyenlo's leaders about the evacuation of the compound. When Gyenlo resisted this, the army made plans to move on the compound on the morning of 26 February if Gyenlo still hadn't agreed by then. However, Gyenlo complicated matters by calling for its supporters to join them in the compound to help defend it. Many hundreds and perhaps as many as several thousand came. Gyenlo also sought support from Beijing, and, just as the army was preparing to attack, the Gyenlo leaders in the compound were informed that a telegram had arrived from the Central Committee in Beijing, clearly accepting them as a true revolutionary organization. This was a major victory for them, since they felt it meant that the army could not suppress them as counterrevolutionaries. The following comments of the head of Gyenlo in the newspaper compound, though obviously biased, give a glimpse into a revolutionary leader's thinking:

> Well, actually, things were still complicated after we took the power [on 5 February]. The attempt to reseize power, the fighting among the people, and even fighting with weapons, all these problems eventually led to the Central Committee's order to institute military control.
>
> We were simply following the orders of the Central Committee to take power and were not prepared for all the problems. We definitely had no idea [of their military plans] when the Tibet Military Region Headquarters came to take control from us. They had received permission from the Central Committee. I was then in charge of the publishing house and had to negotiate with the army. I told them that we would hand over power if they could show me their orders from the Central Committee. The army, to tell you the truth, favored the other side and deliberately refused my request. It could have been very simple—they show me what they have, and I give them what they want. However, they just didn't do it that way. [Laughs.] Well, I then said, "Fine, I believe that you have the okay from the Central Committee, and we'll get out of here immediately."[61]

However, as will be seen in the following continuation of the narrative, Gyenlo certainly did not agree to leave unconditionally.

Q: When did this happen?
A: It was in 1967, probably on 26 February. . . . [T]he person who negotiated with me was Wei Ke. He was utterly unreasonable. I told him that I believed him, and my men would leave right away. However, it was already too late.

Q. How many people did you have in the publishing house then?
A: About two thousand to three thousand.

Q: In the publishing house?
A: Yes. Well, how should I put it? . . . People came to the publishing house of their own will. They were there to protect the publishing house, to protect the fruit of the Great Cultural Revolution. [Laughs.]

Q: How long had you been there before the negotiations with the army? . . .
A: Well, I was in charge at the publishing house since we took the power. . . . Not that long. About twenty days or maybe just ten days. So it was getting complicated after we took the power. We mainly published information about the Cultural Revolution and some local news of course. We organized people to write for us, and I myself wrote for the paper. We couldn't leave blanks on the paper. [Laughs.] You can imagine, life was pretty hard for us. We had to find people for the Tibetan version of the paper. I don't know Tibetan, but those who were in charge of the Tibetan version always came to me when they had problems. . . . We hired some temporary workers for that. Most of them were Tibetan; a few were Han.

. . . It was on 11 January that we took the power, and the army came on the 26th. After the negotiations, the army did not let us go, and we were kept there till late that night when a telegraph was sent to us from the Central Committee. We had our people in the post office, and they read the telegraph first and then sent it to me. . . . We had a party to celebrate, because the telegraph was addressed clearly to "the revolutionary masses in Lhasa." The telegraph ordered us to establish the "revolutionary three connections" with Zhang Guohua, so we were being addressed as a revolutionary organization. We were very happy at that time, and we even had a parade inside the publishing house. Using the parade as an opportunity, we organized our people and were ready to leave. However, we were stopped. The army literally surrounded us.

It appears that once the telegram arrived, Gyenlo wanted a guarantee from the army that they would treat the faction as revolutionaries and not suppress them. The army, however, apparently did not agree but still wanted to avoid a massacre so surrounded the compound and did not let the Gyenlo people leave. The Gyenlo leader continued the narrative:

They didn't let us leave on 26, 27, 28 [February], 1 March, or on the 2nd. . . . [Finally] [o]n 2 March I said that we shouldn't let it go any further. First of all, [the army] didn't allow us to get food from the outside, and the food stored in the publishing house was limited. I could have only one steamed bun for a whole day. Second, our communications with the outside were cut.

Q: They didn't allow anyone to go out?
A: No, none of us could go out. However, they did allow people to come in, so more and more people gathered at the publishing house. We had

trouble providing food for all the people and couldn't reach any agreement with the army. So I decided on 2 March to surrender myself along with a few other leaders. Then when we went out, we were immediately seized by the army.

Q: Whose order was that?
A: It must have been the Military Region Headquarters. She Banqiao was the army's chief of staff. . . . [W]e knew each other. I thought I could find a way out by communicating with him. However, that guy was swollen with arrogance because he had the order from the Central Military Committee.[62]

When the Gyenlo leaders finally agreed to leave unconditionally, they quickly learned that the army would not treat them as revolutionaries. To the contrary, it immediately detained almost one hundred of the Gyenlo activists. The Gyenlo leader explained:

We went outside and were immediately seized by the army. . . . They had actually assured us that if we left, we would be freed after being searched. [Laughs.]

Q: Nyamdre told you that?
A: No, the army did. They used their loudspeakers. . . . [Instead] [t]hey tied us up, . . . but they couldn't get anything [from me] after half a day's interrogations. They wanted me to say that we were being used by someone "backstage" and to tell them who exactly was using us. It was an easy question, and the answer was "those leaders [in the Regional Party Committee] who follow the capitalist road." [Laughs.] Actually I would have been happy if I could have named some backstage people and then have been set free. I just couldn't do that. Those people I worked with were not my backstage controllers. Most of the time they needed to consult me before making any decisions. [Laughs.] . . . We were first taken to the East Suburb Prison, where we spent about eleven days. Later we were transferred to a detention center. They talked pretty nice, saying, "We'll transfer you to a better place, since the conditions at the East Suburb Prison are terrible." [Laughs.] We were then put in the North Suburb. What they really wanted was more information from us.

Q: How long did you stay in the prison?
A: . . . Seventy-one days . . .

Q: Besides you, how many people were put into prison?
A: I can't recall the exact number now. Probably more than a hundred. The detention center was full. People like me were considered important criminals and should have been kept in private rooms [solitary confinement]. However, it was simply impossible. I shared a room with two other people.

Q: Did they beat you?
A: Not really. . . . There was no solid evidence of our "crimes." . . . They repeated to me that I would be freed if I could name one or two backstage supporters. [Laughs.] We thought at that time that the Central

Committee would rectify this for us. However, we can see now that that was a naive idea.

Before the incident at our publishing house, an incident occurred at the publishing house of the Qinghai Daily, where the army under Zhao Yongfu opened fire and killed more than one hundred people there. We didn't know exactly what happened in Qinghai, but we heard that the army had surrounded the Qinghai Daily. Zeng Yongya [a top leader in the Tibet military region] later teased me, "You were so brave! If the Central Committee had allowed the army to open fire, you would have lost your lives!" [Laughs.] It was Premier Zhou [Enlai] who said that bloody struggles like the one in Qinghai should not be allowed to happen in Tibet. That was why the army didn't fire at us. However, the army did scare people by shouting through their loudspeakers, accusing us of keeping weapons inside the publishing house. After we surrendered, they started to say that we were hiding the weapons in a well. Actually they later found out that we didn't have anything hidden there.[63]

The Tibet military region also received approval from the State Council and the Central Military Committee to implement military control over key offices, such as the Public Security Bureau, the Procuratorial Bureau, and the Tibet People's Broadcasting Station.[64] At the same time the military also arrested many Gyenlo activists. Thus, from the beginning of March 1967, the army gradually established military control offices in Lhasa and in the other main cities and counties in Tibet.

For Gyenlo's leaders, the events of February and March were a stunning and unexpected defeat that led to the desertion of many of its own fighting units. From one thousand members at the start in December 1966, Gyenlo had grown to an organization of more than three hundred combat teams and more than fifteen thousand persons. (They themselves claimed they had thirty-five thousand members.) However, after their loss in February, one after another of the combat units left, and by 1 April they had declined to three thousand people. By contrast, Nyamdre had increased to about thirty-eight thousand members and became the more powerful faction in the continuing conflict between the two.[65]

The extent of the army's repression of Gyenlo at this time can be seen in the written self-confession (dated 5 September 1967) titled "Preliminary Examination of the Mistakes I Made in Supporting the Left" (i.e., Nyamdre), by Yin Fatang, a top army leader and Nyamdre supporter:

> After 5 February, . . . I regarded the contradiction among the people as
> one between the enemy and us. I regarded "Specially Attack," a [Gyenlo]
> revolutionary mass organization that included Red Guards and ordinary

cadres, as a "reactionary organization"[66] and regarded certain revolutionary actions of Gyenlo General Headquarters as "counter-revolutionary
actions of a small handful of persons," thus confounding right and wrong
and black and white.

After 9 February . . . I suppressed and attacked the revolutionary masses
and revolutionary cadres within the Army and placed some good comrades
under arrest. After 26 February, I proceeded with suppression and attacks
outside the Army, banned "Specially Attack," and placed some revolutionary people, revolutionary cadres and revolutionary young fighters under
arrest. They were beaten and thrown into prison. Mentally and physically
they suffered great pains. The "oath-taking" rally held on 5 March put
forward some wrong slogans and made some wrong approaches. In particular, it did not permit Gyenlo Headquarters to attend meetings. These
methods had very bad consequences. Around that time, some wrong notifi-
cations, open letters, and propaganda materials were put up and distributed. As the spearhead was directed against the wrong target, Gyenlo
General Headquarters almost disintegrated. . . . The revolutionary masses
of Gyenlo General Headquarters and the revolutionary cadres supporting
Gyenlo General Headquarters were repressed.

The great "April" directive once again embodied Chairman Mao's
boundless trust and care of the revolutionary masses and revolutionary
young fighters, showed the bearings of the movement, and gave us a chance
to correct our mistakes. But I obstinately adhered to error and failed to
mend my ways. I maintained that the circumstances in Tibet were special,
that the mainstream actions of February and March were good, and that
everything would be all right if some things were corrected. The result was
that the work of vindication [of Gyenlo] was delayed.

Further, for a long time I mistakenly regarded "Rebel General Headquarters" as a mass organization manipulated by the Party capitalist-
roaders in authority. I thought that by calling it a revolutionary mass
organization I would be treating it with favor. It was not until June and
July [1967] that I recognized it as a revolutionary mass organization.[67]

The violent purge of the pro-Gyenlo members in the army is vividly described by one worker in the Military Region Headquarters:

I am an ordinary member of the cultural workers' group in the Tibet
Military Region. . . . After getting up on the morning of 10 February, I
found that the building housing the cultural workers' group was almost
empty, having only a few persons in it. Later in the lavatory I saw many
armed fighters holding rifles and guarding the rear of the assembly hall.
At that time I felt it was quite strange because such a sight had never been
seen in large compounds in the Military Region. Then, when I went over
to the parade ground, it gave me a great shock. There were 72 trucks neatly
parked. Armed troops ready to charge with bayoneted rifles were everywhere in front of the meeting hall as well as on the parade ground. A tight
cordon was posted around the meeting hall.

Not knowing what had happened inside it, I waited outside the hall. Suddenly, out of the main entrance came four fighters pushing and pulling a person who, when I got closer, gave me a fright. The person was none other than Comrade Lan Chikui of our Military Region's combined corps. He was bare-headed with both hands tied behind his back. Then more than ten people rushed up from both sides (they were all members of the head-quarters of defending Mao Zedong's thought), surrounding Comrade Lan Chikui and giving him a savage beating. Some of them pulled his hair, some grabbed him by the neck and some struck his head violently with their pistols. Tens of fists landed on his head like a shower and hit his cheek and back. In a moment blood flowed straight down his face and he became a mass of flesh and blood. His clothes were torn to pieces and his face was swollen out of human shape.[68]

This was the beginning of the deep enmity between Gyenlo and the army that would worsen in the next two years and play a significant role in the Nyemo incident. However, although weakened by the army's action, Gyenlo continued to compete with Nyamdre, and factional fighting did not stop in 1967–68. In Lhasa, the western and northern sections of the city came to be controlled by Gyenlo, whereas the center was mostly controlled by Nyamdre. Normal work and life in Lhasa were literally brought to a standstill.

A Han eyewitness who was the twelve-year-old son of a surgeon at the People's Hospital at this time recalled this period. He had been studying in Chengdu at a school for the children of cadres working in Tibet but was called home by his father when the Cultural Revolution fighting there became too dangerous. He returned to Lhasa in February 1967 and went to school in Lhasa for a month or so before things also became too dangerous in Lhasa. At that time serious fighting was going on between the Gyenlo-held People's Hospital and the Nyamdre-held Potala and the People's Daily Office, which were located, respectively, on the hospital's west and east sides. He recalled:

> The doctors and staff in the hospital couldn't defend themselves from the Nyamdre combat units, which were located on both sides, so they brought lots of Gyenlo fighters from the Large Vehicle Repair Workshop (ch. *da xiu chang*), which was located to the north of the hospital, to come and live in the hospital.
> Nyamdre shot down into the hospital compound from the buildings on the east side of the Potala, and [those at] the People's Daily shot at us from that side. They shot guns and fired homemade cannons. My family and I lived in a single-story building near the Potala side, so when I went out I had to run fast across an open area between my building and the hospital's outer wall, since until I reached the safety of [being close to]

the wall, there was a danger of being hit by gunfire coming down from the Potala.

On one occasion, when Nyamdre was shooting a lot of homemade cannon shells at the hospital, my mother was so afraid that one of them might hit and collapse the roof of our one-story house and injure me that she took me to stay in the three-story out-patient building, which she felt was safer. I had to sleep on a patient examination table on the first floor.[69]

Military control was formalized on 11 May 1967, when the Central Committee established the Tibet Autonomous Region Military Control Commission and appointed Zhang Guohua as director, with Ren Rong and Chen Mingyi as deputy directors.[70] All were strongly anti-Gyenlo.

However, fighting between Gyenlo and Nyamdre continued and actually increased in the second half of 1967. Beginning in 1968, the situation further deteriorated when both factions began to use guns. These were ostensibly stolen from the army, but it appears that in reality supporters in the army turned a blind eye to such "thefts" by revolutionaries, if they didn't actually aid in them. In addition to acquiring the military guns, the factions also started manufacturing bombs and other weapons in their workshops.

Beijing was concerned about the worsening situation in Lhasa and was eager to restore some semblance of calm there so that it could replace the Regional Party Committee with a new form of government that it called a Revolutionary Committee government (tib. *sarje uyön lhengang;* ch. *gemin weiyuanhui*). However, before it could do this, both revolutionary factions not only had to stop the violence but also had to agree to the membership of the new Revolutionary Committee government. Consequently, as early as February 1968, at Beijing's behest, the Military Region Headquarters made an unexpected overture to Gyenlo to this end. A leader in Gyenlo recalled this event:

On 3 February 1968, the Military Region Headquarters decided to form the (Three-Way) Great Revolutionary Alliance (ch. *geming da lianhe*) with us.[71] They came to talk with us, carrying the flag of the army. I was very surprised. I didn't understand why those of the Military Region Headquarters changed their minds in such a short period of time. And even today, I still don't understand this. Maybe history will give me an answer in the future. Of course, they said that they were sincerely supportive of us and that it was we who denied their support. Although I was the general leader of our faction at that time, I was not able to control the situation, and some Red Guards from Beijing made things worse by verbally attacking Yu Zhiquan, the deputy commander of the military region. He was the one talking with us. Vice-Commander Yu, as a military commander, was not good at debating and almost dozed off at the meeting. Finally, the army men got up and angrily left the meeting, saying that we had humiliated the flag of the army. I didn't understand why they felt that. However, I knew that things were getting worse, for it was very rare to see the army men come out with their flag and then have the negotiation that day turn out to be such a failure.[72]

As a result of this debacle, Beijing acted quickly and summoned the top leaders of Gyenlo and Nyamdre to Beijing at the end of February for a "study class," again to end the factional violence. More than three hundred cadres attended, including top leaders such as Tao Changsong of Gyenlo, Liu Shaoming of Nyamdre, and Ren Rong of the military region.[73]

The rationale that leaders in Beijing presented to the delegates was simple. Times have changed, they said. At the beginning of the Great Cultural Revolution, everyone rose up to revolt against the capitalist-roaders, but since that time the capitalist-roaders have been exposed. Now is the time to establish revolutionary committees, which are the true tool for creating the dictatorship of the proletariat. Consequently, any further factional conflict would only serve to decentralize revolutionary power and weaken this effort as well as negatively impact Tibet's war readiness (against India). Thus, the assembled delegates were told that they had to agree to end factionalism, because if it were to continue, the revolution itself would be crippled.[74] However, achieving such an agreement meant bringing about a new positive relationship not only between the two revolutionary factions but also among them, the army, and the cadres. In particular, it meant establishing some agreement about who would hold what positions in the new revolutionary committee of the Tibet Autonomous Region.

On 5 May, Zhang Guohua, who was in Beijing, met with the representatives of Gyenlo and Nyamdre and told them that Zhou Enlai had just phoned, instructing that the delegates must send a report on the establishment of the new revolutionary committee within the next two weeks.[75] However, even pressure from this level did not work, because the two factions could not agree to compromise on this committee's membership.

A month later, there was still no agreement, so on 6 June 1968, China's top leaders, including Zhou Enlai, Jiang Qing, Chen Boda, and Kang Sheng, interviewed the top party committee members of the military region (Ren Rong, Chen Mingyi, Zeng Yongya, Wang Chenghan, Lu Yishan, Liao Buyun, and Yin Fatang) along with others in the Regional Party Committee, instructing them to come to an agreement about the formation of the new revolutionary committee. Their comments were the same as those that Zhang Guohua had made to the representatives of the mass organizations, but they pointedly added that the army should not have been engaged in "supporting one faction and suppressing the other faction."[76]

However, despite Beijing's continued pressure to push the representatives to reach an agreement in Beijing, the violent struggle continued in Lhasa throughout the first half of 1968. Gyenlo at this time also pushed to increase its strength outside Lhasa, where the PLA, which they felt tacitly supported Nyamdre, was not stationed in force. As a result, Gyenlo sought to proselytize in the countryside to increase its numbers and power. As we shall see, Nyemo was one of the counties where Gyenlo's local leaders made a major attempt to increase its manpower and political control.

In the midst of both the chaotic revolutionary violence in Lhasa and the still ongoing study class in Beijing, a signal event took place on 7 June, the day after China's leaders stated that the PLA should not have supported one faction and suppressed the other. In a major breach of the army's neutrality, two Gyenlo strongholds in Lhasa—the Jokhang Temple, in the heart of Lhasa, and the Financial Compound (ch. *caijing dayuan*), near Gyenlo General Headquarters—were attacked by armed PLA troops.

At this time, Gyenlo activists physically occupied the top floor of the Jokhang Temple and had set up loudspeakers on the roof, making it a major platform for Gyenlo propaganda. The Financial Compound also had loudspeakers on its roof. The stream of derogatory and insulting broadcasts emanating from them infuriated Nyamdre and the army, who on 7 June launched a major military strike against both strongholds.

The Financial Compound was chosen as the site of the first army attack because of its strategic position, as one of the PLA commanders involved in the attack explained:

> Before the incident of 7 June, Ding Yongtai told one of his trusted subordinates, "The Financial Compound is the transportation key spot of Gyenlo Headquarters. From there, they can go east to the second command office of Gyenlo, go north to the general office of Gyenlo Headquarters and to the suburbs, and they can also go to the installment team and the experimental primary school. The communications among those units is through the Financial Compound. If the Financial Compound can be captured, Gyenlo Headquarters will be isolated in Lhasa."[77]

The actual plan of attack was originally based on deceit. Gyenlo Headquarters was to be sent a letter saying several trucks were coming to deliver food, but when the trucks arrived and Gyenlo opened the gate to receive the food, three companies of the 159th Regiment would rush into the compound. If this ruse did not work, the troops were under orders to tear down the compound's walls.[78]

The attack, however, was unsuccessful in spite of the plans. The following report on the incident details the failure:

> The soldiers first broke down the door and tore down the wall around the Financial Compound. They entered from different directions and started to beat members of the Gyenlo Headquarters with wooden sticks and gun butts.
>
> Soldiers of the Ninth Company of the 136th Regiment were responsible for capturing the west blockhouse. Soldiers of the First Battalion of the 159th Regiment and the First Company of the 305th Regiment were added to help them. The 136th Regiment started the main attack while the other two companies blocked the masses from coming to join them [Gyenlo]. However, they could not capture the west blockhouse.
>
> Shi Banjiao [the top military commander] then ordered Wu Zhihai, the commander of the troops attacking the west blockhouse, to add two squads from the Second Battalion of the 159th Regiment to the fight. These soldiers used implements such as shovels to dig out the doors and windows of the west blockhouse, trying to enter by force. At about noon, when Shi Banjiao called Ding Yongtai asking about the situation at the west blockhouse, Ding said, "The attack at the west blockhouse has not seen any progress yet, and the scaling ladders were all taken by the Gyenlo followers." Shi Banjiao told Ding, "You seemed like a capable guy, but now you are useless. I put so many soldiers under your control, and you are saying that you cannot get the blockhouse for me." Shi Banjiao then led an armed platoon of the 138th Regiment to the west blockhouse and started to command the attack himself. [However] [l]ater that day, he was captured by the Gyenlo defenders.[79]

A twenty-five-year-old Tibetan PLA soldier who was among those eventually captured by Gyenlo recalled what to him seemed like the "fog of war" that day:

> [The worst incident was] the fight at the Financial Compound. At this time the military headquarters tricked us. . . . They told us to take guns and go to the Financial Compound to fight with some bad elements who were there. . . . When we got there, [Gyenlo] severely beat us up, and we were unable to fire one shot.
>
> Q: *What happened?*
>
> A: After we got there, they [the military headquarters] ordered us to prepare to shoot. We did this, but the order to open fire never came. At this time the deputy chief of staff (ch. *fu canmouzhang*) was captured by Gyenlo. . . . We learned of this, and that's why we were sent to attack the Financial Compound. When we arrived there, the company commander

(ch. *lianzhang*) was also seized by Gyenlo. And they seized several Tibetan soldiers [including me]. I had a machine gun, which they took and beat me severely. I also had three hundred bullets, which they stole. They ripped my clothes off and left me completely naked. Then they took us to the Military Control Commission Office (ch. *jun guan hui*) within the Financial Compound. Actually the Military Control Commission was supposed to stop outbreaks of fighting within the unit. We lost our guns and were taken [into custody], as were our officers. . . . A fat Chinese was there. He said, "Don't seize the common soldiers, just the officers."

Q: Was it Gyenlo who seized you?
A: Yes, it was Gyenlo. That afternoon I didn't know how the battle at the Tsuglagang (Jokhang) had gone. I had been kicked a lot and was unable to walk well. They were not afraid to do this, even though we were soldiers. Then they suddenly said to us, "You lost your guns; now go back."

Q: How many soldiers were there [captured]?
A: More than ten soldiers. All our guns were taken. There were several Tibetans in our group. . . . [We were captured because] [a]fter we arrived there, we were ordered to lie prone on the ground. Then when the Gyenlo people came running toward us, we never got the order to fire. We just continued to lie there. If we had made our own decision to fire and if people had been killed, it wouldn't have been good. So the Gyenlo people grabbed our guns and beat us and took us into custody. That afternoon they told us to go, and we left. . . . They sent us back to the military garrison. At the garrison, they asked us where our guns were. When I said they took our guns, the team leader (ch. *duizhang*) had us all stand in a line and said to me, "You lost the People's Liberation Army's weapons." And then he slapped my face and kicked me. There was nothing I could do but stand there. Then he asked us who stole the guns? I said the revolutionary masses stole them. Then he beat me again because I used the term revolutionary masses.

Q: You weren't allowed to say that?
A: At this time we couldn't call the factions bad people, only revolutionary masses, so I used that term. [But he got angry because I didn't say bad people had stolen our guns.]

They confined all of us who had lost our weapons to the base. They said, "You can't go outside. If you have work, you have to ask permission to leave." Then one day the military headquarters held a big meeting. They told us to come. I was very afraid, because I thought they would put me in prison or execute me. However, they gave us new uniforms to put on, and we went. At the meeting they read my name first to stand up. At that moment I thought I would be executed. However, the officers were nice to us. The officer who slapped me now apologized and said, "Don't be angry with me for slapping you." Really, it isn't permitted for an officer to slap an "enlisted" soldier in the army.

Q: Were you very afraid?
A: There was nothing I could do. I had already lost the gun. So I went up

to the platform and was told to sit on the front of the platform facing the audience. Then they praised me a lot. They said, "You suffered a lot of beatings but didn't fire your weapons. You are really brave men."[80]

On that same day, later in the afternoon, the more famous of the two army attacks occurred at the Jokhang (ch. *dazhao*) Temple. A detailed account of the battle follows:

Tang Shengying then gave the soldiers of the Fifth Company a case of bullets and six rocket shells, and Ding Yongtai encouraged them to occupy the commanding spots of the Dazhao Temple and seize the weapons that the masses of Gyenlo's Fourth Headquarters were keeping there. Soldiers of the Fifth Company then ran [from the Financial Compound] to the Dazhao Temple, ready to start the fight against the Fourth Headquarters of Gyenlo.

. . . The Third Machine Gun Company and the Eighth Company went to the third floor from the connecting bridge in the north. One group of the Second Machine Gun Company and the Seventh Company took the stairs in the northeast corner to the top of the third floor. The military signal was "two whistles." Five veterans guarded the stairs and the door to the second floor. The Fourth Company guarded the door of the Dazhao Temple. The Second Platoon was the backup force. Soldiers were told to tie a piece of white cloth or a white towel to their right arms in order to look different from the masses.

At 6:30 P.M., the soldiers started the fight. Before they started, the commander of the Third Platoon, Shao Guoqing, gave a brief speech. He said, "We have to capture the weapons the masses of Gyenlo Headquarters are keeping, but do not fire without my command. When the fight begins, we will try to assemble at the southwest corner. Do not fire submachine guns from a long distance. You can use machine guns, but do not use more than ten bullets."

The soldiers set off with their bayonets attached and pointing outward. They shouted, "Kill! Kill!" [and] "Lay down your guns and we will spare your lives." At that time more than sixty persons from Gyenlo's Fourth Headquarters were having dinner and studying in the corridor.

All these people, with the exception of one person who was at the broadcast station, stood up when they heard the noise. They surrounded the armed soldiers, some of them waving the red book, some holding rakes. They shouted, "Long live Chairman Mao! Long live the Communist Party!" A few people pointed to their chests, shouting bravely, "Shoot me. Shoot me."

The person at the broadcast unit then started broadcasting "Emergency! Emergency!" through the loudspeakers. Hearing that, the commander of the Third Platoon jumped to the platform and fired two shots into the air. The soldiers of each platoon then started to shoot at the members of Gyenlo Headquarters on the third and fourth floors with semiautomatic rifles, submachine guns, and cannons. Some soldiers of the

Second Platoon went upstairs and shot from there into the revolutionary masses. Five veterans shot at the loudspeakers on the fourth floor.

The gun battle lasted about two minutes. Three loudspeakers were destroyed, and sixty people of Gyenlo were killed or injured. Six soldiers were also killed or injured. More than one thousand bullets and nine hand grenades were used by the soldiers. The soldiers captured one semiautomatic rifle and some guns and hand grenades from the masses.[81]

A Gyenlo member who was just outside the Jokhang saw the attack start and remembered:

> Those people went inside the Jokhang through the Shingra entrance, the place that was used for keeping firewood during the Mönlam Festival. Before that, the woman who was broadcasting from the roof of the Jokhang was shouting, "This is the red rebellion broadcast station (ch. *hongse zaofan guangbo zhan*)." . . . After those people went inside the Jokhang, no voice came from the broadcast station. Probably, they seized that woman.
>
> At that point, I didn't dare to go inside. Some people who had gone inside were saying, "You shouldn't go inside, because when we went inside the people in the Jokhang had burned lice insecticide (tib. *shigmen*), and we felt that we were almost going to die from the fumes." So I didn't go inside, and I didn't see anything. Then I went home.[82]

Another Gyenlo fighter who was part of the group in the Jokhang recalled:

> I was not in the Jokhang that morning. It was a fortunate coincidence that I had gone home. Otherwise I would have been killed. I heard that the soldiers climbed up to the temple of Lhamo and first shot a gun into the sky. Then they started shooting machine guns.
>
> At that point, a girl called Tshamla was shot in the forehead, with the bullet coming out of the back of her head. And there was a boy called Sonam. First his leg was shot, and he fell down. Then the soldiers stabbed him with their bayonets. I had a friend called Kejöla; he was shot twelve or thirteen times. His whole body was riddled with bullets. All together, they killed twelve people in the Jokhang. Then the rest of the people were locked up in the Shingra that night. . . .
>
> The next morning, the rest of the people [who had been injured from beatings with rifle butts] were made to pull a cart and take away the corpses.[83]

The attack also involved Nyamdre fighters, one of whom recalled that the Nyamdre side also fought with insecticides:

> At that time, they gave us the powder for killing lice. . . . [W]e were staying in the compound of the People's Government (ch. *renmin weiyuanhui*) of the Autonomous Region. We were not in our work unit. In those days there was a broadcast station in the Jokhang that was said to be very powerful. So probably they told us that we had to take over that broadcast station.

We were given only the powder for killing lice. We didn't have other weapons. The insecticide was put in plastic. I remember I put that in my pocket. That night, when we climbed up a ladder, they [people in the Jokhang] stoned us. It was just like in the movies of the [early] Chinese Empire, where the people were stoned when they climbed up ladders to scale the walls of a fortress. That night . . . a lot of people were there. They climbed up to the place where the broadcast set was located. I reached the place where the loudspeaker was set up.

There were not many people from Gyenlo. They were hiding, covering their heads with their hands. Some people threw the insecticide at those who were hiding. I told somebody, "Don't throw that at the people who are not doing anything. Why are you throwing that at those people? You have to throw it at the people who are fighting."

I just threw some insecticide [at the people who were throwing stones at us] when I was climbing up. Otherwise, I didn't get any chance to throw it. I thought it would be useless to throw it at the people who were hiding.

Later, Nyamdre seized those [Gyenlo] people and brought them down. I didn't know where they took them. There were men and women; there were not many people. At that point Nyamdre had many more people.

Q: How many hours did they fight?
A: They didn't fight very long. After we gathered together and were brought to the Jokhang, we had to wait in the courtyard (tib. *khyamra*) for about an hour or half an hour. After that we started to climbed the upstairs. The [Gyenlo] people who were on the roof of Jokhang were all seized. Later, we went back to the People's Government compound.[84]

These attacks on the Financial Compound and the Jokhang resulted in the death of 12 Gyenlo activists, the serious wounding of 13, and less serious injury to another 361. Two soldiers were killed, nine were seriously wounded, and six only slightly injured.[85]

One of the heads of Gyenlo talked about the reasons for the attack as well as his role in it:

The army was not happy after the 18 January armed struggle,[86] in which they failed, and the 3 February [failed army negotiations]. And they considered our attacks on Zhang Guohua as the worst offense, so [I felt] they would seek revenge sooner or later. And they also had failed in other armed struggles, because our side had many workers who were a powerful force in armed struggles. Although [the army] had weapons, they still couldn't win. You know, sometimes during the fighting their weapons might end up in our hands. [Laughs.] And as I told you, our factories also made weapons. So finally the army decided to do it [attack us], although they still used the name of the Central Committee. At the Jokhang Temple, the broadcast station . . . [t]hey could have just taken the power from us, so why should they shoot at us? At the Jokhang Temple, if I'm not mistaken they killed ten of us. Some of those were shot at the stomach, some in the head, and ten died right away. A few others were injured.

Q: Why did they want to take over power at the Jokhang?

A: . . . [T]hey said they were there to "take over military control." . . . Of course, they didn't like our broadcast station there. They shot at us without hesitation, not just at the Jokhang Temple, but also at the Financial Compound. I was in Beijing then [attending the study class], and Liu Shiyi phoned me immediately when this happened.[87] He asked me what we should do. I stayed cool when hearing this. I said, "Don't fight back. Let them shoot." I knew things would be even worse if we fought back. So I told Liu to let the army shoot and that it didn't matter how many people we lost. Therefore, we lost ten people at the Jokhang Temple and two at the Financial Compound; there was a path linking the Financial Compound to the Second Guest House [the main headquarters of Gyenlo], and the two were killed there. Many others were injured. Ai Xuehua, a photographer, was trying to take pictures as evidence during the shooting and was shot at the back. He didn't die but was paralyzed. . . .

The reason why this happened was that the other faction [Nyamdre] had been losing the game time and time again, and the army decided to help them. Anyhow . . . , we were proud that we properly dealt with the incident. Of course, some of us were very upset when this happened and were ready to fight against the army. I knew it was not right. A few people even suggested bombing the electricity factory in the northern suburb to leave the whole city of Lhasa in darkness. I said that was even more ridiculous, and we couldn't do it. Liu Shiyi was very nervous when he phoned me and couldn't even talk in complete sentences. After talking with Liu Shiyi over the phone, I said to the military leaders at the study class that it was not right for them to kill our people. Those leaders pretended not to know anything about it.[88]

This attack clearly showed Gyenlo Headquarters that the army was now openly siding with Nyamdre, and, of course, it also put the Gyenlo faction on the defensive. Gyenlo, already at a disadvantage because it possessed fewer guns than its rival, was outraged by this blatant breach of rules by the army, which was supposed to maintain a neutral stance in revolutionary factional disputes, not shoot and bayonet members of the revolutionary masses. The already existing anger and enmity Gyenlo felt toward Nyamdre, the Regional Party Committee, and the army leadership now soared exponentially. However, despite the defeat, Gyenlo's spirit was not broken, and its members became even more determined to fight back as best they could against their enemies.

Ironically, a few days after the killings, on 12 June 1968, an agreement between the factions was actually signed in Beijing by the participating delegates, who were still there at the study class. In theory the agreement ended the factional conflict, saying, "Both sides guarantee that [henceforth] there will be no violence of any kind. Shooting guns and cannons will cease, and in the future both sides must not instigate violence or participate in violence on any pretext."[89]

However, not surprisingly, the agreement was ignored once the Gyenlo leaders returned to Lhasa. In the ensuing months, the situation in Lhasa worsened substantially, and the central government convened another meeting in Beijing in late August 1968, at which the leaders of Gyenlo and Nyamdre were to meet the very top leaders of the central government and the Central Great Cultural Revolution Group, resolve the factional conflict, and agree to work together under the new Revolutionary Committee.[90] On 26 August in Beijing, the top leaders questioned the Gyenlo and Nyamdre representatives closely, and Premier Zhou Enlai tried to mollify Gyenlo by saying, "It was wrong to send in the army on 7 June. It was not approved by the Central Committee, and the Standing Committee of the Military Region has admitted its mistake."[91] At the same meeting, a strong self-criticism written by the Party Committee of the Tibet Military Region was passed out, and the Gyenlo and Nyamdre representatives were told to read it overnight and discuss it the next morning.[92] Addressed to the top leaders in China, it is a remarkably frank statement intended to placate Gyenlo, illustrating how intently Beijing wanted to settle the conflict.

THE WRITTEN SELF-CRITICISM ON THE MISTAKES MADE
BY THE STANDING COMMITTEE OF THE PARTY COMMITTEE OF
THE TIBET MILITARY REGION REGARDING THE WORK OF
SUPPORTING THE LEFT

To: Chairman Mao, Vice-Chairman Lin, the Central Committee, the Central Military Commission, and the Central Great Cultural Revolution Group:

First, we wish that our great esteemed and beloved Chairman Mao lives forever. We also wish that Chairman Mao's intimate comrade-in-arms, deputy general, and vice-chairman Lin stays healthy all the time.

At the key time of seizing the all-round success of the Great Proletarian Cultural Revolution, the leaders of the central government decided to invite the representatives of the two organizations of the revolutionary masses and the leading local cadres and cadres of the army to Beijing to study the thought of Chairman Mao. During the time of this study, our great leader Chairman Mao and Vice-Chairman Lin interviewed us several times.

This was the best care, the best education, the greatest encouragement, and the deepest motivation that Chairman Mao and Vice-Chairman Lin gave us. It was also our greatest honor and happiness. The leading cadres of the central government separately interviewed the representatives of the cadres of the troops and the Standing Committee of the Tibet Military Region four times, on 18 September last year, and on 6 June, 17 August, and 26 August this year. And they gave very important instructions to us. They gave us a very profound education. And they gave us great encouragement. They further defined our orientation, made us recognize our mistakes, and strengthened our beliefs.

Since we joined the local Great Proletarian Cultural Revolution, our PLA who are stationed in Tibet did a lot of work in the campaign of the "three supports" and "two troops," using the guidance of Chairman Mao's revolutionary line and the wise leadership and intimate care given by Chairman Mao, Vice-Chairman Lin, the Central Committee, the Central Military Commission, and the Central Great Cultural Revolution Group and the vigorous support and help of the broad revolutionary masses and the revolutionary young militants and cadres. We complied with the great leader Chairman Mao's call to fight, which was, "The PLA should support the masses of the left."

However, we still made a lot of mistakes in the work of supporting the left, because the members of our Standing Committee of the Party Committee of the Tibet Military Region did not fully understand the revolutionary line of Chairman Mao and did not carry it out completely. The main mistakes we made were that we *"supported one group and suppressed the other group"* and *"were close to one group and estranged from the other group."*

At the end of January last year [1967], during the time we joined the local Great Proletarian Cultural Revolution, it was also the critical moment that the Great Proletarian Cultural Revolution entered the stage of seizing the power. The masses were mobilized. The situation was good. However, because we were lacking in mental preparation for this Great Proletarian Cultural Revolution, we could not correctly deal with the masses. We could not distinguish the main current of the movement. We made wrong analyses of the situation. We confused two different kinds of contradictions. We mistakenly regarded the revolutionary mass organization Gyenlo Headquarters as the bad organization controlled by "a handful of counterrevolutionary elements." We severely attacked and suppressed this organization. We arrested and interned some persons in charge, some members of the revolutionary masses, some revolutionary young militants, and revolutionary cadres of this organization. Some of them were suppressed as "counterrevolutionary elements." We seriously dampened their revolutionary enthusiasm. At the same time, we made a series of mistakes in propagandizing inside and outside the army. We also put political labels on this organization, such as "antiparty, antisocialism, and anti–Mao Zedong thought."

We did wrong deeds that were meant to disintegrate this organization. The revolutionary masses of Gyenlo Headquarters were severely hurt politically. Gyenlo Headquarters almost disintegrated. The most serious thing we did was that we also prepared for a second attack. We tried to ban several fighting teams of Gyenlo Headquarters. We tried to arrest and intern more people. Our real purpose was to suppress Gyenlo Headquarters completely.

In February last year, during the time that the organs of the military region further developed "the four basic elements," we did not trust the masses and had fears, so we mistakenly regarded the combat teams as bad organizations, and we attacked them. On 9 February, when the combat team attacked the Military Region [Headquarters], we mistakenly thought that the combat teams inside the army and outside colluded with each other. We thought they wanted to usurp the power and were trying to rebel. Under the influence of this wrong thinking, we sent a force to surround the revolutionary masses of the combat team, who were holding a rally at that time. We arrested some revolutionary comrades under the charge of being "reactionary and bad elements." We made a series of wrong propaganda pronouncements. We held a so-called investigation and an exhibition of "evidences of a crime." We also prepared to convict the combat team as a "reactionary organization." In politics, we severely struck at the revolutionary masses of the combat team. They were discriminated against for a long time, in both their work and their lives.

In general, during February and March last year, we directed the spearhead at Gyenlo Headquarters and the revolutionary masses of the combat team among the troops. We violated the revolutionary line of Chairman Mao and made a mistake of orientation. We sidetracked the Great Cultural Revolution in the Tibet Region. We damaged the Great Cultural Revolution. We were a bad influence.

Chairman Mao has taught us, "If you make a mistake, you should admit it without any hesitation. You should correct your mistake as soon as possible. The more completely you correct it, the better it will be. You cannot be bashful and hesitate. Furthermore, you cannot persist in your mistake and make more mistakes." After the instruction of 1 April by the Central Committee and the assignment of the "ten items" by the Central Military Commission, we should have corrected our mistakes quickly and completely. However, because we were self-assuming and opinionated, we did not analyze and inspect the mistakes.

We always thought that our mistakes were not so serious and always forgave ourselves. So it was only very late when we recognized our mistakes. We corrected them slowly and wrote a self-criticism very late because of our poor consciousness. We did not rehabilitate the revolutionary comrades who were arrested and interned. We let them be discriminated against in politics, in their work, and in their lives. Our attitude toward the comrades of Gyenlo Headquarters and the combat team did not change for a long time. We did not give them enough support in their revolutionary movement. We could not accept their correct opinions. We underestimated their contributions, and we overemphasized their problems. We violated Chairman Mao's instructions on how to deal correctly with the masses. We seldom approached the revolutionary masses of Gyenlo Headquarters and the combat team. We estranged them, and the relationship between them and us was always very tense.

On 7 June this year, we put pressure on the revolutionary masses of Gyenlo Headquarters again. We mistakenly sent troops to the Financial Compound, where the Eleventh Headquarters of Gyenlo General Headquarters was stationed. We occupied the west blockhouse by force. We published the open letter and announced the proclamation of martial law. And we made the conflict between the revolutionary masses of Gyenlo Headquarters and us worse than before. As a result, the serious bloody incident happened. Some branches of the troops opened fire and killed and injured some members of the revolutionary masses of Gyenlo Headquarters. This deviated from the revolutionary line of Chairman Mao, violated the glorious tradition of our troops, worsened the relationship between the soldiers and the masses, disturbed the great strategic plan of Chairman Mao, and postponed the foundation of the Revolutionary Committee in the Tibet Autonomous Region. It had a very bad influence on the masses. We seriously damaged the Great Proletarian Cultural Revolution. We feel distressed about this, especially since this incident happened after receiving the new instructions of Chairman Mao, who said, "Whether to protect or to suppress the broad masses is the basic difference between the proletariat and the Guomindang. It is the basic difference between the dictatorship of the proletariat and the dictatorship of the Guomindang." So this mistake was really serious.

The [Jokhang] incident of 7 June did not happen by chance. It was our fault that it happened. It completely exposed our uncorrected mistakes of supporting one group and suppressing the other and being close to one group and estranged from the other. It completely exposed our lack of discipline. It happened because we did not correctly deal with the revolutionary masses of Gyenlo Headquarters. It was also the consequence of our failure to fulfill the instructions concerning the struggles between two lines in the troops. After the incident of 7 June happened, we did not recognize the gravity of our mistake. We did not deal with it very seriously. And that was more serious. . . . We, the leaders of the Military Region are responsible for the mistakes above. The broad commanders and soldiers have no responsibility.

The main reason we made mistakes in the work of supporting the left is that we did not grasp the essence of the works written by Chairman Mao. And we did not apply them very well. We did not understand well the revolutionary line of Chairman Mao. And we did not adhere to the important instructions of Chairman Mao, the Central Committee, and the Central Cultural Revolution Group. We thought that the 26 February telegram sent by the Central Cultural Revolution Group to Gyenlo Headquarters was just a telegram to the revolutionary masses and did not pay attention and study it. Consequently, we did not correct our mistakes in time. We did not learn well about the important instructions, such as [those issued on] 18 September last year and 6 June this year by the leaders of the Central Committee and the Central Cultural Revolution Group. We did not understand them completely and did not implement them well. In addition, we were not united in our understanding of these documents.

We did not recognize that some of the comrades of Gyenlo Headquarters were still oppressed. Some comrades did not admit that Gyenlo Headquarters was still oppressed after the instructions of 18 September were given. So the mistake of supporting one group and suppressing the other group and approaching one group and estranging the other were not corrected. This is evidence that we were not loyal to the proletarian headquarters led by Chairman Mao and Vice-Chairman Lin.

Chairman Mao had instructed us, "We should trust the masses. We should depend on the masses. We should respect the creative initiative of the masses. We should go all out to mobilize the masses. We should let the masses rise to revolution by themselves. Let them educate themselves. Let them manage themselves. Let them emancipate themselves." We deviated from this instruction of Chairman Mao.

Our attitude toward the masses was not appropriate. We were always afraid of many things. We did not trust the masses. And we even attacked and suppressed the revolutionary masses. We made big mistakes regarding our attitude toward the masses. As to fighting the enemies, our sense of their situation was not well developed. In some problems we dropped our guard. In our thought we were self-assuming and lacked self-criticism. We did not accept the criticism of the masses. We had serious bureaucracy in our leadership. We were far away from the masses and seldom communicated with them. We dealt with the problems according to old standards and rules. In the final analysis, the main reason we made mistakes was that we did not handle affairs according to the instructions of Chairman Mao and violated the revolutionary line of Chairman Mao. This was evidence that we were not loyal to Chairman Mao.

Our mistake is serious. The lesson is heavy. We did not accomplish the honorable mission given us by Chairman Mao. We are unworthy of the instruction and trust of our great leaders Chairman Mao and Vice-Chairman Lin. And we disappointed the trust and the expectations of the broad revolutionary masses. We are very sorry about that. We apologize to Chairman Mao and Vice-Chairman Lin. We apologize to the Central Committee and the Central Cultural Revolution Group. We apologize to all revolutionary masses.

Complying with the instructions of Chairman Mao to "correct a mistake when you make it, and the more quickly and more completely you correct it, the better it will be," we make a promise that we will completely rehabilitate the revolutionary masses, the revolutionary young militants, and the revolutionary cadres. To those revolutionary organizations that we oppressed and attacked, we apologize. We have decided to comply with the instructions of Chairman Mao. We have decided to obey the series of new instructions from Chairman Mao and [those] from 18 September last year and 6 June, 17 August, and 26 August this year issued by the leaders of the Central Committee and the Central Cultural Revolution Group. We have decided to completely correct the mistake of supporting one group and suppressing the other group and approaching one group and estranging the other group. And we welcome criticism from the revolutionary masses.

In our future work of supporting the left, we will obey the thought
of Chairman Mao. We will work hard on the writings of Chairman Mao.
We will regard "fight privatization, criticize revisionism" as our principle.
We will try our best to run study classes on the thought of Chairman
Mao. We will study hard and fulfill the new instructions of Chairman
Mao. We will adhere to the great strategic plan of Chairman Mao. We
will support and protect our broad revolutionary masses with our enthusi-
asm. We will correctly deal with the two revolutionary mass organizations
in Tibet. We will further persist in developing revolutionary criticism. We
will completely criticize a handful of capitalist-roaders in the Communist
Party and their deputies, such as Zhou Renshan, Wang Qimei, and so on.
We will deeply criticize them and fight them. We will clean the class ranks.
We will uncover all the rebels, spies, and counterrevolutionary elements. We
will attack all the class enemies steadily, accurately, and severely. We will
uphold the movement of "support the army and love the people" more
extensively to strengthen the solidarity between the army and the people
and the solidarity among the nationalities. We will strengthen the instructions about the struggles between the [political] lines within the troops
to try to heighten the sense of the discipline among them. We will try to
enhance the solidarity inside the army. We will try to "manage revolution,
promote production, advance work, and promote combat readiness." We
will smash the damage done by class enemies and their provocation both
inside and outside our country.

At this time, the Great Proletarian Cultural Revolution is in good shape
all over our country. The situation in Tibet is good. We have decided to
unite with one another more intensely around the proletarian headquarters
led by Chairman Mao and Vice-Chairman Lin. We will unify our thoughts,
steps, and behavior with the leadership of the proletarian headquarters.
We will completely criticize the schism of right-deviation. We oppose the
bad behavior of complying in public but opposing in private. We will try
to achieve new success regarding the work of founding a revolutionary
committee in the Tibet Autonomous Region and achieve complete success
in the Great Proletarian Cultural Revolution.

*The Standing Committee of the Party Committee
of the Tibet Region Military Headquarters*

27 August 1968[93]

With this statement in hand, the Gyenlo leaders in Beijing had no choice
but to say they would end the fighting and agree to the membership composition of the Revolutionary Committee. Consequently, on 5 September 1968, the TAR's Revolutionary Committee was formally established,
with both factions and the army agreeing to cease all fighting.[94]

However, in Lhasa, the animosity still ran deep, and the conflict did
not end. One Nyamdre delegate and his wife recalled what happened
when they returned to Lhasa from Beijing:

Husband: After we returned [from Beijing] they said there should be no factions and ideologies. . . . We went to speak to the members of Nyamdre and Gyenlo. I said you must come together, and we told them about the instructions from the leaders in Beijing. . . . We went from Beijing to Lhasa by airplane. When we arrived in Lhasa many people from both factions were waiting to welcome us back. They took us immediately to the military headquarters. I didn't even go home first. However, after we entered the gate of the military headquarters, the two factions started fighting.

Wife: It couldn't be stopped. When they [the delegates] first came back to Lhasa, [representatives from] all the offices and the masses were sent to welcome them in front of the Potala. We got up early to go, but they didn't arrive until noon. So we waited. Nyamdre and Gyenlo sat separately, singing songs back and forth, each side trying to sing more loudly than the other. The offices brought along drums and cymbals, and the two factions put their drums and cymbals together and banged them loudly. They [the delegates from Beijing] arrived at noon. We welcomed them, and then they left. At the time, the two factions were supposed to leave and go back to their factories. But they [the delegates] weren't even in the military head-quarters when we started fighting. People took the flags and put them on their waists and starting fighting with the flag poles.[95]

At the same time, in rural counties like Nyemo, the factional conflict escalated when Gyenlo, outnumbered in Lhasa, moved to gain control of the countryside, where only a few troops were stationed.[96] In chapter 2, the plans to mobilize the Nyemo peasant masses in 1968 are examined.

Gyenlo and Nyamdre
in Nyemo County

While Gyenlo and Nyamdre were competing for control of offices and other workplaces in Lhasa, branches of both factions proliferated in other counties and prefectures throughout Tibet. In Nyemo, most of the leading Tibetan and Chinese cadres belonged to Nyamdre, and the overwhelming majority of villagers followed their lead, clearly making it the dominant revolutionary group. As in Lhasa, each faction, although passionately disagreeing about the other's approach, actively carried out the core Cultural Revolutionary campaigns, such as destroying the "four olds" and holding struggle sessions against class enemies. One young lama from Nyemo whose family had served as managers for the estate of an aristocrat,[1] recalled his family's persecution from both factions:

> We suffered lots of difficulties during the Cultural Revolution, especially from Gyenlo, since many of its leaders in the past were our servants . . . so they treated us very badly. . . . If Nyamdre told us to do work they would tell us to do very heavy labor, such as cutting firewood . . . and then in the evening they would beat us harshly [at struggle sessions]. Then the next day, Gyenlo would order us to do some hard work for them, such as harvesting, and in the evening they too would beat us. We had to work for both Gyenlo and Nyamdre [whenever they ordered us], but neither of them gave us food or wages. . . . When we were being beaten by Nyamdre, they said we were supporting Gyenlo, and when Gyenlo was beating us, they said we were supporting Nyamdre.[2]

As the competition for power between Gyenlo and Nyamdre intensified in Lhasa, it did also in Nyemo, where Gyenlo Headquarters made a conscious decision not just to carry out the core Cultural Revolution campaigns, as mentioned above, but also to mount a campaign to displace Nyamdre from its position of control in the county. Gyenlo, in a word, set out to take control of Nyemo County itself.

To do this Gyenlo's leaders understood they would have to convince large numbers of rural Tibetans to switch allegiance, join their organization, and fight for them. Since this would mean persuading villagers to go against the authorities in power, mobilizing them would not be easy. However, at that time (in late 1967 and early 1968), Gyenlo had something critical working in its favor: the countryside was rife with anger and apprehension stemming from the way that the Democratic Reforms (tib. *mangdzö jügyur;* ch. *minzhu gaige*) were playing out.

Democratic Reforms was the term used by the Communist Party for the set of interlocking reforms that were implemented in Tibet in 1959 to begin the transformation of the "old" society into a new socialist system. These involved creating a new social hierarchy in which the "poor" were now valorized while the former elites, such as lords, estate managers, headmen, and monastic leaders, were vilified and persecuted as class enemies. In this new hierarchy, individuals and families were classified according to class criteria, such as the amount of land the family held, the amount of labor they hired, whether they had been money or grain lenders, and whether they had been lords or agents of lords.[3]

At the same time, the traditional manorial (feudal) system was abolished, and the fields and property (for example, the manor house, livestock, furniture, and farming equipment) of the lords and monasteries were redistributed to the poorest, usually landless, households.[4] All in-kind extractions imposed by the traditional system were also ended, and peasant families no longer had to provide corvée labor to their lords. For aristocratic and monastic serfs in the traditional society (before 1959), this had meant sending at least one person to work without pay for his or her lord every day and more at times of harvest. The elimination of such obligations was generally welcomed by the peasantry, especially by those who had been mired at the lower levels of traditional rural society. And those villagers who were classified as "middle" and even "rich" peasants retained possession of their fields and property, since collective farming was not instituted, and the extended family continued its traditional role as the main unit of production and consumption.[5] On the other hand, for Tibetan Buddhism the impact was disastrous. Organized religion was terminated, and monasteries ceased to function as centers of religious study and prayer. Monks and nuns basically were sent home.[6]

This change affected all regardless of class. In general, however, for all but the top elite, whose land and property had been confiscated, and monks and nuns, who could no longer live in religious communities, life initially became materially easier.

But that did not mean that no government extractions occurred in the new system. In the economic sphere, two new taxlike obligations were created that soon caused problems. One of these was euphemistically called "patriotic government grain" (tib. *gyeje shungdru;* ch. *aiguo gong liang*). It required households to "donate" some amount of grain to the government. Some villagers explained this as a kind of lease fee to the state, which ultimately owned the land they farmed, but the donation was clearly not voluntary. A second, more onerous obligation was called "sales grain" (tib. *tshongdru;* ch. *gou liang*). It required households to sell a portion of their grain yield to the state at government-set prices.[7] In theory, this was "surplus" grain the farmers did not need for subsistence, but in reality they had to sell this whether or not it was surplus.

Initially, these new extractions were modest, even for the middle and rich farming households, which were required to sell proportionally more than the poor households. However, after a few years, the size of these extractions began to increase, in part because the state took a larger percentage, but primarily because the cadres in charge overreported the size of the total yields to demonstrate "socialist progress" and improve their own performance records. Since the percentage of grain to be given and sold as patriotic and sales grain was pegged to the size of the yield, inflated yields meant proportionally larger transfers to the government, even though the actual yield may not have increased or may even have decreased. By the start of 1968, this began to create artificial food shortages, and there was talk that the situation would become markedly worse in 1969, when households would be left with only 12 *khe* (168 kilograms) of grain per person for both their food consumption and for sale in exchange for all other necessities, such as tea, salt, and clothing.[8] Many peasants feared that, if this came to pass, their families would not have enough food, and they did not know what would happen, since monasteries and rich aristocratic families from whom they could borrow grain no longer existed since 1959. Coming after the initial good years of private farming with minimal tax extractions, this was seen as a breach of the new society's norms established in 1959–60, and people were angry. Many believed this was the fault of local leaders who were corrupt. For the villagers, this was not a question of looking back to the old feudal society but rather looking back to the new socialist economic system implemented in 1959, which they had liked. Since almost all of the key local and county leaders were Nyamdre members, Gyenlo saw this discontent as a perfect opportunity to attack Nyamdre and to win villagers to its side.

A 1974 TAR government report on the causes of the Nyemo incident that is the subject of this book talks about this issue and how Gyenlo in Nyemo used this to recruit new members from the masses:

> Since 1967, Zhang Yongfu [the head of Gyenlo in Nyemo] . . . and some other people have been taking advantage of the problem of grain to viciously attack the party's policies. They said, "The grain policies are Liu Shaoqi's policies.[9] The policy of grain and oil purchases by the state [and] carried out by the . . . county party committee . . . was implementing the reactionary capitalist line. Now, it is up to the people how much grain and rapeseed oil they would like to hand in, and if they want, they can hand in nothing. Before liberation, every person could get eighteen *khe* of grain, but now every person can only have twelve *khe*. If a person joins our organization, he can get eighteen *khe* of grain, and we will not have people's communes." . . .
>
> Instigated by these [Gyenlo] people, many meetings were held [by villagers] to attack our party's policy of rapeseed oil and grain purchases by the state. They said, "Nyemo County has made us suffer 'the three empties' (ch. *san kong*)—empty houses, empty pockets, and empty stomachs. We have been suffering from hunger for about three or four years. The warehouses of the county are filled with the grain of the rich and middle-class peasants. In the past, we had dissatisfaction deep in our hearts but dared not speak out about it. Now it is time for us to rise up. Our revolt is to stop the oil and grain collections and purchases by the state."[10]

Another report, written in 1987 by a work team sent from the Lhasa Municipal Party Committee, also blamed the heavy extractions in grain for the disturbances:

> [W]e can see that after submitting grain and butter to the state, each person had only about six hundred *jin* of grain or rapeseed on average for [food and] seeds, fertilizers, and other daily necessities, such as salt, and to pay their debts, so it was very hard for them to live on such a small amount of resources.[11] Therefore, when the bad elements [Gyenlo] promised to give them "eighteen *khe* of grain and some tea," people were easily fooled. Nyemo was always sensitive to the problem of grain.[12]

But it was not just official reports that stated this. Virtually all Nyemo interviewees also emphasized this issue. For example, one villager explained the new exploitive extractions:

> They were saying that we got yields that we didn't actually get. . . . After the threshing was over they would come to calculate [the yield]. . . . We

didn't have any chance to say no. They would just tell us, "You got this yield, so you should deliver this amount of patriotic donation grain and sell this amount of sales grain." ... No matter whether or not we had that much surplus grain, we had to deliver it. That was the way the government collected the grain.[13]

Another Nyemo villager explained:

[Regarding the sales grain] [a]fter the harvest, we had to tell our leader the amount of yield we had harvested. The leader usually said that I must have gotten more grain than the amount I said and should add some amount to the yield I told him. I would say that my figure was the real harvest output, but he [wouldn't listen] and would say that he would give me more time to think about the yield. I didn't have anything to think about, but I left him and sat outside his office and took snuff. After a while, he would tell me that I had to add a certain amount to my yield. Even though I told him that I did not produce that much output, he added some number to my total harvest yield and on that basis did the accounting of how many *jin* of grain I should pay as the donation grain and how many *jin* of grain I should sell to the state as my sales grain duty. I had to do these two things. There was no choice. It was mandatory.

So since the output was increasing [on paper] every year, the donation grain and sales grain were also increasing every year. Usually the patriotic donation tax was reasonable, but the sales grain tax was very heavy. Because of this, the rebellion of 1968 and 1969 arose. Because the sales grain obligation had increased so much, many people became poorer and poorer and ... participated in the rebellion and became counter revolutionaries.[14]

Three other villagers similarly remembered:

The root reason for the rise of Gyenlo was that Gyenlo said that it was not going to [make people] pay either the patriotic donation grain tax or the sales grain tax. [It said] that the so-called sales grain was oppressive, and the patriotic donation grain should be just a small quantity, like the small fees paid for leased land in the old society.[15]

At that time, Gyenlo mobilized people by telling them that if they joined Gyenlo they would be given eighteen *khe* of barley. They raised the anger of the masses.[16]

Gyenlo said, "Even in the dark and cruel old society, servants were paid eighteen *khe* of barley as wages, but now in the era of the revolution, we have only twelve *khe* of grain as rations. So we are correct to rebel. It is no crime to make revolution." Because of talk like that, Gyenlo became larger and larger in Nyemo.[17]

Nonvillagers who were living and working in Nyemo at that time also indicated that the grain extractions were the key factor motivating the villagers. One of these, a Tibetan People's Liberation Army (PLA) soldier who had been stationed there (and who was associated with neither Gyenlo nor Nyamdre) explained, "[T]he masses had to rise up because they thought if they had [only] that amount to eat, they would have nothing. Because of that . . . the leaders, the ordinary people, the rich, and the poor people all rose up."[18] And another pro-Nyamdre Tibetan who had been educated at the Xianyang Nationalities Institute and had come to Nyemo after the violence to translate for the PLA's interrogators recalled what the people they interrogated had told him: "They said that they wanted to pull down the people who were embezzling from the state and who were not implementing [Mao's] policies [correctly] for the masses. That was the primary ideology of Gyenlo. Their secondary ideology was that . . . there was a shortage of *tsamba* [the staple flour made from roasted barley] everywhere, because the state was taking the grain, so they said that the state should leave the grain with the masses."[19]

Gyenlo's strategy for recruiting large-scale support among the Tibetan villagers, therefore, was to play on the villagers' fear and anger by criticizing the Nyamdre "authorities" (cadre) for imposing incorrect and self-serving economic policies and by promising the masses an alternative economic program that would allow households to retain 50 percent more grain per year (eighteen *khe* per person as opposed to twelve *khe*) as well as greater flexibility regarding loans and labor. Gyenlo, however, also adopted a pragmatic and sympathetic approach to another key issue that concerned the masses: collectivization and communes. The villagers had heard, correctly, that a new system of agriculture was imminent in which all the villagers' fields would be taken away and farmed collectively. Individual households would no longer have any control over either production or their labor. This, of course, was widely unpopular and greatly feared. Gyenlo, not surprisingly, made use of this by telling villagers what they wanted to hear, namely, that when they took power in the county they would not implement collective farming. Gyenlo, of course, did not say that the institution of communes was bad but rather that conditions were not yet appropriate for this step in Nyemo. One Nyemo villager recalled this: "Gyenlo said it was too early to change the Mutual Aid Team [system] and set up revolutionary committees [which included the commune]. In short, they said that to set up a big organization like the people's communes without first having the appropriate local conditions would impoverish the livelihood of the people."[20]

Gyenlo was well positioned to implement this anti-Nyamdre campaign, because its leaders were not only pragmatic and opportunistic but also knowledgeable about local conditions and attitudes. Zhang Yongfu, for example, was an unusual Han cadre. A short man who wore glasses, he spoke Tibetan well and was at ease in the villages, where he often stayed with Tibetan families and ate Tibetan *tsamba* and butter tea.[21] Gyenlo Headquarters also had a number of Tibetan cadres from Nyemo and other regions. The most important of these, Rangjung, was a local grassroots-level cadre who later was the main bridge between the nun and Gyenlo, as well as the field commander of Gyenlo's Army of the Gods.

Rangjung, however, was not some religiously pious Tibetan from a formerly upper-class family. He was completely a product of the new society. In the traditional society, he had been at the bottom of the status hierarchy, a landless "lifetime servant" (tib. *tsheyog*) to a family that served as the manager of the local estate of the aristocrat Shatra. As a youth, he was very aggressive and liked to fight and throw his weight around, using the name and authority of his lord. Although he was illiterate, his status after 1959 as a member of the elevated "poor class" and his experience doing tasks for the estate manager served him well, and he became a grassroots-level official, serving for a time as the head of the security office in Nyemo *xiang*. In that position he was known for cruelty and violence toward class enemies, including monks and nuns. He was one of the first Tibetans to join Gyenlo and quickly became a leader. Rangjung and Zhang Yongfu lived near each other and were friends.

A former incarnate lama from the family of Rangjung's lord gave a firsthand glimpse of his aggressive and violent character, albeit an obviously slanted glimpse.

> From the time he was young he was a very bad person, and we regarded him as the worst of our servants. . . . He liked to use violence. . . . I really do not know how the Communist Party was duped by this person. They allowed him to do whatever he wanted. He was bad. For example, sometimes in the summer when he went to graze our family's cows, he would seize other people's cows and put them into our courtyard, saying that these cows had eaten our crops [the crops on our fields]. We never asked him to do such things, but he wanted some gifts from both sides—the owner of the animals and us. I heard he got lots of things, such as eggs, by doing this. And during harvesttime, he used to steal grain from the threshing ground at night and send it to the nomads, from whom he got meat and intestines. . . . Rangjung . . . was illiterate, but because the government gave him power and allowed him to do whatever he wanted, he became very famous. He did not have any education and did not have any ability.
>
> *Q: When Rangjung acquired power [after the Democratic Reforms were instituted in 1959], did he treat your family badly?*
> A: Yes, he treated us very badly. What he did cannot be explained in a few

sentences. . . . He made us suffer a lot. Both the Nyamdre and Gyenlo factions beat us up and put paper hats on our heads and paraded us around the streets. . . . They said that we were running dogs of Liu Shaoqi and Deng Xiaoping. . . . Rangjung and his partners had power and said whatever they wanted. Today the government says we should "seek truth from facts" (tib. *ngöthog dentsö;* ch. *shishi qiushi*), but at that time we didn't have the chance to seek the truth.[22]

Food and collectivization were not the only things irritating villagers. They were also angry about the campaign against the "four olds," especially the new prohibitions on all forms of religious practice. Notwithstanding the suppression of organized religion (monasteries and nunneries) after 1959, individuals had still been permitted to practice religion on a private basis. That freedom ended with the onset of the Cultural Revolution in 1966, when all religious activities were prohibited and local Red Guards systematically searched houses to collect and destroy religious paraphernalia, such as statues, icons, and prayer wheels. At the same time, the Red Guards and activists mobilized villagers to tear down most temples and monasteries. The above-mentioned 1987 government report also commented on the negative consequences of this:

> Another example [of mistakes and shortcomings] was the party's policy on the freedom of pursuing religious beliefs. We used to talk too much but do too little to help people with their religious needs. We put too much emphasis on opposing religious beliefs. Especially during the Great Cultural Revolution, religious beliefs were labeled as one of the "four olds," and nobody was allowed to practice any religion. People did not like our policies, and once something tempting about religion appeared, the masses were easily fooled.[23]

Consequently, at the end of 1967, villagers were angry about a number of things, including the physical destruction of monasteries and the ban on private religious practices. However, organized religion had already been destroyed in 1959, and the immediate and pressing problem on which they were focused was not the restoration of monasteries but the *hunger* they feared they would experience after the coming year's grain extractions. That is what Gyenlo set out to use, and that is what drew the masses to join and support Gyenlo.

Zhang Yongfu, Rangjung, and other activists, therefore, increased their efforts in 1968 to persuade villagers to join Gyenlo and to induce those who were members to take action against the Nyamdre officials in power. Specifically, they sought to persuade villagers to disrupt the 1968 tax collections of grain by attacking the collection meetings and subjecting the presiding Nyamdre officials to struggle sessions in which they would be forced to admit their crimes and mistakes. In the process, of course, the villagers would free themselves from having to pay the grain tax or provide sales grain. In Gyenlo's plans, if this could be accomplished, the next step would be to seize control of the county administration itself.

Gyenlo rationalized this for villagers, as suggested above, by presenting such action in revolutionary ideology, namely, claiming these were positive actions in agreement with Mao's call to "bombard the headquarters." They were correct actions that opposed Liu Shaoqi's reactionary policies, which the Nyamdre cadres were wrongly enforcing. Gyenlo assured the villagers that because Chairman Mao himself had stated that "[t]here is no crime in making revolution; there is a reason to rebel" (tib. *sarje chebar nagnye mey; gyenlo chebar gyumdzen yö;*[24] ch. *geming wuzui; zaofan youli*), they had the revolutionary right, even a duty, to rebel against these capitalist-roaders who had sneaked into the party. The language of "seizing power" was used so commonly by revolutionaries like Gyenlo that this remarkable idea seemed perfectly normal and reasonable.[25] Rebellion against the authorities running Nyemo, therefore, was not something illicit and dangerously reactionary but, to the contrary, something laudable.

From the villagers' vantage point, this was appealing. For the first time since 1959 they felt able to oppose the authorities openly and without fear of reprisals, because they were now acting as part of a Maoist revolutionary organization. They were, in essence, fighting under orders from Chairman Mao to purge the cadres and policies they felt were then impoverishing them and were about to ruin their futures by taking back their land and animals for communes. Consequently, Gyenlo provided them a ready-made framework or agenda for doing something to change the rules on the ground. Members of Gyenlo understood that it was not in their interest to specify in too much detail what would change after they seized power, so villagers could read in whatever they wanted regarding the postvictory society.

This agenda and rationalization found ready ears among the villagers, as one Tibetan PLA soldier who was involved in the later interrogations recalled:

> All [the villagers involved] said we rose up in order to receive the eighteen *khe* of grain [that Gyenlo promised], and in doing this we were obeying the orders of Mao. . . . They said that the cadres in the county can't remain in [charge in] the county. They called the county officials "blue pigs." They

said that they were going to assign people to the county government from among themselves. They said that they were going to have freedom to trade and to lease land and hire servants to work their land.[26]

Gyenlo's strategy to seize power from Nyamdre, therefore, was bold and resonated well in rural Nyemo in 1968. And it clearly had nothing to do with the now famous nun named Trinley Chödrön. Gyenlo's move to wrest power from Nyamdre started well before the nun from Nyemo was involved, and it certainly would have continued with or without her presence. Moreover, at this time, Gyenlo's strategy was not about religion or nationalism; it was about Gyenlo defeating its rival revolutionary faction with the support of village masses who were willing to join in this venture because Gyenlo was promising them that they would benefit by being allowed to keep more grain, by ridding themselves of officials they saw as corrupt and avaricious, and by stopping implementation of the collective system. Given these attractions, it is not surprising that Gyenlo's tactics were successful and many new recruits flocked to join this faction. Included among these was Trinley Chödrön, a young nun from Phusum *xiang,* a rural township about ten kilometers from the Nyemo County seat.

THE NUN TRINLEY CHÖDRÖN JOINS GYENLO

In 1968, Trinley Chödrön was thirty years old. She was the oldest of eleven siblings in what had been a middle-level (taxpayer [tib. *treba*]) farming family named Bejang on an estate of the Lhalu aristocratic family.[27] Since about age twelve, she had been a nun in a small Kagyüpa nunnery named Thaser in a Phusum village, where she had lived in a small one-story house (tib. *shag*) together with an older teacher.[28] She was not highly educated and could not write, but she was able to read a few simple prayer texts, such as Demön.[29]

Like the lives of the rest of Tibet's vast monastic and nun population, Trinley Chödrön's life underwent a total transformation in 1959, when the imposition of the Democratic Reforms ended organized monastic life. At that time, monks and nuns were forced to attend "study classes" and struggle sessions, at which the basic ideas of Buddhism were ridiculed and denigrated and monastic leaders and lamas were criticized and humiliated. The rapidity and intensity of the changes were stunning, and within months almost all the common monks and nuns had returned to their villages to start new lives. Most gave up their vows and married, but some did not, including Trinley Chödrön, who continued to consider herself a nun. After the initial phase of attending study classes, Trinley Chödrön worked in the village during the day but returned to her nun's house beside the nunnery (which, of course, was no longer functioning as a religious institution) to live with her teacher.[30]

An interview with a Tibetan who had been a poor monk (from another area) illustrates vividly the dramatic and traumatic manner in which the lives of monks and nuns were turned upside down in the first months after the failed 1959 uprising and the flight of the Dalai Lama.

Q: In 1959 how many monks were in your monastery?[31]
A: About five hundred. A work team came to our monastery and they held meetings [study classes] for all monks in the monastery. . . . [32] The classes went on daily. Teams comprising about ten monks were formed, each having a team leader (ch. *zuzhang*). All members of the team . . . were made to learn the points introduced in each of the [daily] classes. After about twenty days of such sessions, this introduction to class struggle was finished. We knew and accepted the existence of classes, such as the lords (tib. *ngadag*) and so forth.

One day after that . . . the leader of the work team called the names of the higher-ranking monks . . . and told them to attend a seven- to ten-day political study class [in another building]. They were told to bring their own mattresses and bedding and were permitted to be accompanied by a servant. Their food had to be provided from their own monk households (tib. *shagtsang*). Each of them was kept in a separate single room, and although they were told that they were attending a study class, in fact, they had been arrested. . . .

Q: What happened to you after those people were separated from the other monks?
A: We had to continue attending the study classes. For the common monks [like me], we had classes every day. They were a substitute for the prayer assemblies that we had previously held daily. [Those had ended.] . . .

Q: What actually did the study classes consist of? . . .
A: Normally, topics were introduced in the morning session and then discussed after the lunch break. The person who ran these meetings was Chinese. He had an interpreter who would translate what he said. We were taught to discuss the topics presented to the group in the morning. Then after a break for lunch, which was provided to us where the class was held, we would continue our afternoon session. A topic would be introduced for the afternoon session too. Anyway, the topics were mainly slogans like "oppose three and exempt two" and the "exploitation and oppression of the three lords" [the aristocrats, the monasteries, and the government]. We had to discuss these and give the reasons for them, but this was quite hard to understand, because there were so many new terms.

Q: Were you surprised to hear those lectures? What did you think at the time?
A: . . . I always wished that I would be sent home, because my food (tsamba)

was running out. Moreover, unlike the older monks, who understood things, young monks like me didn't understand much of what was being said.

Then, just before I left the monastery, a one-day struggle session was held against the higher lamas and monastery leaders. [This was the first struggle session in his monastery.] Ten days before the struggle session was to be held, rehearsals were organized on how to conduct a struggle session. It was very difficult to learn.

Q: What kind of training did you receive?

A: . . . The monks were divided into several small groups, each of which was told that we would struggle against this and that person. The group members were seated in a circle with several big tsamba bags set up in the middle. Each tsamba bag was said to represent one particular higher-ranking lama or official. Every monk then had to stand up and point at those tsamba bags and rehearse and practice his accusation dialogues against them.

Q: What kind of accusation dialogues were you made to rehearse at the time? . . .

A: . . . In the dialogues one would say things like, "For the past thousand years you lords were standing on the shoulders of common people and poor monks, and you were exploiting and oppressing us. Now, under the leadership of the Communist Party, you are in our hands and should be brought down." Actually, just a few monks went through the motions of saying the words that we were taught. The rest of the monks just watched and kept quiet. Therefore, it didn't seem very useful.

Q: How did the actual struggle session go?

A: After the small group-training sessions, we had to practice in a larger meeting together with the majority of monks who had been studying the same methods. The monks who were brave and verbal were selected from the smaller groups and rehearsed and practiced the accusation dialogues in the larger practice meeting. I was not selected for this. . . . The monks like me were not selected, as there were many monks. The older [poor] monks who were eloquent and knew reading and writing were selected over us. Then one day . . . we were told to show what we had trained for. They selected who would speak first, and who would be second, and so forth.

The actual struggle session was held in the monastery's assembly hall on the stone floor. All the monks had to attend this, as did the masses from nearby villages. The moment the higher-ranking monks and lamas were brought to the front of the meeting by PLA soldiers, one person in the audience started shouting out slogans such as, "So-and-so should be destroyed!" The audience then raised their fists and responded saying, "Destroy them!" The atmosphere became so tense that I was really scared.

There were several lamas like Risur Rimpoche and Botön Rimpoche, who were in their sixties and seventies. Those higher-ranking monks had never heard of or experienced a struggle session, so while some of them were a little scared when the soldiers brought them into the meeting, others had no idea what was going to happen to them. They were lined up at the front of the stage [platform] and told to stand with their heads bent at the waist [their body bent at the waist so that the torso was horizontal with the ground with their head facing downward]. In the beginning, some of them did not know what a struggle session involved and were confused. They kept on standing up and looking around. . . . Some of them were not frightened and looked at people's faces rather than bending over at the waist. . . .

Q: *What did you feel seeing others act this way? When you had to raise your hand and yell at the lamas on the stage, what did you do?*
A: It was a fearsome experience, and I was not able to look up at the faces of those lamas. Those lamas were the lords of both monks and lay people, and they were my lords too. They became the lords of this area not through being appointed by others but by their own capabilities. And they were from our own Shalu Monastery, not appointed from other monasteries.

Q: *Did the lamas really have bad reputations?*
A: When the rehearsals were going on, it seemed that everybody was able to accuse them of something, but when coming face-to-face it was different. At the actual meeting we were told that it was voluntary for people to stand up and accuse the lamas and leaders, and for some time nobody had the courage to stand up and accuse them directly to their faces. That seemed to annoy the people in the work team and the teachers of the rehearsal/training sessions, so they told the people from the [prepared] list to stand up [and speak]. The leader of the work team said, "Today, there are hundreds of poor monks and poor masses who want to criticize and denounce the monastery's leaders. However, since we do not have enough time, we will let only a few people criticize and denounce them." And then he called the name of the first person on the list to stand and make his accusation. It took a while for that first person, who was a monk, to stand up. I thought he must be scared to be the first person to accuse them. The audience had to wait silently for a while.

When the monk finally stood up, he looked a little nervous in the beginning and paused for some moments before saying anything, as it was the first time for him. Then he calmed down a little and started to yell, ordering those lamas to look down [not to look directly at the audience]. He accused them one by one according to what he had learned in the training sessions. The scene was very strange, because he was accusing no one in particular, for he couldn't distinguish who was who. But step by step, he made accusations according the history of each target person.

Some of the lamas still looked up at the audience and tried to see who that monk was. I guess they still did not realize how serious the situation was. The person who was the local [lay] lord was beaten severely by the monk, much worse than the others. I think that was because he had possessed the power to bully people in the past, so people now used this opportunity to get revenge. After accusing each one of them, the first monk concluded his speech by saying, "Now I would like to stop my speech here, because there are many others who also want to accuse them." He was one of the most verbal of those in the training sessions.

After this monk sat down, the name of a young village girl was called by the work team, and she stood up. I think she was from the upper Shalu area. The girl was very verbal and harsh. She accused each of the targets of a lot of things. Sometimes, when she got angry, she put her knee on the back of the lamas and lord to force them to bend over [more at the waist]. Sometimes, while she was speaking, both her hands grabbed the lamas' upper shawl (tib. *sen*), so some of the lamas' clothing were torn to bits. By this time, those lamas realized what a struggle session was about. And all of them were very scared. . . .

The masses meanwhile were shouting, "Bend your head down!" . . . and "Why are you still looking at us, the masses?" "Your time to look down on us is finished." "Why are you not looking down?" And they pressed them down with their hands [pushed down on their backs so they stayed bent over at the waist], and some of them fell down [when they were pushed that way].

After the girl, there was a long break when no one went up to the stage [to accuse them]. After some time passed, the leader of the work team must have felt that no one else would come forth, so he announced, "Today, the struggle session will be stopped here. From now on we must struggle against these lords month by month and year by year until they are completely destroyed." And then the PLA soldiers took all the lamas back. It seemed that the monastery leaders were very frightened by the session. Not only was the monastery head beaten a lot, but also his shawl was torn to pieces. . . . I saw his monk clothing torn to pieces at the meeting.

The next morning, I heard some people yelling outside that someone had jumped out the window of a building. I went outside to see who that person was, and I saw that same lama lying on the stone-paved ground. He had not died yet and was still breathing weakly when I got there. After a moment, he stopped breathing and died. He had jumped through a glass window on the fourth floor of the building. That day all the lamas were moved to the first floor of the building and were not subjected to any further struggle sessions. . . .

Q. *Did he commit suicide?*

A: Yes, and because of that, the other lamas were all moved on the same day to the Garkhang Prison in the fort of Shigatse. After that, the lamas weren't subjected to any more struggle sessions. And shortly after that, the young monks were allowed to leave the monastery.[33]

The shock of study classes and struggle sessions was only the beginning. Monks and nuns then returned to their villages and had to find a new life, as this monk explains:

Since I was a young man, the work team let me go back to my home village. At the time, the work team announced that all monks had the freedom to choose whether to continue to stay in the monastery or to leave. However, if one remained a monk and stayed in the monastery, no one would support his livelihood; that is, he would not receive a salary as before. In addition, by the time the study classes had finished, most of us monks had run out of *tsamba,* so we had no food reserves that would have enabled us to stay in the monastery longer. . . .

Q: *How did you feel about leaving the monastery?*

A: I was happy, because my situation then was bad. When my guardian-teacher died, my share of the monk household's tsamba was not given to me [because of a dispute with the teacher's family], so I didn't have anything to remain in the monastery for. Therefore, I returned home. I left the monastery at age eighteen. I was really happy about that, because when I was in the monastery I had suffered lots, and then after my guardian-teacher died, there was no one I could depend on. . . .

When I was going to return to my village, it was said that we could not wear monk's clothing anymore, so I took off the monk's upper shawl, and one of my monk friends gave me a shabby Tibetan (layman's) dress. Although its color was a little reddish, it was different from the ordinary monk's clothing and good enough to wear outside. My village was located on the other side of the mountain, so I climbed the mountain and went back home. When I arrived, the people in the village were also having political study classes every day. . . . I had already experienced much stricter sessions in the monastery, so I did not find the village's study classes hard. This time I felt comfortable, as I understood the new terms and new ideas. . . . [34]

Q: *What did your mother say when you returned?*

A: Not much, as she understood the situation [regarding the monasteries]. . . . I found that the food my family was eating was better than before. They had as much food as they wanted, since this was being provided by the work team. Consequently, most of the young men . . . were having a very good time, because there was plenty of barley beer to drink every day. They got drunk every night. . . .

Q: *What jobs did you do after returning from the monastery?*

A: In the beginning I attended the study classes. Then when the Democratic Reforms were launched, land was allocated to us. All the servants who had worked inside the lord's manor house were given farming equipment and rooms. My mother, sister, and I received a small inner room and a room with two pillars on the third floor of the lord's manor house. . . . Each person was also given 2.1 *khe* of land.[35] That amount was given to every person equally. . . .

Q: *How many people in the xiang received land at that time?*

A: Not more than three hundred to four hundred people received land shares. At that time they distributed only the land that had belonged to the Samling aristocratic family. The fields of the middle-class farmers, the taxpayer households, and the rich farmers were retained by them. Actually, the taxpayer households were the middle-class farmers. The poor households were the ones who didn't have much land or good houses to live in. The serf-servants (tib. *trenyog*) didn't have any property or place to live; hence they received more land and other items than people from the other strata.

Q: *When you returned to the village, had the system of class statuses already been determined?*

A: No. At that time study classes were being held. During that time it was quite a chaotic atmosphere, with dancing and other such things going on hand-in-hand with the political study classes.

Q: Were the people who were teaching the study classes Chinese?
A: The people who taught the classes were all Chinese cadres. However, there were also quite a few young Tibetan interpreters who had studied in China.

Q: At that time were you happy to receive the land share, et cetera?
A: Yes, I was. As they said, the time had arrived for us to be owners of our own land, and all the people felt very happy to take a share of land and cattle. However, on the day following the distribution, everyone returned to the work team, asking them to please take back the animals they had been given, since they did not have any place to keep the cattle and also did not have hay to feed them. It was very comical to have a family with only one small room trying hard to tie up a huge dzo [a hybrid yak and cow] it had received. . . . Consequently, many wanted the work team to take back the cattle they had received. Of course, the work team sent the people away, giving them a scolding, and later many sold their animals for a very low price. . . . Many of the middle-class [former] taxpayer households bought them.[36]

This former monk also recalled that although the elderly in his village were happy to receive their own land and apartments, they were sad about the fate of religion:

After the elder people heard at the study sessions that they could be the owners of their own land, they became very happy. They were also happy because they were told that they didn't need to perform any more corvée taxes and be serfs anymore. . . .

Q: What was the common people's response to the heavy persecution of monks in monastery?
A: It was mostly the older people who saw the persecution of lamas and all others as very bad. Many became very sad and even cried. Of course, it was obviously dangerous to cry and show one's emotions openly, because they would then be criticized by the work team. But for younger people, it hardly had any effect. They were not attentive. And as for the younger monks, since the work obligations they previously had to perform had ended, they were actually happier. Otherwise, the elders were more affected, for they were more devoted to the lamas.

Q: Did it prove very difficult for you to farm and do cultivation after all those years of monastic life?
A: Yes, it did. Of course, first of all, I was inexperienced in cultivation work. And not only were there the actual farming tasks, but there were lots of other manual labor tasks a farmer should have mastered, of which I knew nothing. For example, I didn't know how to sew my own shoes at all. But through experience and learning from others, it gradually got

better. In the beginning, though, it was difficult for me to do even a minor task, such as putting a saddle on a donkey. At times, I would be made fun of by others; for example, once when I asked them how to irrigate the fields, they said, "You should irrigate from the lower place to the upper place." Though I was an adult physically, I seemed like a complete fool at those times. . . .

Q: Had you thought of marriage?

A: I was actually married at age nineteen [the year after I returned home]. The woman I met was a nun from Gyangön Nunnery. At that time all the monks and nuns from Dujüng District were ordered to come together for a political study session here in Sogang. That gathering actually ended up being more like a matchmaking affair for marriage than a political study session.

All the monks and nuns had gathered from different places, and since being a nun or monk no longer had any future, we were encouraged to find partners whom we found interesting. I was back in the village at that time and went. I met my future wife there. At the time nothing happened between us, but later her family asked me to move to their home as a move-in bridegroom (tib. *magpa*), since my sister was already living with my mother [in our household, and it would have been difficult to have two couples of the same generation].

Q: What did you think about that? Did you see her at the session?

A: Yes. I felt that I would not be a monk in the future, and it was just a matter of time before I would look for a wife, so why not?[37]

Trinley Chödrön was among the thousands of monks and nuns whose life as part of active monastic communities ended suddenly like this. However, unlike the Shalu monk who was happy to leave the monastery, she was angry and bitter at the new policies and brooded over the end of organized monastic life. Her isolation increased a few years later when the older nun (her *gegen,* or guardian-teacher) with whom she was living died.

The onset of the Cultural Revolution's campaign to destroy the four olds in Nyemo pushed her over the line. Her younger brother says that she became more despondent and disoriented and at the same time was incensed about the Red Guards and activists' attacks on religion and about the new rules preventing all manifestations of private religious practice. She was also agitated because her own family's class status had been reassessed negatively from middle farmer (tib. *shingdring*) to upper middle farmer (tib. *shingdring gongma*) without justification and because Red Guards had ransacked their house searching for religious texts and objects.[38] The force of these shocks appears to have unbalanced her, and she was soon acting mentally disturbed. Her younger brother recalled:

She was like a crazy person (tib. *nyönma*). Sometimes she did not eat food. Sometimes she drank dirty water from puddles on the road or from cesspools (tib. *dzabdong*). Sometimes, she did not stay in her house but went into the mountains and spent nights or days there alone.[39] At this time she was considered crazy and did things that made no sense (tib. *khunglung dilung mepa*). And she would dress in a disorderly way and wear a fox fur cap, and she did not really understand what was going on around her (tib. *hako diko meba*). At the same time she had also become passive and somewhat dazed. She had no friends and "always followed whatever other people said. For example, if we put a cup of tea before her, she drank it. When anyone came, she would follow whatever he or she said."[40]

A neighbor in her village added, "She had mental problems (tib. *sem mathangwa*). She lived by herself and used to yell and scream at people who walked back and forth on the path [in front of her house]."[41]

Disoriented, angry, and bitter, she began to have hallucinatory dreams and visions of people and strange cloud formations. She talked of birds landing on the monastery to bring her messages. The same neighbor recalled, "She would say that she saw something, and we would see her talking to [imaginary] people whom normal people could not see and hear. She told people many different stories, but it was the talk of a crazy person. It was all hard to believe. She did this for several years."[42]

According to some, Trinley Chödrön's immersion in this imagined world of hallucinatory visions and conversations included the Dalai Lama appearing in clouds or on birds. It is not absolutely clear when her imaginings moved to a new level wherein she believed that gods were possessing her, but at some point that is what happened.[43] Her younger brother, who was then living with her, recalled how this began. After Trinley Chödrön had been acting crazy for what he thinks was about a year, she became very sick and so weak that she could hardly walk or do housework. At this time she acted as if a god was trying to possess her, but she was unable to accommodate the god, and she felt that was why she had become ill.

In the Tibetan religious tradition, being possessed is very different from having a dream or a vision, since experiencing a trance follows a culturally scripted process in which the body shakes and the person huffs and puffs (symbolizing the god entering the body). People whose bodies are possessed by gods for short periods of time were traditionally called *lha phenyen* or *lhaba*—in English, mediums.[44]

Mediums played an important role in traditional Tibetan society, linking the realm of the gods to the realm of humans, and were frequently consulted at times of illness and other major decisions. (And they still are.) At the highest level, there were official state mediums, such as Nechung, who were consulted by the Dalai Lama and the Tibetan government at difficult times, but mediums were also found throughout the countryside, where scattered villagers—male and female—functioned part-time as religious specialists able to summon deities to possess them. In the Tibetan tradition, the god who was invoked took such complete control over the medium's body that the medium was not supposed to remember anything the god said after the god left and he or she came out of the trance. Mediums, however, led normal lives when not in a trance; they were not in any way perceived as mentally ill or unbalanced because they could summon deities into their bodies.

After their initial spontaneous possession (tib. *tongbeb gya*), mediums usually could summon one or more gods. Dressed in a special costume, a medium typically would bang on a drum while doing a kind of ritual dance to summon the god to enter his or her body. Once a god had entered the medium's body, it could be asked questions and would speak and give answers that Tibetans considered prophecies (tib. *lungden*). Sometimes the voice or language used by the "god" was so stylized that it had to be "translated" by an assistant, although in the case of the nun, her statements were easy to understand.[45]

Going into a trance the first time was a major event for which it was customary to consult a lama to seek ritual empowerment so that the link could be controlled and the god could later be summoned on demand. This was typically done through a ritual called *tsago che* (literally, opening the door to the vein). The lama at this time would typically determine whether it was a god or a demon or a ghost that had chosen to possess the person spontaneously. Because of this, the nun asked her brother to take her to see one of the local lamas, and despite the risk of consulting a lama during the Cultural Revolution, he agreed.[46] He recalled,

> She acted as if she were almost going into a medium's trance, but she couldn't complete this and as a result was getting very sick. . . . For three days she looked as if she might even die. Then she asked to go to see one of the three lamas living in the area, and since she was so sick I agreed to take her.
> We left the village after dark, since going for such a visit was dangerous to do during the daytime. It was very difficult for her to walk, so at first I had to support her, but then after some distance she became more active and talkative and was able to have a conversation with me and walk herself. . . . [S]he went ahead straight to the house of the lama named Chamba Tenzin.

> I just followed behind her. Chamba Tenzin was from Ru Monastery in
> Phusum, just near the nunnery, but was then living in the county seat.[47]

The lama did the *tsago che* rite, reading some pages of a religious text
and then placing it on her head. He told her that it is correct for her to
serve as a medium. Chamba Tenzin also gave the nun a protective string
(tib. *sungdü*), which he told her to wear when she went into the
medium's trance.[48] In an interrogation document, her brother said that
in addition to this the lama Chamba Tenzin told her, "This country originally belonged to the Dalai Lama, but since he failed to manage it, he
gave the power to Chairman Mao. Chairman Mao is the one who distributed material wealth [as at the time of the Democratic Reforms],
while you are the one who distinguishes between good and bad people."[49] Later, when the nun went into public trances, she sometimes said
versions of this, and the same language appears again in her famous 1969
written statement, which will be discussed in a later chapter. It appears,
therefore, that Chamba Tenzin, who was executed in 1969, played a role,
perhaps a significant one, in shaping some of the key ideas of the nun.

Trinley Chödrön's visit to the lama was a success and led to a marked
improvement in her health and behavior. Her brother recalled, "She got
much better. She started talking and walking like a normal person and
was again able to do normal housework jobs. In addition, she now started
to go into trances as a medium."[50] Her brother said that she initially went
into a trace alone in her own house: "The first time . . . she came out of
the room (inner room) in a trance and offered me some holy water (tib.
chabdrü). After she came back from the lama, she went into a trance like
this [privately at home] six or seven times. No one else knew."[51] One
Chinese report on the Nyemo incident cites a date of May 1967 for the
initial onset of the nun's trances,[52] but the evidence indicates that she
started practicing as a medium only in the summer of 1968, after seeing
Chamba Tenzin.

Notwithstanding Trinley Chödrön's problematic mental state and
imagined world, she was aware of the conflict between Gyenlo and Nyamdre and in April 1968 sought to join Gyenlo. This happened when several Tibetans from her village went to Gyenlo General Headquarters in
the seat of Nyemo County to join. The comments of Trinley, one of the
villagers, to the leaders of Gyenlo conveys the widespread anger mentioned earlier toward the cadres who had ruled in Nyemo since 1959 and
the perception in the nun's village that Gyenlo was giving the villagers a
vehicle to speak out:

The red sun rose in our town in 1959. However, black clouds blocked the sun the next year. The head of the *xiang* (ch. *xiangzhang*) and other leaders acted just like the three lords (ch. *san da lingzhu*) [in the old society]. They [the new leaders] issued orders and rode roughshod over us. Every time the government purchased cooking oil and grain, they overreported our production by a lot. These leaders are like dogs and infuriate us in our hearts, but we dared not say a word.[53]

After Gyenlo Headquarters accepted them as members, this same villager asked the Gyenlo leaders whether someone a little bit crazy could join Gyenlo.[54] Li Yongchang, a Tibetan cadre from Kham (Chamdo), was initially dubious and answered that only people who were citizens with full rights could join (which excluded class enemies and people who were mentally incompetent). Li recalled this conversation:

> In early April 1968, Trinley . . . from Phusum *xiang* came to the county to see me, asking what kind of people could join Gyenlo Headquarters. I answered everyone could join Gyenlo Headquarters except for those who were part of the "agents of a lord" class. Trinley then asked whether crazy people could join Gyenlo Headquarters, and I told him, "No, people who are crazy cannot join, since they have no right to vote [as citizens in society]." Trinley then asked me whether people who are dumb [in the sense of unable to speak] could join. . . . Several days later, Trinley came to my home and told me that he had a female relative who was a poor peasant. He said she sometimes appeared to be crazy, but she wanted to join our organization. I asked Trinley how serious her mental problem was. Trinley said she was not seriously mad, so I said she could join our organization.[55]

Another account of this same event was given by Xiao Yong, a Tibetan cadre in Gyenlo Headquarters in Nyemo who had studied in Beijing:

> In February or March 1968, several people, including Zhang Yongfu and Trinley from Phusum *xiang*, went to Li Yongchang's home. When I came there, they had already finished talking, so I asked Li Yongchang and Zhang Yongfu what those people wanted. Li and Zhang told me that they had come to join Gyenlo Headquarters. When I asked why they wanted to join, [he repeated what Trinley said above]. . . . Trinley, Wujinlaqing, and another person then went to Xu De'an's home . . . [and] I went with them. Li Yongchang told him, "There is a crazy person in Phusum *xiang* who loves Gyenlo Headquarters. Can she join us?" Luo Boqing and Xu Lide said, "No. Lunatics have no right to vote, so we cannot accept her." Trinley then said, "She is not insane. She is just dumb." Then Luo Boqing and Xu Lide agreed to accept her.[56]

At this point, Gyenlo's leaders had no idea who this young nun named Trinley Chödrön was, let alone any thoughts of using her to help their group fight against Nyamdre. It was just part of their strategy to increase support in the farming countryside.

There is no record of why someone who was deeply religious, like Trinley Chödrön, would have wanted to be part of a revolutionary mass organization that was fighting to carry out Mao's call for the new Cultural Revolution. These were, of course, the very kind of leftists who had carried out the Democratic Reforms and struggle sessions she abhorred. The answer, we believe, is that she, like so many other villagers, saw Gyenlo through a different lens. For her, Gyenlo shared many of her own thoughts and represented the first opportunity for change since 1959. Like herself, it was deeply opposed to the county's leading cadres—the same ones she hated—and appeared to hold compatible ideas about what the new society should be like with regard to taxes and collectivization. Gyenlo, moreover, seemed a realistic force for change, since it asserted that rebellion against the "bad" things that had happened since 1959 was ideologically okay, because these were misrepresentations of the true views of Mao Zedong. Supporting Gyenlo meant it was okay to rebel against the status quo.

Trinley Chödrön actually had talked favorably about Gyenlo even before she joined, telling villagers that they should side with Gyenlo rather than Nyamdre.[57] Further evidence of her predisposition to Gyenlo comes from statements of Phusum villagers who were adamant that she wanted a Gyenlo armband (ch. *xiu zhang*) when Gyenlo agreed to admit her, and later she actually often wore it publicly.[58] Ironically, this was more of a problem than her mental state, since Gyenlo Headquarters had no extra armbands at that time, so one of the leaders sent her his own personal armband.[59]

Consequently, in about April 1968, Trinley Chödrön became a member of a revolutionary faction that was organizing villagers to seize power from its Nyamdre enemies. Within a few months, the nun also began to go into trances with powerful gods and developed a following in the rural countryside as a medium. Over the next year, this seemingly incompatible and incongruous relationship with gods on the one hand and Marxist revolutionaries on the other intensified and ultimately created the unique texture of the 1969 Nyemo incident.[60]

When someone is spontaneously possessed, a key question is, Which deity is doing the possessing? Sometimes the lama who performs the *tsago che* rite identifies the god, but other times the god identifies himself or herself after entering the medium's body. Initially it appears that Trinley Chödrön claimed that several gods possessed her, including a local mountain deity and Jowo Rimpoche, the Shakyamuni Buddha of the Tsuglagang Temple in Lhasa.[61] However, in Tibetan Buddhism, enlightened deities like the Buddha *never* possess human mediums. As the anthropologist Diemberger explains, "The deities who most frequently possess local mediums are territorial deities—those who inhabit mountains, rock, lakes or springs. . . . From a Buddhist perspective these deities are considered to be of low stature, belonging to the worldly sphere and still involved in mundane affairs."[62] Because of this, the nun's claims of being a medium were not taken seriously by many who had a more sophisticated knowledge of religion. One incarnate lama from Nyemo commented on this:

> When the nun went into trances in Thaser, I heard she said that she was going into trances with Jowo Rimpoche. At that time, we could not talk about it publicly because they [the nun's people] would have skinned us and killed us if we had, but we talked among our family and friends, saying that it is absolutely impossible to go into a trance with the Buddha of the Tsuglagang because he is the Tathagata Buddha (tib. *theshin shegba*).[63] So how could she go into a trance with this Buddha? This was just a lie. Of course we did not say such things in public.[64]

At the same time, the nun also said bizarre things such as, "I am the right shoulder [hand] of Chairman Mao" and "Chairman Mao will not treat us badly, since he is an incarnation of [the Buddha] Manjuśri (tib. *jambeyang*). It is the internal [local] people who are the worst."[65] Such claims and comments reinforced many people's belief in her mental instability and enabled her to go into a medium's trances in the midst of the Cultural Revolution, when religion, even private religion, was otherwise prohibited. Her younger brother explained, "At first, when this started, neither the people from our village nor the officials from our *xiang* paid her any attention, since they considered her to be crazy. . . . Later, however, . . . people came to her to ask her to perform as a medium."[66]

Other villagers from her area also recalled that she was not stopped from doing religious activities, because she was considered to be insane. "She wore a fox fur hat and carried a small bow hanging from her neck. . . . People said she was mad. It was the time of the Cultural Revolution, so people were not allowed to burn incense, and all statues had been destroyed. But the nun continually burned incense, and no one stopped her doing so because of her madness."[67] A former local (Nyamdre) official also commented on her behavior: "Trinley Chödrön showed signs of being mad. She went around carrying bows and arrows as if they were children's toys. At that time, she said lots of [strange] things in public."[68]

Despite this, some local people who heard about her trances began to come quietly at night to consult with the gods about illnesses, as they traditionally had. For example, one person whose arm was contracted and could not be stretched out became normal after the nun went into a trance and the inhabiting god just touched his hand. And when some other sick people came to her, they were healed after the god hit the part of the body that was ill. As a result, her fame grew, and more and more people came to consult the god through her, although initially most of the people coming to see her did so discreetly at night. One Gyenlo village activist recalled going to see her for his own illness:

> At that time she gave true prophecies and could predict things extremely accurately, so many people believed in her. . . . I had an illness in my leg and visited her about that. . . . She told me that some deities and *nagas* (tib. *lhalu*) were causing my leg problem. . . .
>
> Q: Did everybody trust her?
> A: Yes, everybody trusted her.[69]

As a result of instances like these, word gradually spread that this nun was an authentic medium whose prophecies (i.e., her deities' responses to people's questions) were accurate and whose healing powers were great.

Of the various gods the nun claimed to be possessed by, the most important was Ani Gongmey Gyemo. In Tibetan tradition, this goddess was the aunt and adviser of the famous deity-king Gesar, who in the past had descended to Tibet from the realm of the gods (tib. *lhayü*) to wage a series of bloody wars to save Buddhism from the demons and devils ruling Tibet.[70] In the story, the goddess Ani Gongmey Gyemo remained in the gods' realm and did not accompany Gesar to Tibet, but she played an important role advising Gesar through prophecies after he had descended to the human realm in Tibet. Symbolically, therefore, Trinley Chödrön was now assuming the persona of the goddess who advised Gesar in his war against the enemies of Buddhism in Tibet. Thus, Ani Gongmey Gyemo's return to Tibet through Trinley Chödrön had powerful symbolic and political significance because, for Tibetans, Gesar and Ani Gongmey Gyemo were not some mythical figures in folktales, nor were they simply local mountain deities; they were real and powerful deities famous for fighting for Buddhism in Tibet.

It is not clear whether the idea that Gesar's aunt was the main god possessing Trinley Chödrön came from the nun herself or from the lama Chamba Tenzin. Her brother insisted it was her own idea, saying, "I always went with her to meet those high lamas, and I never heard any of the lamas say it is this or that god. It was she herself who said who the god was."[71] But if this is so, it is difficult to understand how she knew about this, since Gesar's story, as her brother also explained, was not popular in Nyemo: "The King Gesar story is popular in the north [in the Nagchuka area] but not much in Nyemo. My sister definitely had not read the story in book form. At this time she talked a lot about this story, but nobody checked up to see whether what she was saying was really part of the story or not." However, what she said was accurate, so the question of where this idea and information came from is still unanswered. Nevertheless, regardless of who initially had the idea about Ani Gongmey Gyemo, toward the end of 1968 she became Trinley Chödrön's main possession deity.

Meanwhile, during the fall of 1968, as the nun's reputation for accurate prophecies increased, more people from other villages started to come to consult the gods she invoked, and as Gyenlo became more powerful in the countryside, this consultation could be done openly. One neighbor recalled, "As for the nun Trinley Chödrön, [I don't know] whether she was a goddess or a ghost, [but] many people came to see her be possessed by gods. She lived near the monastery, so when people went to the monastery, they had to go past our house. Thus, I saw many people go on the road to the monastery to see her."[72]

Interestingly, at this time the nun not only went into trances but publicly praised Mao and Mao's thoughts. For example, a Gyenlo leader in the county recalled, "Zhou Longquan came to my house and said to me, 'Do you know that recently a lot of people have been to Phusum to worship the deity? It used to be done secretly, but now it's open. Do you know the nun? She is young. She publicizes the thoughts of Chairman Mao.'"[73]

The dichotomy of hating the local Communist Party and speaking favorably about Mao is not as incongruent as it seems. During the Cultural Revolution, as indicated earlier, all revolutionary organizations considered that the party apparatus had been infiltrated by reactionaries, capitalist-roaders, and so forth. Thus, opposing the Communist Party in a place like Nyemo did not mean that one opposed Mao and the nation, since Mao himself, in fact, criticized the old party organization and planned to replace it with a new structure called revolutionary committees. Trinley Chödrön, therefore, appears to have been perfectly comfortable simultaneously going into the medium's trances, praising Mao Zedong, and being a member of the Gyenlo revolutionary faction.

Consequently, at the same time that Gyenlo moved to take concrete steps to wrest power from Nyamdre in Nyemo, the nun Trinley Chödrön reconceptualized herself from a simple oracle in a tiny village to a religious figure who had inherited the mantle and charisma of Tibet's most famous militant defender of the faith. In this context, the prophecies of Ani Gongmey Gyemo took on a political tone. Not only did she say things like that mentioned earlier—that Mao was a manifestation of the Buddha Manjuśri—but also her brother recalled that Ani Gongmey Gyemo used to contrast the roles of Mao and herself, saying that Mao was in charge of allocating material things, but *she had come to rebuild all the monasteries, that is, to restore religion.*[74] All of this was plausible and popular, and as one villager recalled, "When the nun was beginning to be possessed by the Jowo Buddha, nobody supported her, but after she was possessed by Ani Gongmey Gyemo, she slowly became more public [popular]."[75]

Although Zhang Yongfu still had no thought of using the nun in his strategy to displace Nyamdre and take power, he understood the significance of the growing popularity of this medium who was a Gyenlo member and pragmatically began to say things to appeal to Tibetans' religious sensibilities. In keeping with his basic strategy to win over villagers by positioning Gyenlo as the group interested in their hopes and wishes, he is reported to have begun saying things such as "Gyenlo supports the freedom of people to worship or not worship the Buddha" and "Gyenlo has no restrictions regarding the practice of Buddhism."[76] Zhang also told Gyenlo's village representatives that they should protect the nun and show her respect. Thus, as Gyenlo increased its power in the countryside, it was actually inadvertently creating conditions that facilitated the nun's more open practice and therefore her ever larger following.

However, it is important to reiterate that the nun did not see her relationship to Gesar and Ani Gongmey Gyemo as inconsistent with her support for a revolutionary mass organization like Gyenlo. Gyenlo was striving to change (improve) the situation in Nyemo and was opposing the same Nyamdre cadre whom she hated, so Gyenlo's success would be her success. One Gyenlo village activist recalled how it was not just religion but also the tax extractions that the nun opposed: "The nun said that the leaders were not fair, so some of the *xiang* heads were beaten by the people. One *xiang* head was even stabbed. She said that the leaders collected grain even though people did not have grain to hand in, and they were not fair about this work."[77]

Consequently, for Trinley Chödrön, Gyenlo offered a heretofore inconceivable opportunity to rectify some of what was then wrong in the "new society" and to restore some of what had been lost, particularly, organized religion. Not surprisingly she rooted this in terms of core Tibetan cultural and religious images, seeing herself as the chosen inheritor of the mantle of Gesar through her belief that Ani Gongmey Gyemo had chosen her as the god's human vehicle to speak and act to restore religion. While this was developing in Phusum *xiang,* Gyenlo Headquarters in Nyemo was moving ahead with its plan to attack Nyamdre physically over the grain issue.

CHAPTER 3

Gyenlo on the Attack

THE 1968 FALL OFFENSIVE

By the start of October 1968, the harvest was winding down and the county was starting to convene rural meetings to discuss the amount of patriotic donation and sales grain to be turned in that year. Zhang Yongfu and Rangjung took this as an opportunity to strike at Nyamdre by attacking the cadres in charge of collection.

Gyenlo's membership had increased substantially in the past year, and it now had hundreds of active members in the countryside. Their plan was to use their numerical superiority to attack the cadres in charge, marginalizing them in the eyes of the masses. These attacks were to be framed in revolutionary terms by putting up big-character posters and forcing the cadres to undergo struggle sessions and other acts of what normally would be "revolutionary" intimidation. A Gyenlo leader's recollection of his urgings to the villagers illustrates this well:

"Are you still sleeping? You should make use of this meeting and send some [Gyenlo village] representatives there to put up big-character posters."[1] I suggested that it was high time that they started the rebellion. They then sent several hundred people to the [collection] meeting in the name of putting up big-character posters. Those people beat [struggled against] Comrade Phüntso, the deputy secretary of the *xiang* party committee. They also attacked and stopped the meeting. The disturbance was quite serious. . . . Eventually, no surplus grain was sold to the government.[2]

86

Another Gyenlo activist recalled the same event:

> In October 1968, Lhawang Tsering held a meeting of the Gyenlo representatives in Sangmu Village. At that time, Basang and Tsijü, the two cadres who headed the district, were busy collecting and buying grain. [At the meeting, a villager named] Phujung said, "Rangjung said that we should kick out the cadres who are collecting grain in each village. Today we will drive out the leaders like Basang, Tsijü, and the Army Propaganda Team (ch. *jun xuan dui*)." . . .
>
> After the meeting, Gyenlo people went to Chöling Village and found that Basang, Tsijü, and the Army Propaganda Team were having a meeting about the grain collection. Drolma [a Gyenlo representative] told Basang, "You people shut up! You have no right to collect grain in our *xiang*. You had better get out of here." At that time, someone from the Army Propaganda Team was speaking, and Basang was interpreting for him. Drolma stepped forward and grabbed Basang, shouting at her, "You've been giving me the evil eye since I joined the Gyenlo Headquarters. We don't need leaders like you now!"[3]

At this point in time, the nun Trinley Chödrön was still not part of Gyenlo's strategy and played no part in these confrontations. However, Zhang Yongfu and Rangjung were planning to launch a larger attack on the county seat in November, and as the time for that drew near, they began to question whether the villagers who were coming for the attack would lose courage when they finally realized they now had to go attack the county seat itself. During a discussion of this, Rangjung suggested that it might help if the nun from Phusum could go into a trance and exhort the villagers not to lose heart. A Han Gyenlo cadre who was present recalled, "On 11 November 1968, Zhang Yongfu said to me, 'If we attack the county now, our force is a little bit too weak, and we may lose the fight.' Then Rangjung had an idea, 'Let the nun from Phusum perform a medium's trance for the people from Angang District [from which a large force of villagers was coming] to bolster their courage.' Zhang Yongfu said, 'Even though this is superstition, at this point we do not need to worry too much about that.'"[4]

Wu Lide, another Han cadre who was a Gyenlo leader, agreed, commenting on the power of religion in Tibetan society: "Tibet is thoroughly imbued with superstition (tib. *mongde;* ch. *mixin*). So, whereas the thoughts of Chairman Mao are our mental atom bomb (tib. *samlö dütren bande;* ch. *jingshen yuanzi dan*), religious superstition is Tibetans' mental atom bomb. If the Dalai were to come back from India, a lot of people would still have faith in him."[5] The top leaders of Gyenlo clearly had no illusions about the way rural Tibetans still felt about religion.

Zhang Yongfu's fear that some Tibetan villagers would lose courage was realized two weeks later on the afternoon of 26 November, when over three hundred villagers from Angang District arrived in Phusum. As the plans for the next day's attack were conveyed, some of these villagers appeared reluctant to march to the county seat. One Tibetan recalled this reluctance: "When people from Angang came . . . they were very hungry and tired. Some of them were afraid that they would not be able to win if people in the county had already made preparations against them. Others did not want to go any farther and decided to go back to Angang."[6]

Rangjung wanted as large a force as possible so now requested that Trinley Chödrön go into a trance and summon her god to speak to the massed villagers. Trinley Chödrön agreed and, after putting on her medium's garb and her Gyenlo armband, invoked the goddess Ani Gongmey Gyemo, who entered the nun's body and proceeded to exhort the unsure villagers to act, as the following account relates:

> [The god said through the nun,] "Comrades-in-arms, you should make up your mind to attack the county. *I'm the god who supports your Gyenlo and promises there will be no casualties. I'll manifest myself as an eagle* (tib. *chala*) *and join the battle.* All the people wearing white woolen *chuba* [the villagers] should unite together to drive out the people wearing blue and yellow clothes [the cadres and PLA troops].[7] The seeds planted in spring have already ripened in autumn [meaning it was time for their attack]." . . .
> She also distributed blessed barley as protective talismans to the people who were going to attack the county. The lama Chamba Tenzin also offered blessed barley talismans and said that these could protect you from bullets if you cast them to the direction of the gunfire.[8]

Coming nine years after public religious rituals of this sort were banned, this was a symbolically powerful event for the villagers. Before their eyes at an open meeting of a Maoist revolutionary mass organization, a young nun went through the traditional stylized ritual of going into a trance with a god while wearing both the medium's traditional costume and the armband of Gyenlo. It was the gods from the old society integrated normatively into the new society under the imprimatur of Gyenlo.

In this context, the language the nun used via Ani Gongmey Gyemo is significant, because it simultaneously asserted her godliness and her unity with Gyenlo. For one thing, Ani Gongmey Gyemo unambiguously asserted her supernatural powers by saying she could transform herself into nonhuman forms and protect the villagers from guns and other harm. And for another, Ani Gongmey Gyemo explicitly linked Tibet's gods to Gyenlo's revolutionary faction by telling the Tibetan villagers that she was *the god who supported Gyenlo* and by urging them to do what Gyenlo had brought them there to do: drive out the cadres and soldiers. Of course, driving out the cadres clearly excluded Rangjung, Zhang Yongfu, and the Gyenlo leadership, who were not considered part of the category of enemy cadres—the blue pigs.

The reluctant Tibetan villagers from Angang responded well to her urgings, as Rangjung had hoped, and the next day hundreds attacked the county seat, where they were victorious. Arriving without warning, they were able to seize, beat up, and detain the officials and then subject them to struggle sessions, at which they were accused of being capitalist-roaders and so on. One Gyenlo village activist who was involved in the attack recalled that day,

> Carrying swords and slingshots, we fought in the Nyemo County seat. The masses rose up, and the cadres lost. The masses seized the cadres and beat them up . . . locking them in the Nyemo *xiang* [building].[9] . . . We stripped them of their clothing and beat them up. . . . We kept them and made them confess their wrongdoings.
>
> However, we couldn't keep them permanently because we would have had to give them food, and we didn't have the power of the Communist Party. After that, we just had to set them free. They ran away to Lhasa, but on the way Rangjung stopped them and beat them up [again]. . . . At that time, we were pure Gyenlo. We said that we wanted to overthrow the people in power in the party, so we were not really going against the party, since at that time the issues between the factions were not settled. [That is, it was a factional dispute between revolutionary groups.][10]

One of the Nyamdre cadres who was the victim of seizure and struggle sessions recalled that same day from his vantage point:

> I was a Nyamdre member and they were Gyenlo, so they held struggle sessions against me, but I never surrendered [my ideology] to Gyenlo.
>
> *Q: How did they hold a struggle session against you?*
> A: At that time they said they were going to destroy us. And we said we were going to destroy them, whether or not we could really have done that.
> *Q: Did they hold the struggle sessions at meetings?*
> A: When Nyamdre lost and Gyenlo won the victory [on 27 November], we ran away. . . . There were some six or seven or ten cadres. So we had to flee at that point.
> *Q: How did they attack? What did they use to hit people?*
> A: They threw stones and broke the glass of the windows and the doors of the district building. . . . When we heard that they had come, we locked the gate and fled from the windows. Some people planned to run far away and took some food with them. Some people went to the mountains, and some people went to hide in the houses of their friends.

The Chinese head of the district (ch. *quzhang*) didn't have any trusted households there, so he ran away and hid in a stack of hay. However, when the people came to the hay stack he moved, so they seized him, tied him up, and held a struggle session against him. I was hiding in the house of my friend when people came in and seized me. They tied me up and held a struggle session against me.

Q: Who informed them that you were hiding there?
A: At that time the Gyenlo people entered all the houses.

Q: How many people were seized?
A: All of the Nyamdre people they could find were seized. Some people, however, were able to flee to Lhasa.

Q: After you were seized, where did they take you?
A: They took me to the place where their people were gathering. Before they seized the people [of Nyamdre], they had already searched the houses and broken things and had beaten people. After that they held a meeting and said [about me], "He is a stubborn person." And they abused me severely. They beat me up severely. That was it.

Q: At that time, what kind of crime did they accuse you of?
A: They said, "Come on. Bring the people of Nyamdre here! What can you people do now? Now it is our choice what we want to do." Then they beat me up and told me to confess my crimes. . . .

Q: Did they hit you with their fists or what?
A: They hit me with their fists, they slapped me, they pointed their fingers at my nose, and they kicked me. They hit everywhere on my body. . . . I was just thinking, What the hell is going to happen? Otherwise, I didn't have any other thoughts. . . . When they were beating me severely I suffered great pain, but I didn't care what happened to me, because I had decided that I would remain in Nyamdre. I didn't join Gyenlo, and they didn't tell me to join them. . . . At that point, I was not settled [as a householder] in this place. I was single and I was not worried about myself. I was thinking that because I didn't have a wife and children, I didn't even care if they killed me. I was thinking, I am young and don't have anybody who relies on me in this place, and I don't know anybody down here, so the only thing I can do is to stay like this.[11]

Another Nyamdre cadre recalled more specific accusations that were made against him in the struggle sessions: "I was put in many struggle sessions, but I was not killed. My title was head of the security office in the *xiang*. . . . They said I collected large quantities of grain and domestic animal taxes and forced people to sell grain to the government. Also, they said that I did not tell the government the real production levels of grain."[12]

Gyenlo's astute and pragmatic strategy to mobilize the peasantry, therefore, worked perfectly, and their November strike was a great success. Most Nyamdre cadres who had not already fled to Lhasa were now marginalized, and Gyenlo became the dominant revolutionary force in the Nyemo countryside.[13] However, notwithstanding the use of the nun-medium, this attack was presented to the villagers as part of the revolutionary movement responding to Chairman Mao's call to clean out the bad elements who had sneaked into the party. In Nyemo, that conveniently happened to be the Nyamdre cadres. It was not Tibetans versus Chinese but "bad" cadres versus "good" cadres, that is, Nyamdre versus Gyenlo.

The November action was also a stunning victory for the villagers because it meant that they did not have to provide the scheduled heavy grain taxes. Most households had actually been willing to fulfill the more modest obligation of patriotic-donation grain, and some still did, but virtually no one handed in any "sales grain," since these taxes were predicated on the false claim that this was surplus grain. Chinese records reveal the impact of this for 1968: "The plan for donation grain from the whole county in 1968 was 510,000 *jin*. However, only 330,000 *jin* of grain [64 percent] were collected. The planned purchase [quota] of surplus ["sales"] grain was 2.1 million *jin*, but the actual purchase was only 110,000 *jin* [5 percent]. And *xiang* like Chöling, Nyemo, Phusum, Sangang, Shuben, and Bagor did not hand in any grain that year."[14] In other words, in 1968 Nyemo farming households retained almost 2.25 million *jin* of grain that would otherwise have been forcibly sold or "donated" to the government.

In an unanticipated twist, the attack was also a tremendous success for the nun and her god Ani Gongmey Gyemo, catapulting them to a new level of spiritual prominence. The question of whether the nun was crazy or divine now seemed to have been answered on the side of the divine. Her (or her god's) prophecies and promises of supernatural protection for the fighters had proven accurate, for not a single villager had been injured. Faith in her powers now soared. As one villager said, "The nun was very important. When she said something, people followed it, because people believed she was giving them true direction. She had said she would transform herself into an eagle to support her followers, so when people saw eagles in the sky that day, they went to the county to fight."[15]

The nun, therefore, was now simultaneously a Gyenlo supporter, ostensibly assisting Gyenlo to implement Mao's revolutionary agenda in Nyemo by seizing power from the Nyamdre cadres, and the new human vehicle for Ani Gongmey Gyemo, who was again directing Tibetans to fight against their enemies, as she had previously done through her prophecies for King Gesar. As will be seen below, many villagers now also started to believe that the nun had supernatural powers of her own.

Gyenlo's utilization of religion—"superstition" in Cultural Revolution ideology—was reactionary from the leftist point of view, but Gyenlo's
leaders were pragmatic and had decided that temporarily making use of
religion would improve their ability to take over the county, so they placed
ideological purity in abeyance.[16] The nun was an effective means to what
they considered a critical and highly valued end.

Consequently, by the end of 1968, Nyamdre had basically been stripped
of its power, influence, and stature. Most of the higher cadres had fled
to Lhasa, and those grassroots cadres who had stayed because they had
families in the villages were vulnerable to being placed in struggle sessions without warning by the Gyenlo representatives. Nevertheless,
Gyenlo still faced serious obstacles to gaining control of the county, since
the county's Department of Armed Forces (ch. *wuzhuang bu*) and its Military Squadron (ch. *zhongdui*) were intact and stood as a potential base
for Nyamdre to launch a counterattack.[17] The next goal for Gyenlo, therefore, was to further solidify its position in the countryside and prevent
future attacks against itself by creating its own new revolutionary army
and administration and then using them to eliminate the small military
presence in Nyemo. These issues were discussed in a seven-day meeting
in January 1969.

THE JANUARY 1969 MEETING

Between 7 and 13 January, Gyenlo leaders held a meeting in Nyemo *xiang*
to analyze the 27 November operation and discuss their next steps. On
the third day of the meeting, Zhang Yongfu asked for opinions about
how the victory had been won:

> Trinley from Phusum stood up and said, "If you ask why we were all so
> brave during this combat, it is because we have the crazy nun in Phusum,
> and she gave us a lot of help. . . . [W]e people from Phusum were very
> brave because we had our god, Gongmey Gyemo, and she told us that we
> would not fail and would win the battle in about an hour. She told us
> no one would be injured in this combat because we had Gongmey Gyemo
> behind us. We won this combat, not because we were capable, but because
> Ani Gongmey Gyemo was supporting us."
>
> Another member said, "The people from Angang and Phusum won the
> battle because they worshipped the god. Their god, the nun, went into a
> trance and danced for them wearing a Gyenlo Headquarters' armband.
> The nun told them, 'Go ahead and be brave. I have blocked their guns.
> You can win the battle if you go. I will transform myself into an eagle to
> go with you and protect you.'" Trinley then [again] said, "This god is very
> powerful. She knows the future as well as the past. People in Phusum believe

in her. People from other *xiang* also believe in her. We could not have won the combat without her help. *It was she and Chairman Mao who helped us win the battle.*"[18]

However, not all Gyenlo leaders agreed. Some were reluctant to credit the nun explicitly in a summary report they were preparing, since this was clearly superstition and they were a revolutionary Maoist group. Nevertheless, after much discussion, Rangjung and Zhang Yongfu agreed with Trinley, and this view ultimately carried the day. The nun had proved she could use the gods of Tibet to motivate Tibetan villagers to fight against Nyamdre, so Zhang Yongfu was unwilling to refrain from making full use of her in their upcoming plans. Gyenlo again pragmatically decided that the end justified the means in her case, despite understanding that this might later make them vulnerable to claims that they were reactionaries.

On the fourth day of the meeting, the issue of setting up a new administrative structure for the county was discussed in detail. Gyenlo members feared that Nyamdre was planning to strike back and wanted to be ready to defend their victory. Consequently, they set up a new defense organization that would be ready "to fight at the first call and be sure of winning every fight."[19] The nun loomed large in their thinking, because they fully expected to have to confront the army in the future:

> [Rangjung] said, "The nun in Phusum is a very good god. She is the god of Gyenlo. With her support, we will be able to beat the PLA and the [county] leadership whenever they cause us trouble."

> [Zhang Yongfu] said, "I'm sure that we will have a fight with the PLA in the future. We should start by attacking the county party committee. The PLA at the county Public Security Bureau will run to the county building to help them. Then our people will use this opportunity to rush into the Public Security Bureau to grab the weapons there. We'll take the Public Security Bureau over when we have weapons."[20]

In the end, the January meeting produced four documents that set out a new alternative organizational structure for the county called the Gyenlo Headquarters of Farmers and Herdsmen (tib. *shingdrog gyenlo silingbu;* ch. *nong mu min zaofan silingbu*). The documents called for replacing the old *xiang* and district offices with new revolutionary institutions. Extracts from them illustrate the new approach:

> [The section called "Guiding Principle" said:] From the day the Gyenlo Headquarters of Farmers and Herdsmen is established, the county government offices are dismissed. All the power will belong to the Headquarters

of Farmers and Herdsmen. Leaders at all levels will also be set aside and
replaced with members from the Headquarters of Farmers and Herders.
All people must obey the orders of the Headquarters of Farmers and
Herders and respect the leadership of the Headquarters of Farmers and
Herders. The headquarters will accept the leadership of both the Lhasa
General Headquarters [of Gyenlo] and the Military Squadron. In order
to fight the enemies inside and outside, branches should be founded in
the county and district (ch. *qu*) under the united leadership of the Headquarters of Farmers and Herders.

[A section discussing the peasants expressed a flexible attitude toward
the rights of the peasants:] Everybody has rights over his own land,
house, and properties and can sell his handicrafts and sideline products.
Those people who have relatives overseas have the right to write letters
abroad as long as they do not have illicit relations with the foreign
country. If it is necessary to strike somebody, search his house, and con-
fiscate his properties, people should do it only with the permission of
the headquarters.[21]

[The section called the "Announcement" said the following:] Under the
revolutionary Gyenlo Headquarters of Farmers and Herdsmen in Nyemo
County, a command center will be established to fight peacefully and defend ourselves militarily (tib. *shigö tragsung*, ch. *wen gong wu wei*). Under
this command center, there will be six branches, one in each of the six districts, and twenty-seven "Gyenlo communes" in each [of the twenty-seven]
xiang.[22]. . . People can borrow money from one another without any interest
or with very little interest. During the proletarian Cultural Revolution, all
activities of the Communist Party and Youth League are not permitted. If a
person tries to organize a meeting of the Communist Party or the Youth
League secretly, he should be regarded as attempting to restore the old system
[that existing after 1959 but before this new one]. Our attitude toward the
PLA is that we will support them if the PLA truly protects the proletarian
revolutionary Gyenlo organization. However, we will fight against them if
they implement the wrong line. Our revolutionary Gyenlo faction follows
Chairman Mao. Whoever opposes us is opposing Chairman Mao.[23]

Interestingly, discussions about the name of the new organization were
spirited and again reveal the importance that Gyenlo's leaders placed on
continuing to motivate the Tibetan masses. One of the representatives from
Phusum initially suggested this new force be called the Army for Defending Buddhism (tib. *tensungmag*), for this is what the nun and some of those
around her in Phusum had in mind. This name was not well received. Not
only did it connote a purely religious goal, but also it had been used by
the Khamba guerrilla fighters in the 1959 uprising against the state, so
most of the representatives opposed it. Another representative, therefore,
suggested that the new headquarters should be called the Gyenlo Headquarters of Farmers and Herdsmen, but here Rangjung disagreed and said

that it should be called Gyenlo's Army of the Gods (tib. *gyenlo lhamag*). When one cadre asked what that meant, Rangjung explained, "When we attacked the county on 27 November, we weren't sure how we could win the battle, but it seemed as if our people were falling from the heavens and emerging from the ground, and we won the battle in no time. Only an army of the gods could do this. And since we are members of Gyenlo Headquarters, we should name our organization Gyenlo's Army of the Gods [to reflect these two components]. Zhang Yongfu agreed with Rangjung, saying, "The success of 27 November came from the thought of Chairman Mao and the efforts of the nun. Why can't we allow people to call this organization Gyenlo's Army of the Gods? I think we should respect the creativity of the masses. Maybe you are afraid, but I'm not."[24] Despite some objections, in the end it was decided that their quest was too important not to use every method, including superstition, so they decided to use the name, but not publicly to other officials:

> Li Yu said, "Zhang Yongfu's idea is understandable. This name came from the masses. It will be fine if we use it, but we should not disseminate it in public. The current situation requires us to seize political power at all levels, so we cannot separate ourselves from the masses at this crucial time. *We can make use of the nun at present and arrest her after the Revolutionary Committee* (ch. *geming weiyuanhui*) *is founded.* Zhang Yongfu said that this nun has power, and I agree with him."[25]
>
> Huang Guojie then said, "It's no big deal if we call it Gyenlo's Army of the Gods, *but . . . let's just use it among ourselves.* I agree with Zhang Yongfu's opinion."
>
> Dong Xue'an then asked, "Does anyone have other opinions? [I think that] [i]f we give it a name like this, our organization will become a reactionary organization. [However,] Yang Songlin responded, *"No one will know about it if we do not announce it publicly. Let's do as Zhang Yongfu said."*[26]

And so, on that day, Gyenlo Headquarters in Nyemo decided to use the name Gyenlo's Army of the Gods inside the organization (and in the countryside) but the Headquarters of Farmers and Herdsmen in public. Zhang Yongfu was selected as the commander-in-chief of Gyenlo's Army of the Gods, and Rangjung and Tsesum (a Tibetan local cadre who was head of Nyemo *xiang*) were appointed as the deputy commanders-in-chief along with several others.

In the months that followed, Gyenlo consolidated its power, marginalizing the Nyamdre grassroots-level officials as it prepared for an attack on the offices of the county's Military Squadron and Department of Armed Forces. It also now maintained close ties with the nun through

Rangjung, who was organizing and preparing the villagers for the coming military operations against the county seat.

A Chinese document reveals how the leaders of Gyenlo not only understood the utility of the nun for their cause but were actually proud of having come up with this unusual tactic of using a religious medium to help defeat their revolutionary enemies:

> At the end of January 1969, Huang Guojie, Zhang Yongfu, and Wu Lide said to Rangjung and other representatives, "We won in Nyemo, but we need to support the neighboring counties to reinforce the triumph. If the neighboring counties are attacked in the future, we should send the nun to do some religious dances [go into trances] to activate the masses. If there is some situation we cannot stop, we will send the crazy one to activate the people once again to beat them [the attackers] back. The masses believe in superstition, so if the crazy one activates them, they will be fearless. That's good! *This is the great invention of Nyemo County. We have to employ her [the nun]. First, we send her to do some religious dances [go into trances], then we drive the masses to attack. The cadres from the Lhasa headquarters agreed with the method we took and indicated that we should use the religious dances to activate the masses to attack.*[27] *Therefore, if we want to attack in the future, we need to prepare for it; the religious dance [trance] of the nun is the weapon to access the masses' mental world.*"
>
> Afterward, Trinley [from Phusum] said, "If someone wants to kill the nun, what should we do?" Wu Lide said that we should send some representatives to live in the nun's place and guard the nun. . . .
>
> In February 1969 . . . some people from Rimpung County came to Nyemo to learn how to attack a county seat. They talked to Huang Guojie and some other people in private, and then Huang Guojie sent Xiao Yong to introduce them to their [Gyenlo's] experiences regarding the 27 November event. He told them that the crazy one was of great use to us in motivating the people, and this is the invention of Nyemo. Superstition prevails now in Tibet, so the nun's religious dances [trances] are really useful. They [people of Rimpung] are now facing many problems and are really in need of these experiences. We need to encourage them, so you [Xiao Yong] should teach them in detail.[28]

In the following month, March 1969, negative feelings against the army were heightened when a theater troupe from Gyenlo General Headquarters in Lhasa came to Nyemo to perform a propaganda play that focused on the PLA's killing of the Gyenlo activists in the Jokhang Temple incident of the previous year. It was highly emotional and not only generated sympathy for Gyenlo but also stoked the desire for revenge against the PLA. A local Tibetan recalled,

> In the show, they depicted how Nyamdre had treated people badly in the city. . . . I remember old men felt sad and cried at the show because of the

bad treatment. Since then the movement increased to a peak. People said that if the people in the city supported Gyenlo, we should follow them and support them. . . . They said that Nyamdre treated our faction so badly in Lhasa, and they cried.

Q: *Did you cry at that point?*
A: Not really. But I was very sad.[29]

GESAR'S WARRIOR-HEROES

Despite the Democratic Reforms and the campaign against the four olds, Tibetans believed in gods and supernatural causation, so the 27 November prophecies of the nun/Ani Gongmey Gyemo were seen as powerful proof of the nun's authenticity. As a result, not only did her reputation and fame soar, as mentioned earlier, but also the identity of the medium as mortal and that of Ani Gongmey Gyemo as goddess began to blur, and more and more local people began talking about Trinley Chödrön as if *she* herself had supernatural powers, which the following comments from three Tibetan villagers illustrate:

> At that time, people exaggerated and said that the nun was able to tell them what they were thinking. I didn't get a chance to go there [to see her], but at that time, people said that when they took the nun some kind of gift as an offering, such as *tsamba*, flour, or money, she was able to tell them what thoughts they had when they were preparing the gift. For example, she would say, "When you were preparing this gift, you were thinking that you didn't really want to give this gift-offering to me, and you left the bigger gift at home and took a smaller one." At that time, the nun was really famous.[30]

> I thought I should try hard to do the things that they ordered me to do; otherwise, I would be placing myself in a precarious situation. At that time, the nun said she knew what every individual was doing both during the day and when they returned home, because she could transform herself into the body of a bird or mouse and visit households. Because of this, even though no outside persons were staying in my home, we did not dare to talk about our real feelings. We were afraid she could understand our feelings. I had to talk with my wife using very low whispers when we needed to discuss some secret things.[31]

> [When the Army of the Gods was fighting and killing people] I thought the nun was correct. I was deceived like that. I used to tell my parents, "I heard that the nun Trinley Chödrön is going into trances, and people are saying her prophecies are very accurate, so we must also go to consult the gods. If we remain muddle-headed (tib. *go thom*) and stay with Nyamdre, one day we may suffer a loss." That was a childish thought, and my father told me, "The nun is not true, so shut up. You should be steadfast [for Nyamdre]."

At that point, Gyenlo was holding meetings and they looked well united and the nun was going into trances. They said that some Buddhas were coming and would manifest themselves [their form] in the midst of rainbowlike clouds. If you have faith, they said, you should put some water in a basin and look at it [i.e., at the sky reflected in it]. I did that, but I could see only clouds in the sky. However, some people who had faith said that they could see the Buddha, so I thought probably I was a person without faith. And I thought it would be better to surrender and stand on the side of the nun and try to have faith.

Q: At that time, did people have a deep faith in the nun?
A: Yes, they did.[32]

Another villager expressed this widespread attitude more succinctly, saying of the nun's powers, "We thought the nun could foresee the future (tib. *ngönshe*)."[33]

While this was unfolding, the belief that the goddess Ani Gongmey Gyemo had returned to earth to guide a new campaign against the enemies of Buddhism led to a kind of "Gesar hysteria," in which a number of villagers, male and female, spontaneously went into trances over a period of a few months, claiming they were possessed by one or another of the great warrior-heroes (tib. *badü*) who had fought beside Gesar in the past. For example, in Jangra District, a villager named Yönden became possessed by the famous hero Bala, Gombo was possessed by Denma, and Tashi Rabden was possessed by Jangdru Yülha. In Bagor, Norbu Samdrub became possessed by Pehar Gyebo, and another villager by Shechen Riwo Pangyong. Exactly how many new warrior-hero mediums there were is uncertain, but there were many, perhaps as many as thirty.

After initially going into a trance in their own villages, these warrior-heroes went to the nun when she was in a trance with Ani Gongmey Gyemo. A Tibetan close to the nun recalled how disturbed they were when they arrived:

They named themselves the *badü*. They came [from other villages], riding their horses. . . . They had started going into trances in their own homes. They came yelling "ki hi" and said . . . they were Denma and so on from the Gesar story.

Q: Did the nun tell them that they were such and such badü?
A: No. They named themselves. For example, Tashi Rabden said he was Jangdru Yülha . . . and so on in the Gesar story. At that time, the people in Phusum were religious people, so they had faith in those things. . . . They initially came when the nun was going into a trance with the god, and then they gave a khata scarf to the god and said they were this or that badü. . . .

They were like mad people yelling "ki hi," and their bodies were shaking, and they were going into a trance. . . . Then the nun/god . . . did the tsago che ritual for them, which calmed them a lot.[34]

By virtue of this phenomenon, a new category of activists (warrior-hero mediums) was created around the nun/Ani Gongmey Gyemo. In Tibetan terms, King Gesar's heroic entourage had now come to join Ani Gongmey Gyemo in Nyemo. The suggestive power of this Gesar hysteria can be seen from the experience of one die-hard Nyamdre cadre (a deputy *xiang* head) who recalled his shock at seeing his own son spontaneously start to go into a trance:

> With all those problems caused by the nun, I deeply resented hearing people say that the medium was possessed by deities (tib. *lha*). I personally thought that the nun was possessed more by devils than by deities. One day, even one of my own children fell into some kind of trance and came running forward to our house. When I saw him like that, I became infuriated and grabbed a stick and started to hit him on his head. That stick had a sharp edge, so his head got injured quite seriously. At that time, a neighbor who was a cadre helped my child and calmed me down. . . . Actually, it was very strange that in our village during those times we had a lot of such cases with people just falling into trances.[35]

These new warrior-hero mediums were very different from the standard Gyenlo members and representatives in that they were the truest of the true believers of the nun. They had complete faith that Ani Gongmey Gyemo had chosen the nun as her human vehicle to drive out the enemies of Buddhism and that they similarly had been chosen as the human vehicles by Gesar's warrior-heroes to assist the nun/Ani Gongmey Gyemo. In this powerful Tibetan symbolism, Ani Gongmey Gyemo was again advising the famous battle heroes of King Gesar to wage a second campaign to destroy the enemies of Buddhism. As such, these warrior-hero mediums were totally committed to fighting and destroying the enemies of Buddhism and became the nun's fanatical followers, directly extending her charisma and influence to their own villages. By May 1969, eight of these warrior-hero mediums regularly stayed with the nun in Phusum as a kind of personal entourage/bodyguard for her, and when the attacks on individuals began in June, it was the warrior-heroes who actually carried out most of the subsequent killings and mutilations (together with some of the Gyenlo village representatives). Gyenlo's pragmatic and self-serving tactic of giving the nun a platform, therefore, had inadvertently helped to propel her and Ani Gongmey Gyemo to a new level of spiritual prominence and practical influence as the center of a powerful and uniquely Tibetan supernatural world projected onto the landscape of Nyemo—in a sense, projected on top of the already powerful and uniquely socialist revolutionary world within which Gyenlo and Nyamdre were contending. The village masses who accepted the nun/Ani Gongmey Gyemo as a deity fighting for Buddhism now had a new and emotionally powerful motivation in addition to Gyenlo's more materialistic issues, such as taxes and land tenure. The Gyenlo leader's previously mentioned observation that religion was the mental atom bomb of Tibetans will become more and more relevant from this point on.

This amazing development, however, did not mean that the nun now had her own separate army and operated independent of Gyenlo. To the contrary, there was still only a single Gyenlo's Army of the Gods, and Rangjung was its field commander. In the months leading up to the 1969 attacks, Rangjung worked closely with the nun and the main warrior-hero mediums. Some even say that Zhang Yongfu secretly rode to Phusum at night dressed in Tibetan clothing at least once to meet her, but this is not confirmed. However, it is clear that Gyenlo's village representatives remained in close contact with Rangjung and the leadership at Gyenlo Headquarters in Nyemo, frequently attending meetings. One village representative talked about such a meeting: "[Zhang Yongfu said,] 'Gyenlo is the best group, and we will win under the correct leadership of Chairman Mao.' He said we should argue and study the Red Documents (tib. *marbö yigja*). These were articles from newspapers that were read at the meetings. He held meetings like this five or six times for the representatives, who then went back to their respective villages and passed along his ideas to the local people."[36]

So despite the Gesar hysteria, Gyenlo's leaders and activists were working together with the nun and the new warrior-hero mediums to take control of Nyemo County, although not with the same end vision in mind. Interestingly, there are no reports of the nun and Rangjung ever discussing what would happen after victory or even what exactly the nun envisioned in postvictory Nyemo, but clearly the nun and Rangjung had a close and harmonious relationship. No hint of discord appeared in any of the interviews or documents. This is not surprising given Gyenlo's tactical pragmatism. It would not do anything to alienate the nun until the final victory was won and would let her think whatever she liked about the postvictory configuration. Throughout the final months, Rangjung, in fact, was careful to cloak his own commands with the nun's prophecies and often sought her agreement to do something in the form of a prophecy from Ani Gongmey Gyemo. The nun, therefore, clearly had no objection to Rangjung's continued organization of the coming fight, and everyone we interviewed on both sides said that Rangjung was the field commander of Gyenlo's Army of the Gods despite the presence of the warrior-hero mediums. So while the emergence of the warrior-hero mediums is significant because they created a kind of radical "Buddhist Red Guards" who were totally committed to restoring the open practice of Buddhism, the mediums, the masses, and the activist Gyenlo representatives all co-existed under the umbrella of Gyenlo.

Rangjung and Gyenlo's continuing central role was made easier because the nun herself did not play an active role in these events. She led a rather cloistered existence in Phusum and never gave public speeches (with the exception of her ritualized medium trances at which Ani Gongmey Gyemo spoke through her). She virtually never left Phusum, even to travel to other villages to motivate and organize her followers. With the exception of her actual trances, all interactions with the masses were done through her closest advisers, including the warrior-heroes and Rangjung, who, we believe, were able to influence, if not mold, her attitudes on issues because of this insular aspect of her personality. One Phusum man commented on this:

> Her representatives would make speeches. The nun herself would not say anything. It was very hard for us to see her. Mostly those people who said they had great faith in the nun would call meetings and make speeches. Several important persons were given names of the warrior-heroes from the Ling Gesar epic. They were the people who made the speeches. They would say this and that was the nun's order. [At the time of the killings] [t]hey were also the people who decided who had faith in the nun and who did not and who should be seized and who should not.[37]

As the time for the final attacks on the county neared, Trinley Chödrön—through the voice of Ani Gongmey Gyemo—issued a wild, rambling, and semi-incoherent statement/manifesto that expounded her views and goals and, in retrospect, was a kind of formal justification for the coming attacks. This statement was dictated to a Gyenlo activist while the nun was in a trance. He recalled that day and his involvement:

> On the night of 4 May 1969 . . . I went to see the nun at her house in Phusum. On 5 May, when the sun was just rising, I was ready to go back home, but Trinley [the nun's supporter] said to me, " . . . [D]on't go yet. First write a letter for us." I said that I didn't have a pen or ink, but Trinley said, "We do. Come with me."
> Trinley took me to Trinley Chödrön's house, where she began to intone

prayers. Then she asked Tsering Chösang [formerly the chant leader of the local monastery] to bring me a pen, ink, and some paper, and she asked me to write down what she said.[38]

This statement, however, is extremely difficult to understand. The original translators into Chinese mentioned that they had difficulty understanding the Tibetan but did not indicate whether this was because the nun was immersed in an imagined world that made little sense to normal people or because they couldn't understand the religious terms and allusions she used. Whichever it was, many of the sections below, which come from the Chinese translation, sound like rantings and make little or no sense.

The Tibetan who took the dictation recalled some of what she said:

[The nun/Ani Gongmey Gyemo] said [to me], "I'm here because there are a lot of enemies here. I, the nun, used to live in Lakabala [?] in the mountains. There, I offered one hundred thousand offerings to the gods. There were one hundred thousand god-kings and one hundred thousand god-queens.

The criminal [evil] lama failed to manage this country and handed it over to Chairman Mao. Chairman Mao also could not control this country, so he gave the power to us, the "Eight Buddhist Guardian Warriors" (ch. *ba da jingang*). The Eight Buddhist Guardian Warriors took over this nauseating country and started managing it from the year of the sheep [1967].

"It is Chairman Mao who distinguishes the poor from the rich [i.e., who is in control of the material world], and it is I, the nun, who distinguishes merit from demerit [good from evil]. . . . This place is worshipped by the believers of religion and hated by those who do not believe. . . . The PLA pays attention to the view of only one or two individuals from the masses [is partial], and the PLA is showing the appearance of preparing to start a war. Fine! We will not eat. We will make war starting on the 10th."

After I wrote the letter, Rangjung and Trinley told me not to say that we would start the war on the 10th, since it would be better to send messengers to inform people verbally to prepare for [the specific date].[39]

Our translation of the nun's full written statement follows below. (The Chinese pinyin is cited in appendix 1.)

The gods (ch. *shen*) descended to this human world to subdue the demons and ghosts who are the enemies of humans.

Chairman Mao is the judge (ch. *caipan*). [However,] for the people who are avaricious and devour things (ch. *tan cai tun cai*) [the cadres], the gods who haven't had the right to speak, that is to say, the thousand god-kings and the thousand god-queens (ch. *shen wang nu shen*), are the judges.

If other people intrude into someone's house, one has to defend himself and fight back. According to what Comrade Jiang Qing [Mao's wife] told us, "We must always firmly defend ourselves and counterattack."

Tenzin Gyatso's (Note 1) country was given to Chairman Mao by the evil lama (ch. *zuie lama*) (Note 2). Chairman Mao then passed it on to the world of the gods (ch. *shen jie*). In the past, because we didn't have the right to speak, it was like having fire in the stomach but not daring to spew out smoke from the mouth.

More than one thousand people came to the Biru area (Note 3) to consult the gods. They were told, "Do not be greedy (ch. *tanlan*) or jealous (ch. *jidu*). Do not talk back to your parents, to whom you should be grateful. Your family should eat good meals. You should be friendly to your neighbors and listen to the party."

Among the people coming to consult the god, more than thirty were good people. The other people will be investigated in detail later. They [think they] can make a Tara statue with [only] one dollar of Tibetan money [one *tranga garpo* is an amount far too little] (Note 4).

You uncle (*ashang*)-PLA soldiers need to understand clearly that if you listen and trust just a few people [are partial] and use guns and swords [against the people], from today on, don't plan to eat food [you will be killed?].[40] From today on, even crazy people (ch. *fengzi*) will not eat.

The whole country is not the country of Chairman Mao or Tenzin Gyatso. It is the country of the gods. Although you do not like it, the gods have taken over the country since the Sheep year [*me lug*, 1967]. In June, you'll see a great show.

Thank you, you uncle (*ashang*)-lay people. You have already repaid kindness with harm. So the "wish-fulfilling stone" (tib. *yishi norbu*) [the Jowo in Lhasa? the Dalai Lama?] and the dharma protector deities will gradually repay your kindness in the future [said sarcastically].

One thousand monks sent Ani Gongmey Gyemo, and she is living in the Jiebala Mountains [?], and she is living well. There are demons and ghosts in this world. In the human world, Chairman Mao is the judge of wealth and material things, and I, the nun, am the judge of whether people are good or bad.

I came here according to the instructions of our great leader Chairman Mao. As for you laymen, your lives are like lights seen through a chimney (Note 5). Some people who are intolerant did great harm to laymen and caused a disaster. When the day comes and the sun rises, the goddess Ji lamu (tib. *ji*[?] *lha mo*) in Majie [?] will come to interrogate and try them. You uncle lay people are thinking quite well, thinking to make a Buddha statue with one Tibetan dollar [an impossibility], but the gods never make groundless allegations. The gods will educate you and return those *khata* scarves you offered to them. Ani Gongmey Gyemo is extremely angry about the evil-minded laymen. We have caught nine or ten people who committed heinous crimes. More people are waiting to be caught.[41]

For those who have religious beliefs, this is the place to practice your faith. For those who don't have religious faith, this is also the place to do

something evil. [But] [w]e will definitely defend ourselves and fight back
[against the evil ones]. . . .
  Note 1. Refers to Dalai Lama, Tenzin Gyatso.
  Note 2. Refers to the big living Buddha.
  Note 3. Biru is the name of a place [presumably in Nyemo, not
          Nagchuka].
  Note 4. A small silver Tibetan coin *(tranga garpo).*
  Note 5. Transient, temporary.[42]

The idea of making a formal statement directly from the realm of the
gods, from Ani Gongmey Gyemo herself, is extraordinary. However, like
much else surrounding the nun, it is not clear whether the statement was
her idea or Rangjung's or to what extent Chamba Tenzin, the older lama
who had previously done the *tsago che* ritual, was involved. But with the
time for the attacks about to start, we think it plausible that Rangjung
asked the nun to have Ani Gongmey Gyemo make a statement, which could
then be distributed to key villages to energize the masses. One Tibetan
local cadre who was not a Gyenlo follower recalled reading it:

> At that time, the nun Trinley Chödrön sent a letter around. I read that
> letter . . . , [which said], "The sinful persons could not be subdued in hell
> so were given to Chairman Mao. Mao could not subdue them and gave
> them to the eight types of gods and demons" (tib. *lhasin degye).*[43]
>
> *Q: What else did the letter contain?*
> A: I don't remember.
>
> *Q: What does the phrase "gods and the demons" refer to?*
> A: It refers to the mediums. She was saying that the mediums could expel
> the people in power and take over the power that Chairman Mao was not
> able to take over. . . .
>
> *Q: In the beginning, what kind of slogans did they shout? Did they talk
> about independence, or did they talk about not delivering the [grain] taxes?*
> A: Generally speaking, in the beginning they talked about the serious
> embezzlement being done by the local cadre such as the *xiang* head and
> so on. They were talking above about opposing the people in power in
> the party committee, and when they were pointing to the lower level, they
> pointed to the *xiang* head and those sorts of people. They didn't talk about
> independence.
>
> *Q: What about later on?*
> A: Later, they still didn't talk about the independence.[44]

It is difficult to assess from the Chinese translation of this statement what
the nun was trying to convey, but there appear to be several points relat-
ing to her vision of the gods and her mission—and of the coming battle
against the county seat.

First, the entire statement is a grandiose assertion of the supremacy of the gods, here meaning the gods possessing the mediums, that is, the nun herself and the warrior-hero mediums. The statement says that they have come specially to the human realm to "subdue the demons and ghosts who are the enemy," which is precisely the Gesar paradigm. The statement also emphasizes the power of the gods by stating that the whole country (which in context means Nyemo) belongs not to Mao or the Dalai Lama but to the gods, that is, to the nun/Ani Gongmey Gyemo and her entourage of warrior-hero mediums. The statement further conveys the new freedom that the nun felt, declaring that previously no one had the right to speak out and had to suffer in silence, but those constraints had now ended. And with this new freedom, it also remarks that society is in terrible shape as a result of the behavior of evil and greedy people.

Second, the statement asserts that taking militant action to protect one's house (i.e., to "subdue the enemy") is correct and then implies it would happen within a month (in June). It justifies this by quoting none other than Mao's ultraleftist wife, Jiang Qing, who said that people have to defend themselves and *counterattack*.

Third, it conveys a political statement by emphasizing a continuing link to Mao (the state). It not only says that Mao had instructed her to come here but also concedes authority over the material world to Mao: "In the human world, Chairman Mao is the judge of wealth and material things, and I, the nun, am the judge of whether people are good or bad." What this distinction meant to the nun/Ani Gongmey Gyemo is unclear, but her choice to make it is significant, because it reveals a desire to emphasize that her goals and actions were to be seen as falling within the Chinese state rather than within a separatist polity.

Fourth, the nun was issuing a general warning to all those who had acted "badly" (presumably since 1959), telling them that they would experience retribution. As mentioned earlier, she thoroughly hated the cadres and activists who had destroyed religion-monasticism and persecuted families they deemed to be class enemies. As her religious prominence increased, she also came to hate other Tibetans who believed she was a fraud, challenging her authenticity and ridiculing her supernatural powers. Her comments were, therefore, also a kind of rambling rationalization for the local campaign of blood and terror she was about to launch.

Fifth, the nun was telling the PLA to stay neutral in the coming struggle, warning them that if they chose to intervene, she and her followers would fight against them. It is important to reiterate that the nun was operating under the "umbrella" of Gyenlo and thus was part of the revolutionary factional struggle in which the PLA was not supposed to intervene and take sides.[45]

This statement was sent from Phusum to Gyenlo Headquarters for translation and comment. The reaction at Gyenlo Headquarters varied. Some seemed incensed at what she had said (in their name) and wanted to send a response to her immediately, but the main leaders decided against this, passing her statement off as something that really wasn't very important so didn't require an answer. Zhang Yongfu was gearing up for the coming final attack against the county seat and did not want to challenge the disturbed nun and risk her deciding not to continue to motivate the masses.

Ten copies of the statement were handwritten. On five of these, the apparently original signature of "Gyenlo Headquarters" was changed to "male and female crazy people." These were used for distribution to government venues.[46]

It should be noted that throughout this period, the top Gyenlo leaders such as Zhang Yongfu, Wu Lide, Huang Guojie, and Li Jianhua worked as higher-level cadres in the county and district and maintained their connection with the nun and Gyenlo's Army of the Gods through Rangjung and the village representatives. They did not go to the villages themselves to organize affairs.

Not long after this statement was distributed, the brutal killings in Nyemo began.

CHAPTER 4

Destroying the Demons and Ghosts

THE ENEMIES WITHIN

As the time for the main Nyemo attack approached, the nun, the warrior-hero mediums, and some of the Gyenlo representatives began a wave of killings and maimings targeting those they called the internal enemies—or, more expressively, the "demons and ghosts." Ani Gongmey Gyemo, for example, is reported to have said prophetically, "[First] [l]eave aside the external enemies and destroy the enemies within (tib. *chidra shane nangdra dor*)."[1] She also used the traditional saying, "Even though the rain outside stops, the leaking inside continues (tib. *chi charbe charthag chegyang / nang thigbe thigthag ma che*)," conveying that the remaining enemies in the countryside (the inside leaks) must be eliminated.[2]

These internal enemies are commonly said to have been the Chinese and Tibetan cadres in Nyemo, and to an extent this is correct, but when we look at this closely, we can see that really several different categories of internal enemies were killed and mutilated. The most numerous were, in fact, the remaining local grassroots-level cadres who had been the main implementers of the Democratic Reforms and the new taxes as well as the main persecutors of the religious and lay elites. These targets fell into two subcategories. The first included those who were to be punished according to a list made by the nun and the warrior-hero mediums (either while in a trance or validated while in a trance). These cadres were actively sought out for punishment. The other type were individual cadres who were in the wrong place at the wrong time, that is, were seized and punished after inadvertently coming face to face with a fired-up mob.

However, it should be emphasized that although the nun generally despised the government cadres for what they had done after 1959, simply having worked as a cadre was not sufficient grounds to be included among the targets. As mentioned earlier, Gyenlo officials such as Rangjung, despite having harshly enforced the Democratic Reforms and class struggle, were never targeted by the nun or the warrior-hero mediums. Nor were Zhang Yongfu and the other Gyenlo Headquarters leaders in the county seen as targets. Given the nun's allegiance to Gyenlo and Ani Gongmey Gyemo's declaration that she was the "god of Gyenlo," this, of course, is not surprising, but it reveals clearly that the nun did not treat cadres as a homogeneous category to be indiscriminately attacked, mutilated, and killed. The cadres attacked by the nun were almost entirely prominent grassroots-level cadres whom she (or another warrior-hero medium) considered either implacable enemies or objects of a personal grudge or animosity. Minor cadres, therefore, were sometimes targeted because of something they had done to irritate the nun or one of the warrior-hero mediums, whereas other more important cadres were not. Almost all were Nyamdre members.

In addition to cadres, a second very important category of victims was composed of local Tibetans who had ridiculed the nun's religious claims and thus questioned her religious authenticity, for example, her claim that the Jowo Rimpoche of the Lhasa Jokhang was possessing her. Some of these critics were Nyamdre activists, but a number were unaffiliated religious figures such as monks and tantric practitioners (tib. *ngagba*). They all, however, in essence challenged the validity of the nun's stature in the community.

Doubts about whether individuals were genuine mediums or fraudulent hucksters preying on villagers was not new in Tibet, and at times the traditional Tibetan government itself intervened in some areas to test mediums in order to punish fakes.[3] However, for Trinley Chödrön, the implications of such challenges at that time were immense: if the nun was not authentic, then there really was no Ani Gongmey Gyemo and no warrior-hero mediums, and the gods had not returned to Nyemo to subdue the demons and ghosts and restore Buddhism. Challenges to the authenticity of the nun and the other warrior-hero mediums, therefore, were challenges to her whole vision of a new Nyemo. Not surprisingly, the nun and the warrior-hero mediums aggressively sought to silence such individuals by targeting them for death or mutilation.

Finally, there was a third category of what we can think of as political killings. In at least one case (discussed below), the target was a powerful local *xiang* head who had earlier switched his allegiance from Nyamdre to Gyenlo but then opposed Gyenlo's use of religion and refused to give Rangjung some weapons the *xiang* head possessed.

THE KILLINGS AND MAIMINGS

The first person killed by the nun was a villager named Lhawang Yeshe. He had made some negative comments about the nun's validity, which he apparently later regretted, because on 3 June 1969 he went to the nun for a consultation, this being a convenient way to show faith in her publicly. This gesture, however, backfired, for when the nun went into a trance, Ani Gongmey Gyemo suddenly ordered him seized and killed on the spot.[4]

Why the individual attacks started precisely when they did on that day in June is difficult to pinpoint. The anger the nun felt about what had happened since 1959 was not new, so while it is an important element, it was not the immediate precipitating factor. The specific trigger, we believe, was a series of incidents that challenged the authenticity of the nun and the other warrior-hero mediums.

The former *xiang* head of Phusum (who had been a member of Nyamdre) recalled several important incidents of goading and ridiculing by local cadres who were Nyamdre activists:

> Once I was called to go to where the nun was staying with two other old women said to be mediums. I went there that evening . . . and found people were gathered near Shilok Tsering's house [a local Nyamdre cadre who was the husband of the woman who narrated the maiming incident presented in the Introduction.] When I saw the old woman medium named Chamba fighting physically with Shilok Tsering, I immediately regretted going there, for I thought a big problem might await me [if I got involved]. But others wanted me to stop them from hitting each other, so [as an official] I didn't have much choice and ascended the hill [to where they were] and tried to stop the fighting.
>
> . . . [Shilok apparently had said that the old lady was not a medium but a demon.] I pleaded with them and also tried physically to stop them. I said, "Please, Chamba, whether or not you are a god, try to calm yourself. And as for you, Shilok, please don't make things worse." In this way, I finally separated them.
>
> Now, looking back, I can see that Shilok Tsering earned a lot of enmity from the nun and others because of that fight. At that time, many of the warrior-hero mediums had not yet started going into trances, so her gang was not that strong [but later when they were, they seized Shilok and hacked off his leg].

Not long after that fight, Shilok Tsering and another man, named Bushön, again tried to irritate the nun by throwing stones at the door of her house and calling for her to come out for a fight. At that time, people in the lower village again asked me to go up the hill and stop them, but I refused, saying, "I can't do anything now, as I might also get beaten this time, so please leave me alone." Shilok and the other man continued to throw stones at the nun's door and to yell at her, and everything was in turmoil. . . .

In a way, these incidents fueled the wild clashes that occurred later. Those men from this village who started to fight with the nun were leftists [Nyamdre leftists], but the nun was very stubborn and was receiving support from the warrior-hero mediums like Bala and Jangdru Yülha in Jangra. . . . Here in our village, those people caused all the later trouble by agitating the nun. Thus, all the killings and deaths in our village following that incident were all because of it.[5]

What happened, or, more accurately, did not happen, after Lhawang was killed set the tone for the mayhem of the following three weeks. This first killing shocked one of the remaining local Nyamdre officials, who reported it to the county government and military office and requested their help. In response, several cadres (including Zhang Yongfu) were sent to Phusum to investigate the incident, but as the following two accounts reveal, Zhang Yongfu chose not to move against the nun, since that would obviously have disrupted Gyenlo's Army of the Gods just at the point when Gyenlo's major offensive was about to start. Two local Tibetans explained what transpired. The first said:

> Two days after Lhawang Yeshe was killed in 1969, Zhang Yongfu and some other people came to Phusum *xiang* to investigate how he was killed. . . . I told them, "Now the female lunatic has started killing people. Please arrest the nun and the warrior-hero mediums and take them to the Public Security Bureau. Otherwise, we will live in darkness in our villages." Zhang Yongfu, however, replied, "We are not here to investigate the matter of the crazy person. So long as the female crazy one is useful to us, we can support her."[6]

The second recalled:

> After Lhawang Yeshe was killed . . . Zhang Yongfu and the three other people from Nyemo County's General Headquarters [Gyenlo] came to . . . Phusum *xiang*. I said to them, "In our *xiang* many male and female crazy people [mediums] have assembled. We want to fight against the nun, but we don't have even a single weapon, so our lives are in danger. What are we to do? Please arrest the nun and take her to the Public Security Bureau." Zhang Yongfu said, "It is not necessary to arrest the nun. She is just a common lunatic. We'll have trouble if we take her to the Public Security Bureau. So don't bother her. She is useful to us. We need to protect her."[7]

Members of the military (who were then functioning also as the local public security) similarly refused to act. They were apprised of what had happened when two *xiang* officials went to the county and told them, "Now the problem in Phusum *xiang* is no longer simply a problem between the two [revolutionary] factions. They are really killing people. . . . Trinley Chödrön is performing the medium's trance dance and uses it to kill people. She does all kinds of bad things, and they are really engaged in counterrevolutionary actions. The few *xiang* cadres here can no longer stay, so please come and solve the problem for us as soon as possible. Otherwise, our lives are in danger." The squadron's political commissar, Zhang Diantong, however, did not want to take sides in the struggle among the "revolutionary masses" and risk precipitating a second Jokhang incident. So rather than help, he actually criticized the two *xiang* leaders for themselves engaging in factionalism, passing the incident off by using a common slogan of the time, "You should go back home immediately and 'promote revolution and push production.'"[8]

Given the absence of any restraining response, the nun and the warrior-hero mediums now went on a three-week wave of maimings and killings, several examples of which follow. The maiming incident described in the Introduction, in which a woman's hands were cut off, was motivated by both challenges to the nun's authenticity and personal animosities. That woman's father was a respected tantric practitioner who was neither associated with Nyamdre nor a cadre. However, he considered the nun a fraud and had ridiculed her claim that Jowo Rimpoche was possessing her, telling people things such as "[What the nun says] is ridiculous. The Buddha Jowo Rimpoche would never possess a human body. There is no custom for a Buddha doing this. She is telling lies."[9] He was referring to the previously mentioned belief that only worldly deities possess humans. Since Buddhas have already obtained enlightenment, they would never return to the human realm to possess a human. As a result of his challenge, he was attacked and had one hand cut off. He survived that incident, but the nun sent people back to attack him again, and this time they beat him to death with rocks. It was at this point that his daughter and her husband, Shilok Tsering, ran away to the nomad area.

The nun also despised Shilok Tsering and his wife, both of whom were Nyamdre grassroots cadres. The husband, as we saw, had harassed and goaded the nun, and both he and his wife had been brutal in enforcing class struggle in the years after the Democratic Reforms were instituted. The nun's brother conveyed the anger the family felt toward them, saying, "They [cadres] made me suffer a lot, and all our household's things were confiscated. After this, Shilok Tsering and others came to our house and broke and smashed whatever had not already been confiscated. We were left without even a pot to eat from."[10]

Another instance of religious disagreement occurred between the nun and several monks from the nearby Sharam Monastery. One former monk recalled the murder of a monk colleague of his.

> Q: What did the [ex-]monks or nuns think about the nun?
> A: We were always arguing with her. . . . They [the nun and the warrior-hero mediums] said that the monks and nuns had been given to "the eight kinds of gods and spirits." However, one monk said that if you were truly the eight kinds of gods and spirits, you should be able to take the essence of my heart from my body. The nun was not able to take his heart. . . . Because of this [ridicule], he was [later] tied spread-eagle on a window frame and stabbed to death. . . .
> Q: Did the nun say that she represented the eight kinds of gods and spirits?
> A: Yes. She said the monks and nuns had been behaving badly and were destroying the Buddhist religion (tib. denba). She said that Chairman Mao was not able to control the monks and nuns and gave them to us. However, that monk said if you are truly the eight kinds of gods and spirits and if we monks were given to you, you could take away my heart. He said such things to her, and it caused his death. On the day when they argued like that, the nun and her followers did not do anything bad to him, but later he was tied spread-eagle on a window frame and killed.[11]

Another monk who was attacked had spoken against the nun's authenticity, saying that while many mediums had lived in the old society, never had one ordered people killed or their limbs amputated.[12]

However, despite such skeptics and critics, most villagers believed in the nun's powers and did not lose faith. A Gyenlo activist, for example, explained how he was able to reconcile the conflicting dimensions of the nun, who was both a religious figure and a maimer and murderer of other religious figures: "Mostly we thought that the gods probably knew the inside of people's minds, and those people probably had very ugly thoughts. We did not think cutting off arms and legs was correct but we truly believed in her, and we thought that she knew the correct decisions. At that time . . . we were fooled. We trusted her. Because of this, we did not consider carefully why those people were killed. I really thought those people were bad."[13]

Several other oral history accounts conveyed the range of people singled out for attacks during the killing spree. The first of these is from a Tibetan who went to consult the nun/medium in Phusum and reveals not only how feared the nun had become but also the capriciousness of her decisions to amputate limbs:

Q: Why did you go to see the nun?
A: Since people were saying she was doing great things, I went there. I [also] heard that the deity [the nun in a trance] was chopping off people's hands.

Q: Were you afraid?
A: Yes, I went there because I was afraid.

Q: At that time, had you heard that she was cutting off arms and legs?
A: Yes, she had already cut off many hands and legs.

Q: Did you go alone?
A: No. I went with many people. . . .

Q: When you first saw the nun, what was she like?
A: She was wearing the costume of a medium. She was wearing a yellow satin Tibetan dress. . . . We requested that she bless us by putting her hand on our heads (tib. *chawang*); otherwise we didn't do anything. Many people were with me.

Q: Did she ask you anything, like where are you from?
A: She didn't ask anything, but she gave the appearance that she liked Gyenlo.

Q: How?
A: She said that Gyenlo will be victorious.

Q: What did she say?
A: She said, "Gyenlo will win the victory. However, you should be careful." Actually, we didn't have anything to be careful about.

Q: When you got there, were you able to meet the nun right away, or did you have to request it through other people?
A: We didn't need to go through other people. We had to go inside [her chapel room] slowly. People like Bala [the warrior-hero medium] were carrying swords and standing near the door.

Q: How many people were there carrying swords?
A: About four people were standing there.

Q: Did all of them have swords in their hands?
A: Yes, and they had swords stuck through their belts.

Q: Was the nun alone inside?
A: Yes.

Q: What was the condition of the nun's house?
A: The house was not so big. It was small.

Q: At that time did you ask her to go into a trance?
A: She was going into a trance already. It was just like going to a temple for worship (tib. *chönje*). The medium was asked to go into a trance by the public [in general], so individuals didn't have to do anything. After they said the trance was over, then we had to leave.

Q: At that time, were you afraid of getting your hand cut off?
A: Yes. And on that day that actually happened to someone. There was

a Nyamdre man who came with us. . . . They left him tied up for the whole day.

Q: How did they know he was Nyamdre? Did he tell them that he was Nyamdre?
A: Probably the secret was revealed by other people.

Q: How did they seize him?
A: They seized him immediately. They had three stakes in the ground, and they made him lie on his stomach, and then they tied his legs to two stakes, and tied his hands to one stake. Then they placed a chopping board and a small axe near his hands. At that time, I was so scared that I almost fainted.

Q: What did he say?
A: He didn't say anything. When they beat him with the blunt side of the swords, he was sort of hopping up and down. Bala was acting as if he were mad. He was rubbing his sword on his hands showing that he was going to cut the hand of the person who was lying there. At that moment I thought that something bad was going to happen.

Q: Weren't any of the other people who had come asking for mercy?
A: Who the hell would dare to ask for mercy [and risk being linked to that "demon"]? After it was finished, all the people went back home. . . . I heard that they cut off his hand that evening and put it in the pouch of his dress.

Q: Since he was Nyamdre, why did he go there?
A: He went there not because he liked them but because he feared that he might lose his hand or his life if he did not go there [that they would come to get him]. At that time people were afraid of losing their hands and lives [if they didn't go]. . . . People were afraid and felt they had to go there to see the nun [to show they believed in her].[14]

Another example of extreme violence was the case of a female grass-roots cadre from Jangra named Trinley Drolkar. She was a branch party committee member (ch. *wei yuan*) and was both an ardent supporter of Nyamdre and a sharp-tongued denigrator of Gyenlo and the nun. She had been an activist in 1959 and had angered many by telling the PLA the whereabouts of Chushigandru guerrilla forces at that time. Her daughter narrated:

The day after they cut off the hand of the director (ch. *zhuren*) [on 13 June], my mother was staying at home. One of her relatives had been killed over there [in Bagor], so she was trying to go there, but the mother of the Khangsar family told her to stay quiet and go back home. However, soon after that, a group of people came yelling and entered our home. . . . We placed the children behind us and hid in a room we used to store dung. We stood in front of the children. . . .

At that point, I thought, "Now everything is finished." They said the female demon (tib. *dümo*) was hiding here, and then the person called Lhagong Wangtob dragged my mother by her hair. I tried to beg for mercy,

Figure 2. An axe and "cutting board" used in cutting off limbs in Nyemo during the incident in June 1969.

saying, "Please. Please. [Don't do that.]" At that time, Phüntsoling Gyatso and one of my mother's relatives . . . said, "Drag her away face down," and they hooked a rope around her neck and dragged her away through the gate. I begged for mercy from Gyatso, who was the brother of Bala, one of the warrior-hero mediums. I said, "Please," but he responded, "Shut up." . . .

As they were dragging her like a dead horse, the warrior-hero medium called Shechen Riwo Pangyog . . . said to her, "You female demon. You destroyer of Buddhism." Then they dragged her to the house of the village head whose name was Thondrub Ling and tied her to some trees.

At that point, people said it would help if I prostrated myself before them, so although prostrating was superstition, I did it and begged for mercy. I prostrated myself so many times that sores developed on my forehead and my knees. . . . [Then they left], and since nobody was there [where my mother was tied up so], I asked her, "Shall I untie you? Nobody is here."

Q: At that time, had her hand already been cut off?
A: No. But there was an old man called Phurbu, who was said to be a spy. He was a little bit far away looking at us and then told me, "Don't try to untie her. If you didn't have children, the two of you might be able to run away, but since you have children, you won't be able to flee."

Then just before it became dark, they again came yelling. . . . I heard that the household called Drongme had given them a chopping block. Then

I heard two sounds, "dag dag," and my mother's hand was cut off. At that point, it was dark.

Q: Who cut off your mother's hand?
A: That was Gyatso, the brother of Bala.

Q: Did he cut her hand off with a knife?
A: They used long swords. I didn't see it clearly because it was dark. They struck her with a sword twice and then buried her hand in front of her. I took some tea, melted butter, and a shirt made from raw silk to stop the bleeding. When I arrived, she was just squeezing the wound on her right arm with her left palm. She asked me, "Did you bring anything to wrap the wound?" I said, "Yes." Then I wrapped her wound with the raw silk and served her tea. When we came home, the children were not there. My mother said that they [the attackers] had called her a demoness, "so they cut off my hand and now really made me a demoness."[15]

The rationale behind the amputations was never explained by the nun, but it was a well-known Tibetan punishment for recidivist criminals, who were thereby usually rendered harmless without the need to imprison them. An additional reason mentioned by some was that the victims allegedly had "long arms" for taking others' property and bribes, so cutting off their hands was appropriate punishment.[16]

Individuals were also attacked in other ways, as the incident of Rinzin, an ex-nun from Chöying Nunnery, illustrates.

There was a woman from the Nangwog household who had been a nun. During the Cultural Revolution, she built a house on the site where there used to be a temple in which clay images of Buddha and other deities were kept (tib. *tshakhang*). The temple had been destroyed during the Cultural Revolution. At that time, people said that she was a demoness and buried her alive near the Jangra Bridge. . . .

Q: Why did she build her house on the place where there used to be a temple?
A: At that time I was young [so I don't know], but probably she didn't have another place to build her house, and that site was close to her family's house. . . . Gyenlo called people to bring hoes and shovels to bury a demoness alive. I was afraid, wondering who the devil was and whether it was one of my family members. Afterward, we heard that they brought the nun Rinzin. . . .

Q: Were there any other reasons for burying her alive?
A: . . . They said that she didn't have religious faith because she had built her house where a temple used to be. She had committed a sin, and she was a demoness.

Q: At that point, was she pleading with them?
A: Yes, I heard she begged for mercy, saying, "Please don't kill me, I will rebuild the temple," and tried to get out of the pit. The others, however,

yelled, "Look at her. Because she is a demoness, she is climbing up out of the pit" [into which they had thrown her]. So they speared her in the back and pushed her back down into the pit.

Q: After that they covered the pit with earth, right?
A: Yes.

Q: At that point, nobody dared to say anything, right?
A: Yes. Nobody dared to say anything. Even when one's relative was going to be buried, we had to go to dig the pit.

Q: When you went to have a look, what did you think?
A: From the beginning, when they yelled that they were going to bury a demoness, I wondered who was going to be buried. . . . I was afraid that it might be one of the women of our family.[17]

Another Tibetan who was the servant and bodyguard of two of the warrior-hero mediums also recalled this event:

When they buried the nun [Rinzin], the mediums were yelling. They were kind of going into a trance and went to that place. I followed them. When they brought out the nun, they ordered her to come out of her house. I was on the roof of the house with some other people. They took her down near to the bridge, and the medium Gyatso, who was said to be a hero in the Gesar story, said that we should bury her alive. Actually, they speared her first and buried her in a pit.

Q: The pit was already dug?
A: Yes.

Q: What did the nun say?
A: She showed her thumbs, begging for mercy. She said something, but I couldn't hear clearly. She was so scared that she couldn't say the words clearly.

Q: Did she die when she was thrown down into the pit?
A: Probably; she stopped breathing just after that. She was speared. . . .

Q: Did Gyatso spear her?
A: Yes.

Q: Then they covered her with dirt right after that, right?
A: Yes.[18]

The victim's niece added her own recollection:

In the past Rinzin was the leader of the Mutual Aid Team, and she was the director in charge of security in the district. . . .

When we heard that they were killing people, she hid inside her house. However, when we came back [from the mountains one day], she had been taken from her home. At that time, her aunt was there and told us she had been killed.

Q: They came to her place and took her away?
A: Yes. They said that they were mediums, and they were going into a

trance. Actually, they were not mediums, because they were carrying swords and guns. I have gone to religious mediums to ask for divination [in the old society], and they would say that my illness was this and that. But how could we call people who carried swords and guns mediums? At that time, the masses also carried swords and guns, and the mediums did the same.

Q: *The people who came to take your aunt were from this place, or were they from other places?*

A: They were from this place. Afterward, those people were executed. We are grateful to the state for this.

Q: *Did those people hold any kind of hatred toward your aunt?*

A: They didn't hold any kind of hatred for her.

Q: *Then what did they say was the reason for killing her?*

A: They said that she was an activist and the director of security. At the time of the Cultural Revolution, there was a small temple in which clay images of the Buddha were kept. At that time people were not allowed to become monks and nuns, so she came home from the nunnery. However, she thought that since she wouldn't get along well living together with our family, she made plans to build her own house on the spot where the temple used to be. Because of this, they said that she was a demoness and killed her. They used that as a kind of pretext.

On that morning [when she was murdered], they made me dig a pit, telling me they were going to bury a person there. They were so cruel. The next day they said that I had dug the very pit in which my aunt was buried. Actually, I didn't know that my aunt was going be buried in that pit. . . . If people die from disease, there is nothing to regret, but that kind of death was really the most regretful thing. At that point, my aunt was in her early forties. She also knew how to read and write, and she did quite well in her work. She was regarded highly by the state. At that point, they purposely buried her just near the bridge where her family members had to walk by. . . .

They also came to kill me that day and almost succeeded. . . . I was carrying a basket [on the roof of my house] when I heard them saying that the demoness who was born in the Bird year had come. I was born in the Bird year. They were yelling and holding spears, and then they charged forward toward me, trying to spear me. At that moment, I jumped off the roof of the house and ran away. I was a youngster, but they threw stones at me when I reached the edge of the bridge. . . . After that I didn't go home. I just ran to the mountains. . . .

Q: *Was that the same day your aunt was killed?*

A: Yes. That happened in the morning, and my aunt was killed in the evening. Now, when I am happy [with living conditions], I think that even if her hand had been cut off, she would still be alive and living with us and enjoying a happy life.[19]

A very different kind of calculated political killing occurred in the case of Tsesum, the *xiang* head of Nyemo. He had been a powerful cadre in

Nyemo since 1959 and was notorious for being cruel and unresponsive to the needs of the people. However, as Gyenlo began to mount its campaign in 1968, he switched sides and joined that faction, becoming an active leader. At the meeting in January 1969, he was selected as a deputy commander of Gyenlo's Army of the Gods. However, in the months that followed, he disagreed with Rangjung and Zhang about allowing religious activities and using the name "Army of the Gods," and he increasingly opposed Gyenlo's close involvement with the nun. Tsesum, it was said, had also refused to turn over some explosives and guns that Rangjung wanted for the coming attacks.[20]

Rangjung, therefore, decided to eliminate him before the main attack and did so through the nun and Ani Gongmey Gyemo. One Tibetan involved in this murder recalled:

> Following Rangjung's instructions, I went to Phusum [on 6 June 1969] and talked with the nun [asking her what Ani Gongmey Gyemo had said about killing Tsesum]. She said to me, "We must fight against the enemies inside. There are fifteen ghosts (tib. *dongdre*) in Nyemo. We have already settled with six of them. Nine are left. Among these, Tsesum will be the last to be decided. Killing him would be advantageous to our whole society." I then went back to Nyemo and told Rangjung what the nun had said. Rangjung, however, said that this was inadequate and sent me back to see the nun again, this time requesting that the god [the nun] send three men to help him kill Tsesum. On 7 June, I went to Phusum, and on the following day I returned to Nyemo with two men—the nun's brother Tseden Benjor and Ganden, one of the most active in the nun's close entourage. They killed Tsesum.[21]

Another Tibetan who was involved in this killing added more about what happened on 8 June:

> Ganden told me that the nun had said that Tsesum was like a demon, and it would be best to kill him that day. Consequently, Ganden, Tseden Benjor, and I went to Nyemo. Rangjung was at someone else's house when we arrived, so we sent someone to find him and tell him that the nun said, "Tsesum is a demon, so Ganden and Tseden Benjor have come here [to help kill him]. . . . " The nun also said, "Do not trust people wearing yellow clothes [the uniform of PLA]. They are like a rainbow in summer, which will disappear in no time [the PLA will leave]." Rangjung told me to go back [to Tsesum's house] at once and that he would come right away.
>
> When I arrived at Tsesum's home, I saw that Ganden and Tseden Benjor were already inside and had locked the door from the inside so I could not get in. Tsesum's son was also in the house. Then Rangjung and a few other people arrived, and we all went inside together. Once inside, we hit Tsesum's

head and body repeatedly with stones." When Tsesum was being killed, I also hit him. I climbed to the roof and threw two big stones down at his head through the hole [skylight] in the roof. . . . .

[In the fighting,] Tsesum's son escaped, and Ganden asked me to chase him, which I did up to the county seat, where I lost sight of him. I then went back to attend a meeting where I saw Rangjung lying in bed wrapped in a Tibetan quilt. He said, "Do not tell anybody that people from Phusum killed Tsesum. Just say that Tsesum's son killed his father. Send someone to report to the Military Squadron that Tsesum was killed by his son and that Rangjung was also hit and injured by Tsesum's son. Ask them to send a doctor here."[22]

Ironically, despite this severe beating, Tsesum survived, and Rangjung and Zhang Yongfu soon learned that he had been taken to the Military Squadron in Nyemo, which was preparing to send him to Lhasa for treatment. This worried them, and Zhang Yongfu told Ganden, "We cannot allow them to take Tsesum away. Be sure not to let them transfer him to Lhasa for medical treatment, because if he is sent there, he will work with Chompel, the [Nyamdre] *xiang* head of Tharong *xiang,* and report on the situation here to Nyamdre Headquarters. If he does that, it could be bad for us, so you should tell them that if Tsesum needs any treatment, we can provide it here. He cannot be transferred to Lhasa."[23] Soon after this, Tsesum was taken to the Nyemo county hospital, where he died.

This case is interesting for several reasons. First, it clearly reveals that Gyenlo knew of and accepted the nun's campaign of murder and maiming. Second, it shows that although Rangjung was the commander of the Army of the Gods, he sought to cloak what he wanted done with the charismatic authority of the nun. And third, it suggests that this seemingly chaotic campaign appears to have also had a strategic function by eliminating individuals who were considered a threat to what would be the new order in Nyemo. In fact, although there is no corroborating evidence for this, Rangjung himself may well have encouraged the nun to strike out at the "internal enemies."

Through attacks like these during a three-week period beginning 3 June, the nun's warrior-mediums, together with some Gyenlo activists, killed or mutilated as many as fifteen to twenty Tibetan internal enemies.[24] These attacks on individuals created an atmosphere of fear and terror. As mentioned earlier, many believed the nun had the supernatural power to hear whatever they said outside her presence, so they would talk about her only in whispers in their homes for fear of saying something that would anger her. No one wanted to do anything that might in the slightest result in her people arriving suddenly to drag them off to the "slaughtering grounds," which was the name of the place where they cut off limbs in Phusum. With the blood flowing so easily and the remaining authorities unwilling to intervene, the nun and her warrior-hero mediums felt invincible. However, this invincibility was clearly artificial. As we have seen, Zhang Yongfu could have stopped the nun by mobilizing the Military Squadron in Nyemo to seize her. And the head of the squadron could also have taken action when he was approached for help. Of course, neither did, for the reasons stated above.

In the midst of the nun's killing spree, Gyenlo sought to mobilize its representatives further by holding a ceremony to commemorate the anniversary of the "7 June massacre," the name Gyenlo had given to the PLA's murder of the Gyenlo activists in the Jokhang Temple the previous year. That meeting began with Zhang Yongfu asking the representatives to rise and stand in silent tribute to the martyrs. Then he gave a speech that criticized the PLA's mistakes, and finally he closed the meeting by having the members chant slogans such as "Avenge the martyrs!" and "Blood debts must be paid in blood!"[25]

Within a week, Gyenlo's Army of the Gods marched off to collect that blood debt by attacking the PLA in Bagor and Nyemo.

CHAPTER 5

The Attacks on Bagor District and Nyemo County

By June 1969, Rangjung and Zhang Yongfu were ready to eliminate the external enemies—the remaining pro-Nyamdre cadres, the Department of Armed Forces, and the Military Squadron, the last two of which were then effectively in charge of the county. However, as the time to attack neared, a platoon of fourteen PLA soldiers arrived unexpectedly in Bagor to carry out a propaganda campaign called "cherish the masses and support the army" (tib. *maggur mangje*; ch. *yongjun aimin*), which was aimed at persuading the masses to forsake factional discord. Rangjung decided to attack those troops before moving on the county forces.

Several factors led to this decision. First, if this PLA campaign were to succeed in persuading villagers not to support factions, Gyenlo could lose part of its membership and power. Second, and related to this, these troops criticized the nun and "superstition," saying such things as it was ridiculous for the nun to say she went into a trance (and that she was the right hand of Chairman Mao), because it was impossible for Chairman Mao to depend on superstition.[1] The troops' telling the villagers that the nun was a fraud obviously also threatened Gyenlo's support base. Third, Gyenlo's leaders, as mentioned earlier, harbored deep resentment toward the army for the murder of their comrades in the Jokhang and, in their eyes, for consistently siding with Nyamdre, even in Nyemo. As one activist villager from Phusum put it, "After the whole area became Gyenlo, within the Department of Armed Forces some people acted like the Red Guards who had come to suppress us. . . . At that time . . . we slowly began to feel that they were more likely to support Nyamdre than Gyenlo, . . . and in Bagor District some army soldiers were making the masses suffer."[2] Fourth and equally important, Gyenlo's Army of the Gods was badly in need of modern weapons, and Rangjung saw this as a possible opportunity to seize some, since he had received a message saying that these troops were armed. His hope was to use the weapons he would seize in the main attack.[3]

On 9 June, Zhang Yongfu and Rangjung set this attack in motion by calling a meeting of Gyenlo's village representatives in Nyemo *xiang* and informing them that the time to strike had come and that they should go home and get their weapons ready.[4] Two days later, the representatives of Nyemo, Ritsho, Nyima, and Phusum took their spears, swords, and Tibetan guns to the nun and asked her to go into a trance and bless the weapons. One representative who was present that day said that when the nun went into a trance, Ani Gongmey Gyemo said, "It is the second time for me to come to Tibet to liberate this region. You should fight hard to defend religion. From now on, all power belongs to the Buddha."[5] Another Tibetan villager who was there had a similar recollection: "When we arrived, we were divided into several groups of thirteen people each. We handed our swords and Tibetan rifles to the nun, who chanted sutras and spit on them [a type of standard mantric blessing]. The nun told us, 'You should believe in the gods. We are a collection of gods (tib. *lha*) that are the army to defend religion, so we are unbeatable. All power now belongs to us, the group of gods. . . . These bayonets and rifles [matchlocks] are to kill the demons and protect ourselves.'"[6]

On the next day, 12 June, Zhang Yongfu and Rangjung held another meeting of Gyenlo's representatives and gave them specific tactical instructions. Rangjung also sent a bunch of protective talismans to Phusum to have Ani Gongmey Gyemo bless them for the coming battle. When the nun sent them back, she sent Rangjung a message: "Kill all the people wearing yellow or blue without mercy. With the help of so many protective talismans, we will win the battle in Bagor.[7]

Rangjung's battle plan—using superior numbers to overpower and kill the troops—was feasible because the villagers believed that the nun/Ani Gongmey Gyemo and the other mediums were supernaturally protecting them. Gyenlo's Army of the Gods, therefore, blithely marched off to attack the PLA force, although armed with only swords, spears, slingshots, Tibetan matchlock rifles, and some home-made explosives. One villager explained, "We knew they had guns, but we trusted the gods who said that we would not get hit with bullets. We were encouraged by that. The nun told the people, 'You should visualize that I am on your head.' So the people went there with that kind of confidence."[8]

The villagers, however, did not have to worry about the PLA platoon's firepower, because it turned out that they were armed only with Chairman Mao's little red books. In the tense environment of factional violence, the army thought it prudent to refrain from arming the troops it sent out to stop factional violence, because it feared, with reason, that Gyenlo might manage to steal the weapons, or worse, that the troops would be placed in a situation in which they would fire on the revolutionary masses and precipitate another disastrous incident like the Jokhang killings.[9]

However, once the propaganda troops arrived and set up residence in Bagor, they realized that conditions were chaotic and dangerous and almost immediately sent several soldiers to the Nyemo County Military Squadron headquarters to report the situation and request that they be given some guns for self-protection. This request was refused, as the squadron's political commissar, Zhang Diantong, later explained in a frank self-confession:

> I am guilty of the fact that members of the Bagor Military Propaganda Team were killed by class enemies because they did not have any weapons.
> On 11 June 1969, my suggestions were completely wrong. At one of the meetings, Liang Chao, Director Liu, Deputy Political Commissar Ding, and I were all there. . . . I clearly knew that the class struggle was very intense there [in Nyemo]. However, I was worrying about provoking more struggles among the factions, so I said, "Losing weapons happens very often now. If you carry weapons, the class enemies will find a way to grab them from you. It's better not to carry any weapons. You may bring some cigarettes and candies with you. When people come, you can treat them with something good." So finally we decided not to let them take weapons. . . .
> On the morning of 12 June, when the Military Propaganda Team set off, Deputy Political Commissar Ding reported to me, saying, "Some of them have hidden guns inside bags of rice they are taking back with them." I asked Liang Chao what we should do. Liang was not happy about this, so I sent someone to get the guns back. [Consequently] [w]hen "6/13" came, our class brothers were [unarmed and were] cruelly killed by the class enemies. I have to admit that I was responsible for such an unforgivable crime.[10]

Meanwhile, on the evening of 12 June, Rangjung and the main warrior-heroes led contingents of Gyenlo's Army of the Gods from different villages to Bagor District, arriving early the next morning.[11] Rangjung him-

self led about eighty riders from Nyemo and assumed overall command
of the force, which numbered in the hundreds. On the nun's instructions, the warrior-hero mediums wore white *khata* ceremonial scarves
tied across their shoulder and chest like bandoleers and another *khata*
scarf fastened to their hair, which was combed up into a topknot.[12]
Some also wore medium's paraphernalia. After burning incense as an
offering to the gods, the attackers quickly encircled the Bagor District
government building, which had previously been the old manor house
of the landlord, and charged forward yelling the Tibetan war cry *"ki
hi hi"* and all kinds of other things such as "No submitting grain,"
"No selling surplus grain," "Kill the yellow dogs and blue pigs," "An-
nihilate the demons and ghosts," "All the power to the gods," and "We
want the right to be masters of our own houses (tib. *rangkyim rangda*)."
In addition, several interviews state that some of the mediums also
shouted explicitly separatist political slogans such as "Tibet is independent," and one says that they were carrying the Tibetan national
flag.[13]

When the attackers reached the gate to the compound, it was not suffi-
ciently barricaded, so they were able to break in quickly and hunt down
and kill everyone there. One Tibetan attacker recalled the slaughter:

We left from here in separate groups before it became dark and arrived
there [at Bagor] at dawn. We rode [on horseback] the whole night. . . . A
person called Uchung told us that the mediums had sent a message saying
the nun had told them to kill the soldiers. . . .

Q: *When you got there, were they already hitting the soldiers?*
A: Yes. The groups that were in front had done that. All of the people
of Bagor District had gathered, and the building was full of people. . . .

Q: *When you got there, how many were already killed?*
A: The headquarters of Bagor District was a two-story house [actually three].
Two of the soldiers were running hither and thither and being chased. . . .
All of them held swords. They were yelling, "Ki hi hi," and running up and
down among the crowd of people. Altogether, they killed thirteen soldiers.
Poor things! A couple of cadres and another woman were also killed. It was
the warrior-hero mediums who killed them.

Q: *They were all killed by the mediums [warrior-heroes]?*
A: Some Gyenlo representatives also did the killings. All of them were
killed. . . .

Q: *Did you see them killing the soldiers?*
A: Yes, I saw them stabbing and spearing them. . . .

Q: *At that moment, what were you thinking?*
A: At that moment I was so scared that I didn't have any thoughts. They
were saying [warning us], "There are representatives among the represen-

tatives [of Gyenlo]," and things like "The inner enemy is worse than the
outer enemy, so you had better watch out." In Bagor District two mediums [warrior-heroes] threatened that they were going to differentiate
people [in the attack force] internally [search out those only pretending
to attack].

*Q: So at that moment, do you mean that you had two fears—one from
outside and one from inside?*
A: The mediums [warrior-heroes] said to the crowd of people that so-
and-so is a demon. A person called Ngudrub from Jangra was a Nyamdre
member. He was so scared that he rushed over [on his own] to hit the
soldiers, but the warrior-heroes recognized him because they were from the
same village and told people to seize him. They cut off his hand. [Ngudrub's
own account of this follows.] . . . He thought they would [eventually] make
him suffer severely, so he went to demonstrate [his allegiance] to Gyenlo by
killing the soldiers.

Q: Did you see them cut off his hand?
A: Yes. They attached ropes to his hands, which were held tightly by people
in the crowd. Then they placed his arm on a piece of wood from a juniper
shrub, and the medium [warrior-hero] Tashi Rabden cut off his hand with
a sword. At that time, we could see the inside of his [severed] hand bleeding, and we could hear it was making the sound "si si" while the blood
from the other attached side of his arm gushed out to a distance like that
[demonstrates with his hand].

Q: Did they cut the hand with one hit?
A: They cut off the hand with two hits.

Q: Was he screaming when his hand was cut off?
A: Yes. Then he took his hand and went back. He is still alive.

Q: After they killed the soldiers what were they saying?
A: They said that we should saddle the horses and go back to Phusum.[14]

Another Gyenlo villager recalled the same attack:

On 13 June 1969, Nyima Tsering and Ngawang Tsering told me to go to
kill the PLA soldiers in Bagor. . . .
    After we reached Bagor, we stopped and drank some beer on a small
hill. While there Phujung, Tashi Wangchuk, Ganden, Tashi Rabden, and
Tseden Wangchuk came. Ganden asked me where we were going, and when
I told him that we were going to Bagor, he said, "Let's go together." Tashi
Wangchuk went ahead, and after a while he came back saying, "There are
two cadres who are trying to run away; let's stop them." I went with some
other young people to stop the cadres. Nyima Tsering and Karma Wangdü
caught the two cadres, a woman and a man, and Tashi Wangchuk immediately stabbed the woman with a sword. Later, the tall PLA soldier tried to
talk to us about Chairman Mao's thought, but the medium [warrior-hero]
Tashi Benjor slashed him on the head with a sword. The PLA soldier went
down. I then slashed the woman three times. The woman ran to the district

building, where two PLA soldiers came out of the government headquarters and took her inside.

We then broke into the compound and reached the third floor. Rangjung was on the second floor. He saw a cadre named Danden Dorje, so he slashed at him and almost chopped his hand off. Danden Dorje tried to run away but was stopped by Tashi Rabden [the warrior-hero], who slashed him once again. Danden Dorje fell down but did not die right away. When some of us hesitated to kill him, Tashi Rabden yelled at us, "I can see that some [Gyenlo] representatives are not honest. They are two-faced and are bad elements. I will kill anybody who dares to be dishonest." Saying this, he nudged the people who were near him with his sword [to finish him off]. I didn't have any weapons, so I picked up a heavy stick and used it to beat Danden Dorje six times on the head. Representative Wangchuk Rabden from Nyemo *xiang* then found a flat grinding stone from a mill and pounded Danden Dorje's head with it, killing him.

I went to another room and found that Tashi Rabden, Lhundrup Wanggye, and people from Bagor had already killed six PLA soldiers. Rangjung asked me to search their bodies for weapons and other PLA stuff. I took some cigarettes, candies, and a flashlight. . . . Rangjung then held a meeting and said, "Send people to every *xiang*, telling them that we have won the battle in Bagor. Ask them to burn incense to welcome us." We then went to the nun's house in Phusum.[15]

One Gyenlo representative who was given the task of guarding a window from the outside later went inside and recalled, "The mediums Tashi Rabden and Jangdru Yülha were on the roof, wearing their costumes. When I went up there, blood was everywhere."[16]

These recollections were from Gyenlo activists, but the attack force also included villagers who were in essence drafted into the Army of the Gods. In fact, at this time some voiced the idea that this attack force represented the whole area against the army, not just Gyenlo against Nyamdre. One such former Nyamdre supporter recalled how he had to spear a soldier to demonstrate his commitment:

I ran into the district government's courtyard. Many soldiers had been killed, and ten people were checking to see whether any of them were just pretending to be dead. They said that some soldiers were still breathing. In fact, one soldier had probably survived. . . . [He was] hiding under a bed. . . . Some people said he was breathing, but others said he was not. A lot of different people were standing there, but Norbu Samdrub, a medium [warrior-hero] from Lhajung Village gave me the spear he was holding and told me to spear that soldier. I didn't dare do that, but I was forced. . . . He said I was a person who was two-faced. That meant that I was acting like Gyenlo but was really sympathetic to Nyamdre. He did not believe I was a real member of Gyenlo. Because of that, I feared I

would be killed, so when he ordered me to spear the soldier, I did it. . . .
I had to spear the soldier. . . . The soldiers did not have weapons.[17]

As mentioned above, in addition to all the soldiers, four cadres were also
killed or crippled. One of these, Ngudrub, the cadre mentioned above,
gave his own slightly different version of how he came to have his hand
cut off that day:

> At the time of the Democratic Reforms, I was the official in charge of
> security and a member of the party committee. . . . My duties were to
> mobilize the masses, give instructions about class struggle, and supervise
> the class enemies (tib. *trerim*) [who were officially under the supervision
> of the masses]. Because of this, at the time of the revolt [in 1969] the class
> enemies took revenge and cut off my hand. . . .
>   They locked them [the PLA troops] in the house and killed them with
> stones. The soldiers didn't have weapons and were surrounded. There
> was no way for them to get out. If they had had weapons, they could have
> shot and defeated them [their attackers]. But, since the soldiers didn't have
> weapons, . . . [the attackers] could do whatever they liked, and they stabbed
> and stoned the soldiers. I heard that they hit one woman from the *xiang*
> with a grinding stone and killed her. . . . After those people were killed, they
> cut off my hand.
>
> *Q: At that time, were you staying in the* xiang *because you were the leader?*
> A: I was staying in the village (tib. *trongtso*). . . . I was unable to run away.
> At that time, the *xiang* head told me that we had to go there [to Bagor],
> but in the end he actually stayed behind and didn't go. [I went] and when
> I got there, they cut off my hand. After my hand was cut off, I tried to
> walk home but couldn't make it and had to stay overnight at the end of
> the bridge. . . . I lost a great deal of blood, but I didn't die. That night, my
> son and my relatives came and brought me a kind of soup and tea. When
> I tried to drink this, I vomited. At that point, probably, I was nearing
> death. I had a feeling that I had come to a happy place where there was
> a pasture. . . .
>
> *Q: When you arrived at Bagor, had they already killed a lot of people?*
> A: All of them were already killed when I got there.
>
> *Q: You could have run away but didn't. Did they call you to come there?*
> A: I was ready to run away, but the *xiang* head had told me, "They have
> killed the soldiers, so let's go there." . . .
>
> *Q: Was he saying that you should go to fight?*
> A: He just said that if we didn't go there, it would not be right, so let's go.
> However, he himself didn't go. . . . When I got there, I found that he was
> not there, but the [warrior-heroes] called Bala and Denma were there. They
> were from this place.
>
> *Q: Do you know them?*
> A: Yes. They are from this place. They seized me and cut off my hand with
> a sword so long [shows visually] on a chopping board, and then they said,

"That's enough," and they left. . . . Blood came out from each of the nerves [blood vessels] of my arm. It was like silk threads attached to my arm, and I couldn't get up. After a while, I came along slowly, and I had to stay overnight at the end of the bridge.

Q: At that moment, didn't the villagers living nearby come to help you?
A: No. They were afraid. So I was left there alone. . . .

Q: What did they say when they first seized you?
A: There was a person called Namgang from the household called Khangsar. He came to seize me and said, "Now, it is good [that we have you] (tib. *da yagpo chung*)." He had held a kind of grudge from the time when the Cultural Revolution had just started. After I was seized, [Bala and Denma] came out, and they cut off my hand and said, "We won't kill him. Cutting off his hand is enough for him." . . . The main hatred against me was that I had announced the differentiation of class enemies [in 1959]. . . .

Q: So if you hadn't gone there, they might not have come to your house, right?
A: Probably, they might not have come to my house. At that time, I was unable to run away. Before that, they made me stand up at many meetings and held struggle sessions against me.

Q: Did Gyenlo make you to stand at meetings?
A: Yes.

Q: Did you meet Rangjung?
A: I never saw Rangjung, but once when I had a quarrel with my neighbor, Rangjung came to my house when I was away and called a meeting at which he said he was going to take revenge. At that point, I had gone to the mountains to collect dung, so he scolded my wife and children.

Q: Was he [Rangjung] the leader?
A: He was the main leader of Gyenlo. The reason for taking revenge was that a person who . . . was living below my house had climbed up onto my roof to steal firewood, and the two of us had had a physical fight. [His] house was given to me during the reforms, so he was not allowed to enter my house. But he came into my home, so I beat him up and threw him from my roof down the cliff, where there was a big rock. Then he shouted that he was being killed. After that, he was taken to the hospital in the county.

At that time, a staff officer (ch. *canmou*) of the Department of Armed Forces in the county came to my house and asked me what had happened. I told him about how he came to steal my firewood. The staff officer told me that I had to go and provide support for him in the hospital. Actually, he was a middle peasant and was richer than I, so I told the staff officer, "I don't have anything to support him."

Q: Was he wounded at that time?
A: He was not wounded, but I heard that he hurt his ribs a little when he fell down. They wanted me to pay his hospital expenses, but I said that I didn't have anything to pay them. So then they wanted me to give him a horse, and I agreed. That was why Rangjung came to take revenge.

Q: Was Rangjung friendly with that person, or what was their relationship?
A: It was because they were both Gyenlo. At that time, I was a kind of a leader, and I was Nyamdre. So they said it was not right for me to have beaten up that person.

At the time when Rangjung called the meeting, he criticized my wife, saying, "Your husband can't escape." Probably, he also yelled at the masses. When I came back in the evening, I heard about that. So I thought that the situation was not good for me.

Q: Was he [the neighbor who came to steal firewood] the person who seized you in Bagor?
A: Yes.

Q: He had held a grudge against you, right?
A: Yes.

The wife of another Nyamdre cadre tells the story of her husband's murder at the time of this attack:

We were members of Nyamdre. He was killed along with some soldiers of the People's Liberation Army and some officials of the district government.

Q: Was he an official here?
A: Yes, he was. He was the head of the Public Security Bureau for our area and was also a team leader. He was a very capable person. He had the trust of the government, and when something needed to be done, they used to call him to do it. He was killed in 1969, leaving four children and me. . . .

Q: Where was he killed?
A: He was killed in this village. Many of his colleagues were able to flee, but he did not leave, so some reactionaries who were in this village killed him.

Q: Where did those killers come from?
A: They came from other villages such as Phusum and Gyaram. They broke the glass of the windows of the district building and killed soldiers and officials. Some people were able to flee, but some were not able to flee so were killed there.

Q: Where did they kill your husband?
A: He did not flee to another area. He just stayed in our home. They took him from our house . . . and killed him on the street in our village just outside our house.

Q: Was it the same time that they killed the many soldiers?
A: They killed my husband before they killed those soldiers. After he was wounded, I carried him to our home. At that time he was breathing but only weakly. When I carried him to our home, he said he would not die if someone could send him to the hospital. I was crying and told him, "Reactionaries are everywhere in this village. Who can help you?" I cried a lot. . . .

Q: When they killed people, what did they say?
A: They did not say anything. When they came to kill people, they liked to shout "Ki hi hi." . . . They used swords and spears. They had spears that could cause serious wounds. Most of the time they used swords.

Q: How many wounds did your husband have?
A: He had twelve wounds on his body.

Q: After you carried your husband to your home, how long did he survive?
A: He survived only a short time. I found that his intestines had come out because his stomach had been cut open. It was terrible. He died very soon. The afternoon of the next day, they tied his feet together and dragged his body near to the bridge and threw it into a narrow gorge.

Q: Was he able to say anything before he died?
A: It was very difficult for him to talk. One of his arms had been cut by knives about five times, but his other arm was not injured seriously. So he said he could make shoes for our children with that one hand alone. Just before his death, he was worrying about his children's shoes.[18]

Although no weapons were seized, the attack on Bagor was a stunning success for Gyenlo. Within a few hours, all twenty-two soldiers and cadres stationed there were killed, but Gyenlo suffered no casualties. Gyenlo's Army of the Gods had now shown that they had the courage to face PLA troops as well as the stomach to kill them without mercy. If Rangjung could repeat this in Nyemo, the county would be Gyenlo's.

Following the victory, most of the leaders rode to Phusum to see the nun. A Gyenlo activist recalled meeting the nun at that time:

[W]e all bent over respectfully while the nun went into a trance. Rangjung then reported to the god, "We have accomplished the task in Bagor. Now only a few county offices are left, such as the People's Armed Forces Department and the county Military Squadron. Please instruct us what to do about them." The nun said, "I am the deity Qurenbo (tib. *jo bo rin po che?*). Do not worry. You will solve the problem in about two or three days. Send three to eight capable and reliable [Gyenlo] representatives there in front. Those people who rush ahead in front will never die. Those who lag behind or hide themselves in the corners will be killed." We presented some scarves to the nun, who made two or three knots in each piece. She then put the scarves around our necks and said, "If you wear this, you will never be shot or get sick."[19]

The next day, 14 June, at about 4 P.M., after burning incense as an offering to the gods, a force of about eight hundred villagers under the command of Rangjung attacked the Military Squadron compound, where some cadres and a few soldiers from the Department of Armed Forces had joined with the Military Squadron troops for protection.[20] The Tibetans charged the gate of the building, trying to break it down and rush inside, but, unlike at Bagor, this compound wall was high and topped with barbed wire, and the gate was heavily barricaded, so initially they failed. The PLA was under orders not to fire on the attackers, so they shot into the air and at some of the horses to try to frighten them off. However, since no one was injured, that tactic only reinforced the villagers' belief in the powers of the nun/Ani Gongmey Gyemo, so they continued to try to smash through the gate, pushing and using homemade bombs. One participant explained, "We had broken up pieces of iron that we used for plowing and put them and gunpowder in a piece of cloth, making a kind of bomb, which we threw at the gate. Some people used their slingshots to throw such homemade bombs, but we could not destroy the gate."[21]

While they were struggling like that, one attacker threw a homemade bomb inside the compound, causing damage to a gasoline storage tank and killing or wounding two soldiers.[22] At this point, the PLA troops opened fire with rifles, killing and wounding a number of the attackers. For a moment or two the attackers intensified their pushing at the gate, but as several more fell or were hit, they lost heart, despite the urgings of their leaders to keep pushing. The attack force then broke ranks and fled.

A Tibetan soldier who was a member of the Department of Armed Forces recalled the attack from his post inside the building:

> They were surrounding us, and they were making a lot of noise, so we went to the Military Squadron. At that moment, we didn't care about the material things we had to leave behind in our [Department of Armed Forces] building. We ran away to the Military Squadron's building when we knew they were coming.
>
> Q: How many soldiers were in the Department of Armed Forces?
> A: At that time there were nine, but some had gone on vacation leave, so there were actually only four of us. But nobody ran away, because we were soldiers, and it would have been shameful to do that. . . .
>
> Q: How many people were in the Military Squadron?
> A: About thirty. . . . Most of them were Chinese. Only about four were Tibetans.
>
> We had a very big gate, which they almost destroyed. They pushed against the gate, shouting, "One, two, three" [push]. The gate started moving, and if they could have opened it and gotten inside, that would have been terrible, and many people would have died. We were planning to shoot at them, but the Chinese political commissar (ch. zhengwei) told us not to shoot. He was not a good person.
>
> Q: Was he the leader of the Military Squadron?
> A: No. He was the leader of a branch squadron. If we had shot them at that point, we wouldn't have lost the oil and the grain rations. . . . After that, they destroyed our oil drum, and the oil flowed out like water. . . .
>
> Q: Did they use explosives to do that?

A: Yes. And that made us angry, so we shot them, even though our leader didn't give us the order. . . . I was one of the main persons among the soldiers shooting at them. At that point, we didn't have any choice but to shoot them, because they threw a grenade [or bomb] at our oil supplies and grain. They also . . . had two pistols that they had taken from the Department of Armed Forces building. . . .

Q: *While they [Gyenlo] were making war, what did they shout?*
A: They said that they were going to kill the yellow dogs and blue pigs. The yellow dogs referred to the soldiers, and the blue pigs referred to the cadres. They said that they were going to exterminate these people. . . . They [also] said that they were not going to establish the People's Commune. . . . They thought that if they could exterminate the yellow dogs and the blue pigs, the People's Commune would not be established. . . .

Q: *When they fought with the Military Squadron, did they kill any PLA soldiers?*
A: One soldier was wounded. . . .

Q: *How many Gyenlo people were killed?*
A: About thirteen, but many others were wounded. . . .

Q: *Did they run away after they were defeated?*
A: Yes. When they ran away, I followed them for a while, shooting into the air to scare them. I didn't shoot at them. If I had shot at them, they would have definitely been hit, because I was kind of a marksman. If there had been some ringleaders, I would have killed them, but at that point, not a single ringleader was among them.

Q: *You could recognize those people?*
A: Yes. I could recognize all of them.

Q: *When Gyenlo charged forward, did the soldiers mostly shoot into the sky, or did they target the people?*
A: Mostly, we shot into the air, but some of them were shot.

Q: *Why did you shoot into the sky?*
A: We were just showing mercy on them. If the machine gun had been targeted on them, almost all would have been killed. At that moment, probably, there were about eight hundred people [attacking]. They were coming forward. . . .

Q: *Were they yelling?*
A: Yes. At that time, the mediums [warrior-heroes] such as Bala and Shenba had wrapped white khata scarves around their heads and also wore one khata tied on each side of their torso [like cartridge belts]. They were supposed to be the greater ones. The Chinese did not know who they were, but the Tibetans targeted them in the shooting. I shot one of the heroes who had on the wrapped khata scarf. I aimed at him carefully and killed him. I killed three of the ringleaders in the county and one in the granary office. . . .

Q: *Did you shoot him with a rifle?*
A: Yes.

Q: Who was that?
A: He was Jangdru Yülha; I forget his real name [it was Tashi Rabden].
He was a medium. . . .
Q: In the end, what happened after the fighting was over?
A: Actually, at that moment the nun was not destroyed. After we fought,
we arrested some people from Bagor and interrogated them. . . .
Q: What did they say was the purpose of killing those people in Bagor?
A: They said, as I mentioned above, that they did not want the People's
Commune to be established.[23]

The same failed attack as seen from the vantage point of several attackers conveys the extent to which they really felt protected by the gods and
thus their surprise at what happened. One recalled:

When we arrived at Nyemo [County], they were burning incense on the
mountain, and they were saying that they were great. At that point, the
medium [warrior-hero] called Bala banged a cymbal [going into a trance]
and said, "We should fight right now. I have blocked the mouth of the
guns, so we should charge forward." At that point, the mountain was full
of people. There were people from Nyemo District, Phusum, Shu, and many
other places in Nyemo.

Q: What happened on the mountain?
A: Bala banged the cymbal and said we should burn incense, so we burned
the incense [to the gods]. And then he gave a single grain of [blessed] barley
to each person.
Q: What was that barley for?
A: That was to protect us from weapons. He said that he had blocked the
mouths of their guns and that we should go forward right now. Then all
the people charged down the mountain toward the Department of the
Armed Forces. I was among the people who followed from behind. I was
holding a kind of sword.
Q: What were most of the people carrying?
A: They were carrying just spears and swords.
Q: Didn't they have guns?
A: They had some Tibetan guns.
Q: Didn't Bala have a gun to carry?
A: No, he didn't.
Q: At that point, was Rangjung there?
A: I heard that he had stayed down there [not on the mountain, but by
Nyemo]. I didn't see him there. Then Bala said that we had to go to make
war. After that, all the people charged down. When they arrived at the
front of the Department of Armed Forces [really the Military Squadron],
many people massed at the gate. However, the gate was closed, because
they had barricaded the gate with bricks and big oil drums. They didn't
let people get in, but they were not planning to shoot the people.

Q: What were the soldiers doing at that time?
A: We didn't see any soldiers. They were all inside the house. At that point, a person from Phusum who had an explosive device threw it onto the roof. It, in turn, fell onto the big oil drums, and the oil started flowing out. At that point, the soldiers got angry and started shooting at us.[24] Three people in the front were killed, so I ran away.

Q: What were the other people doing?
A: When the soldiers fired at the people, every single shot killed one person. We heard many gunshots, but it was said those were shots fired into the air.

Q: At that time, how many people were killed?
A: At that point, about six or seven were killed.

Q: Most of the guns were shot into the air, right?
A: Yes. I heard that most of the guns were shot into the air and that the soldiers [later] said that if they had really aimed at the masses, all the people would have been killed.

Q: At that point, what did you think?
A: I was very scared, and I ran away. Later, I heard that the soldiers laughed and watched the people from the roof. A soldier was up there shooting single shots at us. When he shot, smoke rose, and he killed a person with every single shot. But the gun that sounds like a machine gun was said to be shooting into the air. . . .

Q: What did other people say?
A: The people were stunned (tib. *höntor*). They said that it makes no sense to fight like this and that the leaders brought us here to lose our lives. Later, all the people fled. I didn't go to see the medium [afterward]. I just ran away to my home. Some people ran away wearing only a single boot.[25]

A Tibetan who was part of the attack commented on his disillusionment with the mediums: "They said that they could protect people from gunshots and that they had made it so that their [the soldiers'] guns could not be fired. At that moment, the majority of the masses were duped by this. When I recall those things, [I realize] we were really idiots who didn't know how to think. They called the soldiers 'yellow old men' (tib. *bo serbo*), and they said, 'We have made it so that the yellow old men's guns cannot be fired.'"[26]

Yet another recalled both his disillusionment and his continued fear of the nun's supernatural powers:

Q: What was your thinking when they were making war [in the county]? Did you think they would win?
A: . . . I was thinking that the nun had said she had done something so that the guns would not go off, so there probably would be no problem. . . . Otherwise, I didn't think they would win. In the end . . . many people were killed.

Q: When you ran away, what did other people say? What did you think?
A: I was just scared of the nun, thinking that she was still there [in Phusum].
I didn't dare to say that the nun and Rangjung were telling lies. Even if
two people ran away together, we would not dare to say that the nun had
probably been telling us lies. We thought the nun could foresee things, and
we were afraid that the nun would later say, "Why did you say that?" and
she might kill us.[27]

So as the surprised Tibetan villagers fled from Nyemo County, some simply went home while others went to Phusum and Bagor to regroup.[28]

CHAPTER 6

The Capture of the Nun

AFTER THE DEFEAT IN NYEMO

Gyenlo's Army of the Gods dispersed after the defeat at Nyemo. Most of the common, less committed, villagers simply went home, but the main leaders and many of the more committed fighters went to Phusum, where they regrouped under Rangjung's command, and consulted the nun/Ani Gongmey Gyemo about what to do. Her answer was clear. She gave them blessed barley and told them to not worry and to continue to fight because she would protect them. Many fighters stayed in the more defensible upper part of the valley around Phusum, where the nunnery and the adjacent Ru Monastery were located, but Rangjung also sent fighters into the surrounding mountains to keep a lookout for arriving PLA troops and to block the various ways the PLA could advance. At the same time fighters were dispatched to try to destroy roads and mountain passes in order to hinder PLA reinforcements from moving into Nyemo from other areas. At this time there were about several hundred Tibetan fighters in Phusum.[1]

One activist recalled the preparations:

> We hadn't been able to seize any weapons, but the fight had started, and we felt the army would come after us, so we made preparations. Some people went into the upper area in the mountains and some into the lower area. Each of us who went there were volunteers. People like me who had Tibetan muskets went to the mountains, and others stayed in the lower area. . . . We didn't wait for orders or messages as to what

to do. I was in a great position with the mountain behind and only one way at the front for the Chinese to come up from below.[2]

They were, therefore, prepared to fight if the PLA attacked, and as the same fighter recalled, most expected this. "I thought they would come, because the fight was kind of provoked [by us]. We wanted to get some weapons at that time. What should I say? Our people were kind of superstitious or religious. I thought that on one hand maybe we would win the fight, but on the other hand maybe the army would win and we would be killed. But I didn't actually care much about that possibility."[3]

However, the villagers' military tactics were low level and bound up with supernatural causation, as the following recollection illustrates: "[After returning from the Nyemo battle] a warrior-hero medium told me to go to the Shugbula Mountain pass and destroy the road that crosses it. So four or five of us went together. We ran there and then ran back and told the mediums that a crow had arrived there, and it was cawing, so we came back. The mediums said that it was right to come back, because that crow was ours."[4]

At the same time, a portion of the warrior-hero mediums and committed fighters returned to their home area in Bagor and, like those in Phusum, made preparations and then waited to see what would happen. A Tibetan fighter who was involved explained their plan. "We were told to stop them here. . . . After waiting several days, we finally received a message that the PLA was on the way. We waited for them on the roof of the main building. We were ready to fight. We had some homemade bombs with us that had been made from tin cans into which gunpowder and small stones had been jammed.[5] The plan was to let the PLA enter the courtyard of the district building and then shut the gate behind them, trapping them inside."[6] Although firing Tibetan muskets required lighting a wick to set off the gunpowder in the barrel, the villagers were able to load fast and were planning to fire at the PLA in volleys for greater effect. However, when the PLA troops arrived, they set up tents quite some distance from the district headquarters' compound and made no move to attack the compound or anything else. That prompted one Tibetan who was already disillusioned with the nun and the mediums and dubious about the ambush plan to try to make a deal for himself with the PLA. Grabbing a shovel, he left the district compound, explaining to the others that he was going to do some work. However, he actually went to where the PLA troops were camped, as he explained:

They asked me what I had done, and I told them the truth. I said I used to have a good relationship with the People's Liberation Army, but because I found myself in a very dangerous situation here, I had to join Gyenlo. I also told them how many soldiers Gyenlo had killed here and how they had killed them. They asked me what we were doing, and I answered that we were guarding the district building because we thought they would come there. Then they asked me what kinds of weapons they [Gyenlo] had, and I told them. . . . After these questions, they told me to come and eat some food. I used to eat food with them, so I knew that when the PLA offered you food, mostly they trusted you. After I ate, they asked my name and said I should leave their camp and act as if I were a local farmer. I did, and that night those soldiers left this area secretly. No one knew where they went. [They never went to the district's compound.][7]

The sudden departure of the PLA troops in Bagor bolstered the spirits of the fighters, as one cynical, unbelieving Nyamdre grassroots cadre explained. "Probably the soldiers just didn't get permission to fight against the nun [at this time], so they withdrew, . . . but when the people saw this they said, 'Thank God, a crow [sent by the nun] has chased away the PLA. We are grateful to the protective deities.'"[8]

Consequently, despite some disillusionment resulting from the gods' inability to block the PLA's guns in Nyemo, the more committed followers of the nun still clung to their belief that the mediums and gods were real and would protect them in the next round. In fact, one rationalization made then was that if one had deep faith in the protective amulets, they worked better, implying that those who were wounded or killed didn't have enough faith. However, there was also fear that unless the gods really helped them, they would meet certain defeat and probable death. So while the more committed of the fighters were not ready to give up on the Gyenlo agenda and the gods, the less committed, such as the previously mentioned fighter, were thinking of ways to get out and save themselves.[9]

Meanwhile, at Gyenlo Headquarters in Nyemo, Zhang Yongfu and other important Gyenlo leaders were also unwilling to accept that the defeat in Nyemo meant that their plan had failed. Consequently, on 16 June, two days after the defeat, they sent a letter of encouragement to Phusum, criticizing the PLA for opening fire on the "revolutionary masses" and urging the fighters there not to lose hope. Xiao Yong recalled that the letter said:

[To:] The proletarian revolutionary comrades-in-arms at Phusum.
    We saw the soldiers of the Department of Armed Forces [the PLA] open

fire on you. The bullets were like raindrops flying onto the revolutionary members of the Gyenlo Headquarters. The blood of our Gyenlo Headquarters' comrades-in-arms should not be shed in vain. We shall wipe up the blood ourselves and bury the bodies of our companions. Let us hold up the flag of the heroes and stride forward following in their bloodstained footsteps.

The Department of the Armed Forces is implementing not the revolutionary line of Chairman Mao but the reactionary capitalist line. They are implementing the line of Deng Xiaoping and Liu Shaoqi, and the line of Zhou Renshan, Wang Qimei, and Yin Fatang. They treat people in the manner of the Guomindang.

According to Comrade Jiang Qing's instructions, we should use both violent and nonviolent struggle to fight against them. We should reorganize our team. Dear comrades-in-arms, do not be sorrowful. Do not shed tears. We will never give up, even though our enemies are furious. We will never lower our heads when facing the capitalists. We will continue the struggle against the reactionary capitalist line until we die. Success belongs to us![10]

In the meantime, a decision was reached in Beijing and Lhasa that the fighting in Nyemo County must be stopped, and the Tibet Military Headquarters was instructed to send the army at once to reimpose order. However, until these reinforcements arrived, the troops in Nyemo were told not to go on the offensive, so the nun's killings and maimings of individuals in the countryside continued, as the following case of a veterinary doctor traveling to Nyemo for work illustrates:

> I used to receive my grain rations from Nyemo County, so when my supply was exhausted, I had to go there to pick up some more grain. Another cadre from Margyang District named Xiao Dorje also had to go to Nyemo to get a marriage certificate, so we two decided to go there together on horseback. When we reached a place called Yulung, we saw a lot of people there burning incense. Xiao Dorje, who was a cadre in Margyang District, . . . said, "Let's go to have a look," and rode ahead. I was just following him. After that, the two of us were seriously beaten.
>
> Q: Why did they beat him?
> A: At that moment, it seemed to make no difference if one were Nyamdre or Gyenlo. The revolt in Nyemo had probably already started.
> Q: What did you do?
> A: They were beating us up and we were trying to fight back, but we couldn't fight very much. An old man came to spear me. I couldn't see my companion in the crowd of people. Probably, there were about two hundred to three hundred people there. When the old man came to spear me, I seized his spear and pressed down on it so that the spear tip broke from the handle. It was not a good spear, like those made in the past; it was just an inferior one that had been made recently. I broke my pinky doing that. After that,

they stabbed me in my ribs and then they hit me with stones. I couldn't do anything.

Q: *Didn't they ask you any questions?*

A: They didn't say even a single word. . . .

Q: *What did they do to you after that?*

A: They tied my legs and put me in a small room for the night. In the afternoon of the next day, they took me and my companion away. They had stabbed him on his thigh, and there were lumps of blood on both sides of his shoes. He had also been stabbed on his shoulder, and yellowish bubbles were coming out of that wound. I was stabbed here and hit with stones, so I had a lot of swollen bruises on my body. In the afternoon we were taken to Bagor District and arrived there after dark. They tied the two of us to pillars inside the stable and left us there.

At that time . . . I was wearing a blue cotton padded jacket on which all the buttons had been broken and the cotton padding was coming out from all parts of the coat. However, [the coat cushioned the ropes tying me], and I was able to pull my arms out of the coat. . . . I untied my companion, but he had lost a lot of blood and couldn't move. . . . [Then] I ran away. . . . [His partner couldn't flee and died there.][11]

For about five days after the defeat in Nyemo, no PLA counterattack occurred, so from the vantage point of the Army of the Gods, it was beginning to seem as if a decision had been made not to attack them. This conclusion was not inconceivable, since, as we have seen, the PLA was supposed to avoid involvement in factional fighting and normally was under orders not to attack the revolutionary masses. However, on 19 June, that sliver of hope was squelched when more than a thousand troops from the Fifty-third Regiment arrived in Nyemo. Other troops, it was then learned, were also on the way from other areas.

The arrival of these reinforcements prompted Gyenlo Headquarters in Nyemo to meet that very evening to discuss how to proceed. Three main decisions were made: first, to privately warn the people in Phusum that an attack by the PLA was now imminent; second, to continue to try to counter the assertion that this had been a counterrevolutionary *rebellion* by arguing forcefully that it was just a counterrevolutionary *incident;* and third, to distance themselves from the attacks of the Army of the Gods by blaming those incidents on reactionary nuns, lamas, and class enemies, not on the actions of the revolutionary masses. Since the Nyemo County Gyenlo leaders such as Zhang Yongfu had worked through Rangjung and had not been physically present at the attacks or in the villages, they assured the higher-ups that they had had nothing to do with the nun and the mediums. Gao Zemin recalled their discussions about labeling it as a rebellion:

On the night of 20 June [*sic,* 19 June] 1969, we held a meeting at Xu De'an's home to try to unify our ideas. . . . Xu De'an said, "Different terms are being used to describe the counterrevolutionary incident at Nyemo. Some people say that it was a riot, while others from the other faction [Nyamdre] say that it was a rebellion. Also some other people prefer to call it the Bagor incident. My opinion is that we should label it a counterrevolutionary incident and call it the "counterrevolutionary incident of Nyemo" or the "incident at Bagor." The term *rebellion* is too broad and too serious.[12]

Xu De'an recalled that same meeting:

On 19 June 1969, a meeting was held at my home. . . . We talked about the events of 13 and 14 June and about the soldiers of the Fifty-third Regiment, who had just arrived in Nyemo.

Li Jianhua [a Tibetan who was a senior official in Nyemo County] said, "This time I am sure that the army will surround Phusum *xiang* and settle the problem there. Since most of the people in Phusum are members of Gyenlo Headquarters, if the army surrounds Phusum, they will catch many members of Gyenlo Headquarters, and they will say that the incident was caused by Gyenlo Headquarters. We should write a letter to the people in Phusum telling them to leave there and join us here. The letter needs to be burned after they read it." . . . Other people at the meeting all agreed with this idea, and we decided to have Li Jianhua write a letter. When Li Jianhua asked what he should say, Zhou Longquan [deputy director of the Nyemo Agriculture and Animal Husbandry Department] said, "Tell them that the army will surround Phusum, so they should leave the *xiang* and come here."

On the morning of 20 June, Dong Xue'an showed me this letter, which said:

Proletariat revolutionary comrades-in-arms,

The army has already arrived at Nyemo. They have more than fifty trucks and more than one thousand soldiers and weapons. They will surround Phusum in no time. It's not wise for you to fight against them. . . .

After reading it, I told Li Jianhua to revise the first part of the letter and cross out the information about the army's strength. Later, when Dong Xue'an went to see Li Jianhua, Li told him, "Most people in Phusum *xiang* are members of Gyenlo Headquarters, so I think it's fine to call them "proletarian revolutionary comrades-in-arms." The information about the army is not needed, because what we want to do is just tell them not to fight anymore." I agreed with him.

Li Jianhua added one more paragraph to the letter telling the people in Phusum to burn the letter after reading it. I then gave the letter to Xiao Yong for translation [into Tibetan]. Later, Zhang Yongfu came, and Li Jianhua asked him, "Comrade Zhang, could you find someone to take this letter to Phusum?" . . . Zhang Yongfu said, "OK, I'll find someone."

Li Jianhua then said, "This letter should be sent to Phusum *xiang* as soon as possible. It will be too late if the army gets there and surrounds them." I added, "You'd better hurry. If the army gets there first and surrounds the *xiang*, the person taking the letter will not be able to come back."[13]

The letter writer, Li Jianhua, also recalled that meeting:

On 6 June [*sic*, 19 June] 1969, the army came to Nyemo to suppress the rebellion. I went to Xu De'an's home that day. Many people were there . . . and we . . . wrote a letter to Gyenlo Headquarters in Phusum *xiang*. However, if the army had found out about the letter, they would have thought we were connected to the rebels, so I thought we should write a letter but tell them not to tell others about the letter. They should be told that it could be very dangerous if the PLA and Nyamdre Headquarters were to find out about the previous letter. . . . This letter said:

Comrades-in-arms in Phusum *xiang*.

Several days ago, we wrote a letter to you. Please check who has that letter now. Today many PLA troops arrived in the county. They are preparing to march toward Phusum. Do not tell Nyamdre Headquarters and the PLA about the letter we sent you a few days ago. If they find out about the letter, our organization, Gyenlo Headquarters, will be regarded as a counterrevolutionary organization.

I gave the letter to Xu De'an. He added something to it, telling people how many PLA were in the county and what weapons they brought with them. Huang Guojie [deputy head of Nyemo County Security Bureau] added something to it too, namely, "The Central Committee (ch. *zhongyang*) has not yet determined the nature of the Nyemo incident. We don't know whether it will be regarded as a rebellion or not. So do not be afraid. Stay calm."[14]

Xiao Yong, the letter's translator, recalled those events similarly, but he recalled that the letter urged the fighters *not* to give up the struggle:

The main point of the letter was to notify them about the number of PLA soldiers that had come and the number of trucks, rifles, and machine guns they had brought with them. I can still remember three things mentioned in the letter. "1. We should persist in defending Phusum *xiang* until we finally achieve success. 2. If you are outnumbered by the enemy and are having trouble defending Phusum *xiang*, you should go to the mountains and start a guerrilla war. 3. If a guerrilla war doesn't work, dismiss the group and go back home. [However,] [w]e will fight till the end and keep our organization alive forever."

The letter was addressed to "Proletarian revolutionary comrades-in-arms at Phusum *xiang*." Nobody signed the letter.[15]

Consequently, despite some disagreement about what the final letter said, it was clearly a warning to their Gyenlo "comrades-in-arms" in Phusum that the PLA was on the way.[16]

The PLA troops marched out of Nyemo on 19 June and spread out to Phusum and the several other Gyenlo strongholds, including Bagor. The exact chronology of how this played out in Phusum and Bagor is not clear, but it generally took three or four days from the initial arrival of the troops to the final surrender and capture of the nun.

In Phusum, a Tibetan who was with the nun recalled that the main fighters were armed and waiting in her house and in the nearby Ru Monastery, in the upper part of the valley. His account is interesting but also somewhat unclear:

> On the first day, about two thousand soldiers came [up toward our locations]. That day there was a little fighting, and then they returned. Half of the soldiers returned to the county, and half went to a hill near Ru Monastery. But they didn't advance toward us, and we didn't go down [the mountainside to where they were]. They stayed there for two days. The soldiers didn't advance toward us, and we didn't attack them.[17]
>
> Then one morning, as dawn was breaking, the soldiers attacked us. The fighting went on until about noon, . . . [but] that evening they went back to the *xiang* [farther down the mountainside]. The next morning, at about dawn, they came up again, and that day they fought all day long. . . .
>
> Then at about 3 P.M., we could see that many soldiers were shooting a lot of cannons at us, so we had to flee. There were too many explosions. They had sent the soldiers into many different locations, so we were getting bad incoming messages all the time, saying that so many people were wounded here and there. So more and more people came inside the monastery [from their posts on the mountainside], and then there were explosions inside the monastery due to the cannons. . . . Then the soldiers came closer and closer to us, so we worried about this situation. When it was almost dark, we heard their bugles again, and then all the soldiers went back [to the *xiang*]. . . . That night seven people ran away to India with Rangjung. . . . I was the last person to leave. . . .
>
> *Q: When you were surrounded was there a way to escape?*
> A: Many soldiers had come from Kongpo via Tülung, . . . but on the hill behind us there were no soldiers, so we escaped from that side. . . .
> *Q: Did the soldiers use loudspeakers to speak to you?*
> A: Yes. They said that Rangjung and Trinley should come out to talk and surrender. But the two of them didn't go, replying, "We will wage war against you." So then the soldiers attacked. They fired lots of cannons,

and there was nothing we could do. . . . They didn't have heavy artillery, but they fired a large number of shells from mortars. . . . They laid down a volley of heavy fire on us, and for a moment I could not hear anything. The area was full of the echoes of gunshots. They fired fiercely at us, and we fired back.[18]

Ganden, another fighter, also recalled the fighting in Phusum:

At this time I was with two comrades in a house [near the nun's, shooting at the PLA]. One of them had his head blown off by an exploding bomb, and another was hit by a gunshot through the hole that we were firing out from. He was wounded and lost a lot of blood. So only I was left. At that time I had a protective amulet in which I deeply believed. If you believe in these strongly, they work better. . . . Then I put lots of powdered dung in the stove so that it would make a lot of smoke for a long time, so the soldiers below would think that we were still in the nunnery while I escaped.[19]

Meanwhile, when these final battles began, the powerlessness of the mediums became obvious, as one Tibetan from Bagor angrily recalled:

Later when the soldiers came back [to Bagor District] . . . the mediums [in Bagor] could not go into a trance. Each of them said that he didn't have any deity to go into a trance with. . . . At that point the soldiers attacked. There were several thousand soldiers. The whole area around the district building was filled with fully armed soldiers . . . When we asked the mediums to go into a trance, they stood up and just blew their breath once or twice [as they did when in a trance] and said, "Now, I don't have any deity to go into a trance with." The people had been duped. All the people were astonished. The leaders also said, "If the mediums had really gone into trances [in the past], they should be able to go into a trance now and do something when the soldiers are here. Now, not only are the mediums finished, but so are we." After that, we ran away to the upper part of the mountains. We were lying in the caves. We were very afraid of being seized, because we had done those bad things.[20]

The PLA, therefore, systematically amassed a force of overwhelming strength and when it was in place, whatever the exact chronology, attacked. After a few days of fighting, the Tibetan fighters fled. Rangjung, the main leader, fled to the east with seven other fighters, as the nun's brother recalled:

When I fled, I saw the seven people walking up the mountain, leading their horses. Rangjung and those people shouted to us, "The soldiers are everywhere, so you people should leave and escape. Don't flee to the lower area, but go far up into the mountains." . . .

It was the night of the third day. I had seen them [Rangjung and those

with him] making preparations on the night of the second day. They had
packed *tsamba*, butter, and tea, and they had collected Chinese felt and
blankets from the monastery and nunnery and had gathered better saddles
and better horses, but I did not know they were planning to flee the next
day. However, when they were ready to leave, I was unable to go with them,
since I was wounded. I don't know how they could have gone around and
gotten through. . . . They climbed up the mountain facing east.[21]

So then my sister, Ganden, the monk Tsering Chösang, and I fled
up on the mountain. . . . We walked all night, and the second day we
climbed another mountain, and then we stayed for one day in a nomad
household. . . . During the day, we saw that the whole mountainside
was covered with soldiers who had come south through the Shugbula Pass.
Then all that night we fled again. Then we reached Bagor's Phongkhang
xiang. . . . We stayed there for one day also.

On the third day we reached the area called Se, which was part of
Bagor District. That area had a huge mountain called Zingzing, which
had a cave, and we went there. . . . We had only what we carried when
we ran away. . . . Then, because our *tsamba* was running out, Ganden
and I left at night to get more from my house. When we reached there,
my family members said the soldiers were coming, so we went to my uncle's
household in Phusum *xiang.* While we were there, . . . we received a message saying that some people had seen firsthand that my sister and Tsering
Chösang had been captured [back at the cave]. My uncle . . . told us, "Since
your sister has been captured and you are wounded, it would be better if
you surrender now before they capture you." We two agreed with this and
gave ourselves up.[22]

Meanwhile, the PLA had followed the nun and surrounded the cave. Then
on about 21 June, they attacked and captured her. A Tibetan soldier who
was part of that PLA unit recalled the capture:

They told us that the nun Trinley Chödrön was staying in a cave in the
mountains in the inner part of Nyemo. [After we arrived from Margyang
in the west] [w]e stayed on the mountain for two days and nights without
food, watching them. During the day we slept, and at night we scouted
out what they were doing. For one day and night we had no food or water.
Not even a drop of water. We were waiting for an order [to attack] from
the Central Committee [in Beijing]. When the order from the Central Committee came to seize them, all of us soldiers were angry and hungry and
opened fire, but we shot only to scare them, not to hit them. We moved
ahead as in a movie, going and shooting and going and shooting. Then
we arrived above the cave opening.

Q: Did they fire guns at you?
A: They had pistols and [matchlock] rifles.[23] Our deputy platoon leader
was shot in the leg and fell. Then we attacked inside the cave, thinking that
if we died, we died, so we attacked. Inside, there was a big disparity in the
number of people [there were more soldiers]. . . .

Q: How did you seize her?
A: She was called a nun, but she looked like a strong young man. She had short hair and was fat and white. The cave was large inside. . . . We captured them at night. We tied them very tightly and that very night immediately took them back to the Military Area Headquarters in Lhasa. Our orders from the Military Area Headquarters specified that we must immediately hand them over alive. We were not to kill them or let them escape. . . .

Q: How long did the Nyemo operation take?
A: We had to stay on the mountain for two days and nights.

Q: How many of your troops were on the mountain?
A: One regiment (ch. *tuan*) at least. The entire mountain was covered with soldiers. One part came from the Gampa la Pass to block the escape route through the lower part of Nyemo. Everything on the left and right was blocked by troops. The nun had nowhere to flee. . . .

Q: How easy was it to arrest the nun?
A: So-so. They fired some shots at us. But we came down from above and up from under the cave, so they didn't have a chance. It took about one hour. It started about 2:00–3:00 in the morning [on 21 June].

There was a spring nearby. When we soldiers descended, we drank water, because we had not drunk anything for two days. So we drank and carried our guns and ran ahead. At this time there was no one to tell that you were hungry or thirsty. . . .

Q: Was the nun in nun's religious robes?
A: She wasn't wearing nun's clothes. She was wearing a woman's dress but had hiked it up a bit to her calf, so the hemline was higher than a normal woman's but lower than a man's. And she had a pistol tied to her belt. A model-53 pistol. And her belt was a cartridge belt with bullets.

Q: Was it hard to go into the cave?
A: There were two entrances—one at the mouth and one from a hole on top. There was a ladder at the opening on top where they climbed up to look around. We first blocked the top opening, and then we immediately moved into the cave, firing lots of blanks into it from the entrance. They sounded like real bullets. We did this because if we had shot real bullets we would have killed everyone, and we wouldn't have been able to learn the truth about the events there. We were not permitted to kill them. If we were on the verge of losing them, we had orders to shoot them but not above the knees. They told us to shoot at the legs, since this could be repaired even if the leg was broken. If we shot above the knees, we could have killed them, and if they had died, we would have been finished [their mission would have failed]. This was our responsibility. . . .

Q: Was this order the same for all of the people there?
A: Yes. If they flee, shoot only from the knee down. [We were warned,] "If you shoot above the knee, you will be shot. . . . You will be killed." They told us that this was a matter of whether the Tibetan people could become the master of their own politics. They said this emphatically, because

there was a danger the solders would kill the nun, as they were angry and hungry, et cetera. . . .

Q: When you first grabbed her, what did she say?
A: She said, "You have come to kill us. So you don't need to tie us up. Just kill us right here." We didn't say anything. We just tied her up and took her to headquarters. There was no time to say anything, because the work was so urgent. . . .

The nun was very afraid, but however tightly we tied her, she didn't say a word. Not one word. We tied her with a rope across her upper chest in front and then around her arms and then her hands were pulled behind so that they came right up to her shoulder in back, and still she didn't utter even a cry. This creature (*semjen*) was not the usual creature.

Then, when we drove her back to Lhasa, at the bridge by the leather factory, the nun insisted that she had to urinate and that it wasn't right to urinate in the truck, so she had to get out of the truck. She said, "I have to go urinate by myself under the bridge." So we let her go. However, when she didn't return after [some time], we were very nervous. I said, "We should go and watch her urinating. If she escapes, we are in real trouble, and we will all die." So we went to look. [When we did, we saw that] she [was fleeing and] was quite a ways from the bridge alongside the river near the leather factory. She had shackles on her feet, and her hands were tied, although we had loosened them enough for her to pull down her pants; however, she couldn't run very fast, and we caught her at once and tied her up again and put her back into the truck. We then went straight to the Military Region Headquarters. At this time the nun was dripping urine, since she had started running away without first going to the bathroom. She must have thought the men would not come if a woman was urinating. . . . If she had reached the village that was near the leather factory, we wouldn't have been able to find her easily, and all our efforts in Nyemo would have been a waste. And our squad would have gone right to hell. They had told us that this was a great responsibility, so we would have gone right there to hell. We were told to bring the nun alive and able to speak.[24]

As mentioned above, the commander of Gyenlo's Army of the Gods, Rangjung, fled with six or seven others. He vanished and was never heard of again in Tibet or in exile, despite a massive search, including the search his wife was forced to make for him, as one villager recalled: "He [Rangjung] didn't have parents at that time, but he had a wife, who had to suffer a lot because he was the leader of Gyenlo. At the time he fled, his wife had a small child, and Nyamdre told her that they wanted to find Rangjung, so they sent her to search for him in the mountains, carrying her two- or three-year-old child on her back. But how could she find him?"[25] Many in Nyemo think he may have committed suicide by jumping into a river or lake rather than be captured, but neither his body nor any of the others' were ever recovered, so perhaps they really escaped and started new lives.

The PLA/TAR government was eager to bring this event to a close and restore calm without having to shed a lot of blood, so it decided to adopt the position that most of the villagers who had participated had really been duped by the supernatural arguments of the nun and the other mediums. Consequently, it promulgated a policy that offered leniency to almost all of the villagers, saying, "If one confesses one's mistakes, one will be given leniency, but if one is stubborn and does not (confess), one will be militantly suppressed" (tib. *khase shüna guying / tregsung chena tragnön*).[26] The aim of this policy was to persuade people still holed up in the mountains that they did not have to fear a voluntary return home.[27] This strategy worked well, and hundreds of peasants who were involved in the attacks surrendered without further fighting. One of the PLA's Tibetan interpreters explained how they proceeded:

> At that point, we differentiated these people first into those who were guilty and those who were not guilty. After that, we made five different categories among the people who were guilty. The first category was the people who had committed serious crimes, the second category was the people who had committed secondary crimes, the third, tertiary, and so on.
>
> The criminals who could be . . . educated were made to confess their crimes. We educated them and let them find a guarantor and then allowed them to go home.
>
> At that point, the people who deserved to be executed were executed, and the rest of the people were handed over to the relevant counties.[28]

The nun, the warrior mediums, and a few others, such as the lama Chamba Tenzin, were taken away for their subsequent execution. Others who were involved were sent to a "study class," where they were detained and ordered to study Mao's thoughts and, in the government's view, come to understand and *confess* their own crimes. The individuals in such study classes were released depending on their confessions, not after any set term. One Gyenlo villager who did not surrender described his experiences:

> I had been a village representative of Gyenlo so was told to attend the study class. I spent about a month in the class. . . . I was asked about what other people had done and about what wrong things I had done. . . . I didn't have a serious problem [he actually had made explosives for Gyenlo], . . . and I was [let go. but] I was given a political label [hat] of a "rebel" (tib. *ngologba*) and placed in the "reform through labor" program. . . . [This meant mainly that] I had to do public work, like cleaning horse dung and

Figure 3. Lama Chamba Tenzin just before his execution in 1969.

so forth. I was made to do whatever kind of work they needed, and they didn't pay me . . . for this work.[29]

A neighbor of the nun also described his capture, detainment, and release:

> We were sent to block the People's Liberation Army, but we couldn't block them, so we fled. . . . The People's Liberation Army was arriving in large numbers on the plains and on the hills. At about dawn, I heard and saw a signal shell. After this, people said the People's Liberation Army had come, and then the area was full with troops. They fired shells, which lit up the sky, and we were frightened that the shells would fall on us. We had only sticks and *tsamba* pouches, so we took these and fled. When we reached the next hill, we thought we had escaped. Then we looked around and saw soldiers coming down from the upper hill, so we fled again and crossed a few hills.
>
> Some young men who had gone out to defend the mountains were coming back, and they didn't know the Chinese were there. They were fired on with artillery, and some persons were blown away, but others were able to flee because they knew the terrain well. Then Ganden and those who had binoculars looked around and saw PLA troops everywhere. I fled, and when I reached a house I begged some *tsamba* from them and then took it and continued fleeing. Our group fled to the nomad area in Bagor *xiang*.
>
> Meanwhile, the People's Liberation Army troops surrounded the mountains. I kept moving and reached another household and stayed there

that night. I wasn't able to go home, because troops were everywhere, but while I was there a message came from a *xiang* official saying, "You should come down to the *xiang*; there will be no punishment." Fourteen people from my village were with me then. I feared that if I went down they would kill me, but then I looked and saw troops on all the mountaintops, so I thought I couldn't escape. But I also still thought the troops would kill me, so we left the house to keep fleeing. However, as we went, there was more firing, and then the Chinese troops surrounded us on the road. They caught us and asked us many questions.

Q: Were any Tibetans among the interrogators?
A: They were Chinese, but they had Tibetan translators. They asked, "From where have you fled?" and they searched us. I had nothing in my pocket because we had thrown our knives and other weapons into the river when we fled. They took us back to Phusum and left us in a house just near the nun's house. Many people were collected there, and we were surrounded. Then they said that if your home was nearby, you should ask your family members to bring you food, and you should eat. My house was far away, so they told others whose houses were nearby to give me food.

After this, they took me to Parong *xiang* and kept me there for fourteen days. There were about three hundred to four hundred people detained there in a large room. It was like being put in prison. We were guarded mostly by cadres, not soldiers. The cadres said we had to go for study. They asked many questions. During the fourteen days I stayed there, I found the Parong people were worse than the army or cadres. Although they were really a part of us [the masses], they acted as if they weren't and beat us a lot. The [local Nyamdre] officials from Parong also beat us very badly. Some people among us had to confess a lot. The Parong people said that we deserved this kind of treatment, but really they were the same as we were.

Q: What was the main point of the study class?
A: Mostly it was asking questions and reading newspapers. There were no speeches; it was questioning. They said, "If you speak truthfully, we will send you home soon. If you don't, we will send you to a different place [prison]." Some stayed for only six days. They were the earliest ones who were released. I had to stay there for fourteen days. Some people who had done bad things, much worse than I, were released earlier than I was. They were still telling us that if you want to go home, you should confess truthfully, and if you do not, then you will be sent to another place. Several among us had been wounded by gunfire. Others had been beaten by the soldiers with batons. . . .

Q: What did you eat at this time?
A: We were given one ladle full of *tsamba* with one ladle full of tea on top. At first they let family members bring barley beer (tib. *chang*), but then they stopped that. . . .

After fourteen days, another person from Bagor and I were allowed to go home. The rest were taken away.[30]

A Tibetan who had served as a servant-bodyguard of two mediums recalled what happened after he decided to give up:

> At that moment they said, "You don't need to run away. All of you were deceived by the mediums, so you don't need to be afraid. You should come back. There will be no problem. You will not be beaten and killed." So I came back home. Otherwise, I wouldn't have dared to come back, because I was guilty. . . .
>
> We actually hadn't gone far away into the mountains. We were just hiding in the caves in the upper part of the village area. The soldiers told our family members to send messages to those who had fled, telling them to come back home. When we arrived home, the family members told us about that. . . .
>
> I had been called to become the servant of the mediums. Actually, I was their bodyguard. When many mediums were staying in the house, I had to stand guard at the front door. I was told not to let people into the house indiscriminately. At that time, I was deluded and duped by those people. I believed whatever they told us, and I thought I would be protected from gunshots and went with them. Therefore, [later] I had to attend the study session twice. The first time was in the county seat, and I was released after three to four months. Later I was called again, and . . . the Public Security Bureau (ch. *gong an ju*) labeled me [politically as a counterrevolutionary, placing me under the supervision of the masses]. After three years, a work team came here and said that my label had been removed because of my good behavior.[31]

Another account comes from a Gyenlo representative who had not participated in the Bagor killings because he had been instructed to remain in Phusum and make preparations with incense and beer to welcome the fighters returning from Bagor. He also recalled being given a hat (labeled politically) and losing all rights as a citizen (placed under the supervision of the masses):

> Luckily what I did was not given a serious political label. I was given a "hat" and told that I was not allowed to talk with other villagers until the hat was removed. All the village representatives of Gyenlo were given hats. Those who were considered serious criminals were beaten a lot and put into jail. . . . I was not put into jail, but the hat was put on me for a very long time.
>
> *Q: When they investigated the people, did they ask you to attend many meetings?*
> A: Troops of the PLA lived in every village, and we were treated badly. . . . Because I did not have new things to say, I just repeated what the others had said before me, but they did not believe me. They said I had a secret that I was not telling them. They continually said I should think about this. However, if one created some unreal stories for them, one would have to

have some corroborating evidence, and I did not have this. So I repeated what the others had said, and even though they ordered me to consider it more carefully, I said that was everything I knew. They said I still had more problems and if I did not tell them those problems honestly, they would put me into a struggle session before the masses, but I continued to keep repeating my story. If you said something different every day, the "hat" became heavier, because you could not prove what you were saying. So one only admitted what one really did. You could not say something you knew only a little about [to satisfy them], because when they asked many questions about this, you needed to prove what you said.

Q: How long did they hold the study class?
A: For one year. Troops of the People's Liberation Army lived in every village and forcefully questioned us a lot. . . .

Q: How did you feel when you had to attend so many meetings?
A: I was stunned and was worried what would happen to me if I were put into a struggle session. . . .

Q: When they made the final decision, what kind of "hat" did they put on you?
A: Before they made the final decision, I was completely prohibited to speak to anyone.

Q: Could you go home?
A: Yes, I could. I could talk with my family, but I was completely prohibited to talk with other people, not even one sentence. . . . They said I did not have the right.

Q: How many years did you have the "hat"?
A: I had it about two years.

Q: What was the name? They said you were a reactionary, didn't they?
A: I had the "hat" of a criminal. . . .

Q: Did you talk with people [during those years]?
A: I completely refrained from talking with anyone. I was worried that if I talked to a person, that person would tell the authorities that I had talked to him [or her]. So I did not talk to anyone. I just stayed quiet.

Q: Did you have a hard time keeping your mind at ease?
A: Yes, it was very hard. I was always frightened. Fear was always in my mind. I had to do everything very carefully so that I would not fall on either the right side or the left side.

Q: Was it okay to take a trip to Lhasa or somewhere else?
A: No. I was not allowed to leave. I had to stay in my home. I was not allowed to go far away. It was prohibited. If I needed to go to the county seat, I had to ask permission to leave and tell the reason I wanted to go.[32]

Chinese records report that from 2 to 21 June, the nun and Gyenlo killed 54 people, among whom 15 were PLA soldiers, 7 were local cadres, and 32 were grassroots cadres and activists.[33] At the end of the initial investigations, it was determined that 499 people had participated. Of these, 411 were categorized as general rebels, 39 as important rebels, 27 as people involved in killings, 16 as core rebels, and 6 as rebel heads. In the end, a total of 105 Gyenlo local leaders and activists were punished. Of these, 34 were executed, 28 were sentenced to incarceration, and 43 were placed under public surveillance. The rest were released after attending study classes.[34] It is not clear how many Tibetan fighters were killed in battle, but one official TAR report gave a figure of 57, and another 16 committed suicide.[35]

Trinley Chödrön was taken directly to Lhasa, where she remained until the start of 1970. At that time she was brought before a huge public meeting of roughly ten thousand people at Po Lingka Park, where her crimes and the execution order were read. One Gyenlo Headquarters leader who was present that day reported that she said, "Chairman Mao said that it is okay to rebel," taking this as proof that she was not a counterrevolutionary, as she was being charged, but this is unlikely, because no one else mentioned it.[36] Trinley Chödrön was then taken immediately to the sand dune area below Sera Monastery and executed. Many of the other main figures, including all the surviving warrior-heroes and the lama Chamba Tenzin, were also executed.[37]

One Tibetan recalled the cruelty surrounding the parallel executions that took place in Nyemo:

> Four people . . . were executed in Nyemo County. Those were the mediums.
> Q: Did you go to watch them?
> A: Yes, all of the masses were brought to the site where they were to be executed. The people to be executed . . . had wooden placards hanging around their necks and were made to bow down when their crimes and sentences were announced. Then they were put into a truck and taken to the place where they were going to be shot. The masses were also brought there to watch them. That was terrible. They were made to kneel down near a pit that was already dug. Then they were shot from behind.
> Q: Were their family members present when they were executed?
> A: Yes. . . . Some of the family members requested permission to get their relative's corpse.
> Q: Did they let them take the corpses?
> A: Some of them got the corpses, but some of them didn't get them. After shooting them, they buried them in the pit. Probably those soldiers were all from Lhasa, because we didn't know any of them. They all fell down with a single shot. After that, the leader stepped on them. If they moved, they were shot again with a pistol. Probably, they were making sure that they were killed. We didn't dare to go near them. We watched from a distance.[38]

By contrast, the role of the high-level Gyenlo leaders who worked in Nyemo was initially glossed over, because these Gyenlo officials insisted

Figure 4. Struggle session in Nyemo in the summer of 1969.

that they had had nothing to do with the rebels. As mentioned above, they asserted that the Nyemo uprising was separate from the Gyenlo-Nyamdre conflict and that it was caused by a few reactionary figures, including the nun, the warrior-hero mediums, and the incarnate lama Chamba Tenzin, who were all unhappy about the Democratic Reforms.[39] Consequently, for the next year and a half, the Gyenlo officials in Nyemo remained in office as usual.

This changed after 1970, when the head of the TAR military, Zeng Yongya, was removed in favor of Ren Rong, a Nyamdre supporter.[40] Apparently, Ren Rong had wanted to send armed troops to Nyemo earlier but had been blocked by Zeng Yongya, who wanted to send only unarmed forces. Ultimately, after the Central Committee approved of sending in armed troops, Ren Rong blamed Gyenlo's leaders and Zeng Yongya for the incident. A senior leader of Gyenlo in Lhasa explained somewhat bitterly:

> At that time, people were very confused, and I told them at meetings that it was ridiculous to say that forty-two, forty-five, or forty-eight counties had rebelled or attempted to rebel. I wondered whether someone would be happier to say that everyone in Tibet had rebelled against the Communist

Figure 5. Rebels about to be executed in Nyemo in the summer of 1969.

Party, which, he might think, was doing nothing good. This is what I said at the meetings, and, of course, they didn't like the way I put it. They said that the general commander of the 1969 Rebellion was Zeng Yongya, and the vice-general commander was Tao Changsong. [Laughs.] There was an exhibition at the Exhibition Center. Chen Yin, a department head at the Exhibition Center, was very nasty to us. . . . He told the public that the commanding center of the rebellion was just two hundred meters from the Potala.

Q: So he meant the Second Guest House [of Gyenlo] (ch. er suo).
A: Yes, and the Lhasa Middle School. He also said that the general commander of the rebels was a middle-school teacher. It was very clear that he was referring to me. When I heard about that, I was very upset, and I went to meet him with a few roughnecks. I thought I would beat him if he dared to say that in person. Well, he didn't dare to say anything when I got there.

Q: Where were you when they had that exhibition?
A: I guess I was on vacation or something like that. I was not there. When I came back, people told me that those people had said a lot of bad things about me. Problems like this—how should I put it? . . . Those people wanted to make use of problems like this to completely refute our organization. [They said,] "What does your 'Revolt Headquarter' do exactly? You encourage people to rebel." And some of our leaders were sentenced to death. Of

course, later all of them were rehabilitated. I still believe that this [Nyemo] incident will be a problem in the future, though we can't talk about that now. Many of us were sentenced to death, and many others died during the fighting. Now we simply can't count how many people lost their lives during that incident. When the case was redressed, each person who died during the incident was entitled to a payment of two hundred to eight hundred yuan. I used to tell people, "See, a life was worth only eight hundred yuan at most." In some regions, each life was worth only two hundred yuan.[41]

That same Gyenlo leader's explanation of the Nyemo incident is also interesting in the way it even now blames the army.

Q: What do you know about the Nyemo incident in 1969?
A: During the 13 June Nyemo incident, more than ten soldiers from the Military Propaganda Team were killed. I think the army was supporting one side and suppressing the other. . . .

I can't recall the details. We didn't say that those criminals [who carried out the incident] should be excused, but at least they should have been treated properly. . . . I think the incident in Nyemo was an antirevolutionary incident, so we should address it as that. It's definitely not right to call it a rebellion. I believe it was very possible that the Military Propaganda Team was supporting one faction and suppressing the other at that time. The Military Propaganda Team was actually full of problems. Things kept happening in Nyemo and some other areas. What the army did to the local people was sometimes unbelievable. They killed the leader of a certain township and cut off his head. Things like that. . . . I said that both of the factions should do some self-checking. Although those nuns and religious people were "bad guys," the army troops were not that good either. This is my understanding of the situation at that time.

And you know, the ordinary people had not experienced fighting like that before, so they had no choice but to run into the mountains when the army came. However, running into the mountains was a mistake, because they could be accused of waging guerrilla warfare in the mountains, although ordinary people didn't have weapons. Someone told me that a Tibetan county leader . . . used to warn people, "Don't run into the mountains! You'll be tricked if you go!" However, those ordinary people didn't understand and insisted on going. Therefore, the army had a reason to shoot, and many people lost their lives.

Well, of course, I haven't done any thorough research, but I believe that the army did break the rules and did many bad things at that time. I think the army men were killed for reasons, and one of those reasons, I believe, was related to extreme factionalism. Anyhow, it was not right to kill people, and clearly some of the soldiers were killed very cruelly. I've seen pictures of those soldiers who were killed. Some were stabbed with long knives; others were pounded with stones.

As the general leader [of Gyenlo], I actually didn't know much about

what happened at the lowest level of our faction, and I had to tell the
Military Region Headquarters that I would discuss it in Gyenlo Head-
quarters and would work out plans on how to handle this incident. I think
Zeng Yongya used to have a very reasonable way of handling things like
this. He told the army to go to Nyemo without carrying any weapons.
However, he was criticized by the Central Committee. Ren Rong, on the
contrary, insisted on carrying weapons to Nyemo. That was why Zeng
Yongya left office on 14 December 1970 without telling anyone.[42]

After Zeng Yongya was forced out of Lhasa, Ren Rong became the dominant power in Tibet. In 1971, he ordered a reinvestigation of the
Nyemo incident, starting a campaign dubbed "criticize and clear up"
(ch. *pi qing yun dong*). He had concluded that the rebellion in Nyemo
County was caused not only by the nun and other reactionary villagers
but also by Gyenlo Headquarters, so he sent a troop of the Fifty-third
Regiment to Nyemo County ostensibly for "field training" but actually to arrest Zhang Yongfu (who was then deputy director of the
Nyemo District Revolutionary Committee) for organizing Gyenlo's
Army of the Gods. This occurred in February 1971.[43] However, as we
saw, the Nyemo Gyenlo leaders never admitted to organizing the
killings, blaming them on religious reactionaries, including Trinley Chödrön and the mediums. They insisted they were just trying to be good
revolutionaries.

At about the same time, in the name of the Revolutionary Committee
of the Tibet Autonomous Region and the Tibet Military Region, more
than thirty people were chosen to form a work team to publicize the
thoughts of Mao (ch. *mao ze dong sixiang xuanchuan dui*) but also to
reinvestigate the incident. They isolated twenty-two top Gyenlo cadres
(and seventy lesser Gyenlo activists and key members) and sent them to
Lhasa in July 1971 to attend a "study class," which, as mentioned earlier, was really a detention center where the participants were isolated
and not free to leave or have contact among themselves or with people
outside.[44] As one Gyenlo participant put it:

> To go to the study class was like staying in a prison. A whole group
> of fully armed PLA men guarded the study class. There were a lot
> of rules such as "do not meet with guests"; "do not talk with one an-
> other"; "do not go out"; "do not visit other classes"; et cetera. We were
> under surveillance even when we used the bathroom. They opened the
> letters from our families but did not allow us to read them. We had to
> get approval from the study class if we wanted to write letters to our
> families. In the study class, we lost our rights as citizens and had to
> confess our "crimes."[45]

Figure 6. Rebels after their execution in Nyemo in the summer of 1969.

These study class confessions provided the evidence for Gyenlo's role in organizing and manipulating Trinley Chödrön. As a result, every cadre of the Gyenlo Headquarters in Nyemo was punished in some way, including Zhang Yongfu, who received an eight-year sentence.[46] On 24 April 1972, Gyenlo in Nyemo was formally labeled an "organized crime group" (ch. *jituan fanzui*).[47] However, in 1980, after liberalization following the rise of Deng Xiaoping in 1978, the government reinvestigated the incident, reducing the number labeled as involved by over 85 percent, from 499 to just 74. The other 425 were rehabilitated politically, including Zhang Yongfu.[48] Then again in 1985–86 the incident was reinvestigated, and this time the label "rebellion" was eliminated, and the event was reclassified from a counterrevolutionary rebellion to only a counterrevolutionary killing incident (ch. *fangeming sharen shijian*).[49]

In Nyemo, the villagers paid a heavy economic price for this, since the government made every household pay not only what they owed in grain taxes from 1968 but also the new taxes for 1969. Moreover, the government further penalized them by basing the amount owed for 1968, which had been a poor yield, on the crop of 1967, which had been a bumper yield. This, coupled with the start of the collective system, led many households to experience the very hunger that they had feared and tried to avoid by joining and supporting Gyenlo.

In the aftermath of their suppression of the Army of the Gods, the PLA stayed in Nyemo, taking control of the county. This allowed the Nyamdre cadres who had fled to Lhasa to return to their positions of authority, and they used this new authority to unleash their own wave of revenge against Gyenlo activists in the countryside.[50] The anger of Nyamdre activists is illustrated by the comments of one Nyemo woman:

> At that time, the regiment came, and there were also many cadres. After they [the Gyenlo leaders] were seized, they [the Nyamdre cadres] interrogated them and made them more humble than a cat. At that time, I was really glad, thinking that the policy of the party was really profound and those people deserved to be seized. When they held study classes, I raised my head and told them my opinions.
>
> When I was in my twenties and when we were told to hold struggle sessions, I thought I should gouge out their eyeballs, because they had gouged out the eyeballs of our people. But, according to the policy of the party, they didn't let us do that. We were told to enumerate their wrongdoings and not to beat them up.
>
> Q: At that time, did they hold struggle sessions against them [the Gyenlo leaders]?
>
> A: Yes, they held many struggle sessions against them. They let them think for a week and held struggle sessions once a week.
>
> Q: In the struggle sessions, did many people beat them up?
>
> A: Yes, many people beat them.
>
> Q: At that time, did some people who had been Gyenlo members also struggle against them [the Gyenlo members who had been seized]?
>
> A: Yes, . . . they told them, "You deceived me and made me get involved in that matter. Didn't you tell me to come and beat people and kill people?"
>
> After that, the Communist Party distinguished between right and wrong and false and true. It executed the people who deserved to be executed, arrested the people who deserved to be arrested, and educated the people who had been deceived.
>
> Q: What did you think when you heard that they were going to be executed?
>
> A: At that time, some progressives were called to look at the place where they were going to be executed. My father went there. After they were executed, they sent back some photos of the executed people to be stuck on the doors of their families. I thought those people deserved to be executed, because they had killed my relatives, soldiers, and cadres, who hadn't done anything wrong. I also thought that even if we cut their flesh and stuffed it into their mouths, the punishment would still be too lenient.[51]

In the end, therefore, the Nyemo incident was a total failure for both the Gyenlo leaders and the villagers who had supported Gyenlo, and particularly for the nun and the other warrior-hero mediums, all of whom were either killed in the fighting or executed—the notable exception being Rangjung, who vanished. With the army in control, the Nyamdre officials returned to power, communes were implemented, food shortages became the norm, class struggle intensified, and personal religion was forbidden. The light at the end of the tunnel that the Gyenlo agenda had represented was now extinguished, and the darkness would remain until the transformation of China a decade later under Deng Xiaoping.

CHAPTER 7

Conclusions

The Nyemo disturbance was not a spontaneous Tibetan nationalistic up-rising against the Chinese "oppressor," nor was it a revolt aimed at cre-ating an independent Tibet. To the contrary, it was the outgrowth of a careful strategy orchestrated by a Maoist revolutionary faction (Gyenlo) to seize control of its county from a rival revolutionary organization (Nyamdre). Led by a Chinese cadre named Zhang Yongfu, Gyenlo Head-quarters in Nyemo set out to take power by winning over the Tibetan masses and then organizing them to attack the authorities in power, that is, its enemy, Nyamdre. To accomplish this, Gyenlo adopted a pragmatic strategy that played to the widespread anger rural Tibetans felt over the excessive "sales grain" obligation and their fears of the impending col-lectivization of agriculture. Gyenlo's rallying cry of eighteen *khe* of grain per person and its opposition to starting communes at that point in time resonated well among the peasantry. It was clearly this, not issues of re-ligious freedom or the campaign against the four olds, that initially brought villagers into Gyenlo's fold and enabled the group to induce its village recruits to attack the Nyamdre officials and stop the sales grain collection in November 1968.

The Nyemo disturbances, however, would not have been possible had it not been for the state-sanctioned chaos that Mao Zedong unleashed in 1966 with the Cultural Revolution. It created a climate in which conflict and violence could flourish so long as it was "revolutionary" conflict tar-geted at cleansing the party. Mao had called for the revolutionary masses to bombard the party headquarters and destroy reactionaries and capitalist-roaders who had sneaked into the party, and Gyenlo represented itself as seeking to accomplish this. Under the banner of revolutionary struggle, mass organizations like Gyenlo and Nyamdre were empowered to do and say almost anything they wished against those in power (or against each other), since the state had instructed the army and police to maintain neutrality, that is, to avoid using their normal monopoly of force to intervene on behalf of one revolutionary group or the other.

The ensuing factional conflicts destroyed the heretofore invincible unity of the party. Suddenly, the all-powerful party leaders, who, after 1959, had seemed the epitome of communist correctness, were being subjected to struggle sessions much like those the aristocrats, lamas, and estate managers had been subjected to at the time of the Democratic Reforms. For the first time since the end of the old society in 1959, there seemed to be different points of view and different paths within the Communist Party and, in a broader sense, within socialist society itself. The norms of proper "socialist" behavior were no longer unitary. This new ambiguity allowed villagers, including Trinley Chödrön, to see Gyenlo not as dangerous enemies of the state who were launching a counterrevolutionary rebellion but rather as revolutionary stalwarts who were attacking the bad policies of bad officials in accordance with the dictates of Mao Zedong.

Gyenlo's presentation of itself, therefore, gave villagers a ready-made, and to them plausible, *model of* revolutionarily acceptable revolt and at the same time a *model for* actions they could take to rid themselves of the authorities and policies they had heretofore had to endure silently. As the nun/Ani Gongmey Gyemo said in her 1969 statement, "In the past, because we didn't have the right to speak, it was like having fire in the stomach but not daring to spew out smoke from the mouth."[1] Now, by putting on the revolutionary armband of Gyenlo and fighting for its victory over Nyamdre, they could finally spew that smoke out of their mouths and change their lives. Gyenlo, therefore, had shrewdly molded revolutionary goals and rural anger aspirations into a potent *agenda* for action that it dangled before the eyes of the rural farmers, asking for their help in fixing a society that they claimed the Nyamdre officials had broken. In the topsy-turvy world of the Great Proletarian Cultural Revolution, Gyenlo was able to assure villagers that Chairman Mao himself had instructed that it was good to rebel against the power holders who were subverting the revolution, and, in Nyemo, that meant against the Nyamdre cadres. Since most villagers believed the local authorities were venally using their power to bleed them into poverty by extracting excessive grain and forcing them into communes, this made sense and was welcomed.

The armed attacks in Nyemo, therefore, contrasted sharply with the Chushigandru (Khamba)-led uprising of 1959. In the 1959 rebellion, the goal was clearly to drive the Chinese out of Tibet. By contrast, the Gyenlo campaign in Nyemo was aimed only at replacing the individuals in power and reversing some of the post-1959 socioeconomic policies that were deeply unpopular. For farmers worried about not having enough grain for their families and fearful of losing their land to communes, Gyenlo in 1968 was offering them an attractive, and in their eyes attainable, alternative within the Chinese Communist nation.

The first test of Gyenlo's village strategy occurred in fall of 1968, when local cadres started to organize that year's taxes and extractions. As we saw, Gyenlo successfully induced its village members to attack the Nyamdre officials holding grain collection meetings and block their collection of most of the grain due that year, and then to attack the Nyamdre officials in the county seat itself. Gyenlo's mobilization strategy worked flawlessly and produced a major victory. As a result, most Nyamdre cadres in the county fled to Lhasa for safety, and those who remained behind were marginalized. This victory further swelled Gyenlo's burgeoning membership, since many villagers who had remained neutral or pro-Nyamdre now switched their allegiance to Gyenlo. By the end of 1968, therefore, Gyenlo had become the strongest faction in the Nyemo countryside, and in 1969 it started organizing to seize control of the whole county. Its goal was nothing less than a Gyenlo-run Nyemo County.

However, while Gyenlo was finalizing the November 1968 attacks, several leaders worried that at the last minute some of the villagers might have second thoughts about marching on the county seat. Rangjung, Gyenlo's top Tibetan leader, therefore suggested that it might be useful to have Trinley Chödrön, a somewhat unbalanced nun who was developing a reputation as a local medium—and who was also a member of Gyenlo—go into trances and exhort the villagers to attack the county. It was, of course, very unorthodox for a revolutionary organization of the masses to ask a Tibetan religious medium to dress in costume, go into a trance, and summon a god to motivate them to undertake revolutionary work for Chairman Mao, but Gyenlo in Nyemo was pragmatic to the core, and its leaders found it easy to rationalize the temporary utilization of some "superstition" (religion) as an acceptable price to pay for achieving their consuming goal of deposing Nyamdre and taking control of the county.

Gyenlo's suspicions about the villagers' resolve turned out to be well-founded, for on the day before the attack, one group of villagers hesitated. Trinley Chödrön then went into a trance and summoned the goddess Ani Gongmey Gyemo, who exhorted the villagers to go forward by telling them that she was *the god of Gyenlo* and would use her powers to prevent the enemy's guns from harming them. For the villagers, this was a symbolically charged and empowering event, because it was not a secret performance of an illegal and dangerous old society custom; it was the gods from the old society integrated normatively into the new society under the imprimatur of Gyenlo. This young nun went into a trance at a meeting of a Maoist revolutionary organization of the masses while wearing both the medium's traditional costume and the signature armband of Gyenlo. With Mao and the gods now on their side, the future looked bright.

Emboldened by the nun's supernatural promises, the Gyenlo villagers attacked, and Gyenlo won a great victory for itself and for the villagers, who did not provide the grain extractions that year. But it also was a great victory for the nun, who had now demonstrated to her fellow village Tibetans the authenticity of her religious powers. The nun had summoned the god Ani Gongmey Gyemo, who assured the villagers that Gyenlo would win, because the god would use her supernatural power to protect them from bullets and any other kind of harm—and she did. No one was injured!

Gyenlo's tactical decision to use the nun, therefore, brought a new player onto the political scene by raising the status of the nun from that of a part-time village medium whom people quietly visited for advice to that of a prominent figure in Gyenlo's ongoing campaign to seize power in the county. Trinley Chödrön's god, Ani Gongmey Gyemo, was now the god of Gyenlo and had explicitly committed her supernatural powers to protecting Gyenlo's members in their quest. However, this meant that Zhang Yongfu and Rangjung had agreed to bring religion—one of the four olds—into prominence in the Gyenlo strategic program. Gyenlo now told the villagers not only that they were implementing the true views of Chairman Mao, to fight to right the wrongs that had befallen them, but also that they were doing this in conjunction with the powerful traditional gods of Tibet. For the villagers, this meant that, for the first time since 1959, the views of Tibet's gods and Chairman Mao were compatible and that the restoration of religion was now also possible as part of the Gyenlo agenda.

This might not have gone much further had Gyenlo stopped using the nun, but it did not do so. In fact, Gyenlo convened a special meeting of its leaders and village representatives in January 1969 to discuss the success of the November campaign. In reality, this meeting was held to decide whether to credit the nun and incorporate her into the next, more dangerous phase of their campaign: attacking the military establishment in the county seat. Despite some disagreement about openly praising her role even though ideologically it was nothing more than "superstition," the group ultimately concluded that because the nun's role had been so important in Gyenlo's success, the faction should make further use of her by recognizing and incorporating her god into its upcoming campaign. In recognition of this, Gyenlo named its new rural attack force Gyenlo's Army of the Gods.

Gyenlo, therefore, not only decided to give the nun/Ani Gongmey Gyemo a prominent role as the god supporting its faction, but also, by virtue of its 1968 victories, had created a clear playing field on which the nun's religious imagined world could develop without restraint. The remaining grassroots Nyamdre cadres were primarily concerned with avoiding struggle sessions waged against them by Gyenlo activists, not with enforcing the prohibitions on religion and mediums, particularly against an important Gyenlo personality. The nun basically could now practice religion openly.

Mediums were common in traditional Tibet, but this case was somewhat unusual not only because it occurred in the midst of the Cultural Revolution but also because the nun's possessing god, Ani Gongmey Gyemo, was not one of the category of "local" deities who normally possessed mediums. As far as we have been able to ascertain, no one else in Tibet had ever claimed to have been possessed by Ani Gongmey Gyemo, the famous aunt of King Gesar, who lived in the realm of the gods and had advised Gesar in his wars to defeat the demons that were harming Buddhism in Tibet. Consequently, by embracing the nun, Gyenlo was both propping up a medium named Trinley Chödrön and empowering a political-activist deity who was specifically renowned for fighting for a Buddhist Tibet.

In the previous coming of Gesar, a number of key warrior-heroes called the *badü* had fought beside him. In the nun's imagined world, therefore, it made sense for these *badü* warrior-heroes to leave the realm of the gods again and descend to Tibet to assist her, and this is, in fact, what happened. Over a period of a few months, a kind of Gesar hysteria swept through parts of Nyemo, during which time about thirty ordinary villagers, males and females, spontaneously began to claim that they were being possessed by gods, most of whom were identified as precisely these *badü* warrior-heroes. Gesar's famous warrior-heroes had now also come to Nyemo to assist the nun and Ani Gongmey Gyemo. The nun's imagined world, therefore, had now expanded exponentially to include many fanatically committed mediums who believed they were the human vehicle for Gesar's warrior-heroes.

Gesar, Ani Gongmey Gyemo, and the *badü,* it should be noted, were not just characters in a famous Tibetan literary epic cycle. For Tibetans, they were real deities with supernatural powers and strong identities and personae. Consequently, by late spring 1969, the campaign to take over the county had two emotionally charged and intertwined dimensions: the original revolutionary struggle of Gyenlo and the emergent Gesar imagined world of the nun and the other mediums. The Gyenlo movement morphed into a phase somewhat analogous to three-dimensional chess, where the same event would be played out on different, but interlocking, planes.

The arrival of Ani Gongmey Gyemo and the new warrior-hero mediums brought a new dimension to Nyemo. Until then, villagers had seen fulfillment of their aspirations as linked to Gyenlo's secular figures, including Rangjung and the village Gyenlo representatives, but now the gods of Gesar had come and were coexisting side by side with them. This resonated with the majority of villagers, who still believed in Tibet's gods, and the nun found herself quickly transformed into a charismatic champion not just of more food and economic freedom for the villagers but also of the restoration of Tibetan Buddhism. This Gesar hysteria soon produced a wave of killings and maimings led by the mediums, or, in Tibetan cultural terms, the gods who were possessing them.

Zhang Yongfu and Rangjung, of course, were aware that this was happening, since Rangjung and the other Gyenlo village leaders had close relations with the nun and the warrior-hero mediums around her, but for several reasons, they chose to do nothing. First, the nun and the *badü* still clearly saw themselves as part of Gyenlo's Army of the Gods under Rangjung's military command. Second, the nun had turned herself into a perfect weapon for mobilizing the Tibetan peasants to undertake Gyenlo's final and most dangerous push to seize control of the county military entities. The risk of losing her mobilizing powers by confronting her view of the future was simply too great, given that Gyenlo was then so close to success. Third, Gyenlo's cynical and manipulative leaders did not consider her a serious threat, since they felt that once they achieved power the nun would be controlled or eliminated. As the Gyenlo cadre said earlier, "We can make use of the nun at present and arrest her after the Revolutionary Committee is founded."[2] Fourth, and finally, Gyenlo's leaders were also personally invested in the nun as a tactical innovation—as a religious atomic bomb they had invented—and bragged about their innovative "religious" tactic to Gyenlo groups in other areas, inviting them to come to Nyemo to see how this was being done. Consequently, they were willing to ignore Trinley Chödrön's religious notions and goals—albeit temporarily.

In this ideologically fluid situation, belief in the nun's sanctity soared, and by May-June 1969, the identities of Ani Gongmey Gyemo and Trinley Chödrön had, for many, become blurred. Trinley Chödrön had gone well beyond the normal medium's role of being simply a bodily vehicle for a god to enter and answer questions about health and so forth. She had become, in the eyes of many Nyemo villagers, endowed with supernatural powers herself. Consequently, at the time of the final attacks in June 1969, the villagers were not merely following a powerful Maoist revolutionary group advocating changes they wanted but also following supernatural leadership in the person of the nun, Ani Gongmey Gyemo, and the warrior-hero mediums of Gesar, that is, the gods of Tibet who had come to Nyemo. In the end, therefore, although the foundational essence of the disturbances in Nyemo County derived from Gyenlo's quest to seize power from Nyamdre and would not have occurred without the nun, by the time of the final attacks in June, the revolt also involved a major Tibetan religious component aimed at reviving the practice of Buddhism as well as other traditional customs and practices. In fact, by June, a number of cultural practices prohibited during the height of the campaign against the four olds, such as burning incense, intoning prayers, and using *khata* scarves, were openly practiced. Gyenlo's Army of the Gods, therefore, was not a homogeneous and well-disciplined entity with a single common goal. Not only did it operate simultaneously on two conceptual planes, but at ground level it was also an amalgam of at least four different types of Tibetans who shared some, but not other, goals and priorities. These four types were, namely,

1. those who were firmly committed to Gyenlo as an organization and to its goal of destroying Nyamdre and creating a new Gyenlo government in Nyemo. Including Rangjung, these were leftists imbued with strong revolutionary and factional solidarity, and they were the activist leaders (representatives) in the villages. For them, the nun and the warrior-hero mediums were

useful in achieving Gyenlo's ends, so long as they were sub-
servient to the broader interests of the faction.

2. those who were deeply immersed in the imagined Gesar world
   and fanatically committed to the gods. They included the nun
   and the warrior-hero mediums, all of whom were unbalanced
   to some unknown degree, in addition to some common villagers, such as the bodyguard, quoted earlier, who had totally
   accepted the Gesar worldview, both intellectually and emotionally. Like those in the first category, they sought to depose
   Nyamdre and take over the county, but their end-goal society
   was strongly focused on religious freedom and a Nyemo society in which Buddhism dominated. In accordance with Ani
   Gongmey Gyemo's prophecy, "Nyemo belongs to the gods,"
   they were committed to bring that state into being. This category included both those who were the most fanatical about
   wanting to kill and maim the enemies of religion and those
   who harbored a mix of pro-Tibetan and antigovernment attitudes. For example, in addition to yelling slogans such as "No
   more grain sales," "No communes," "Freedom to trade," and
   "All power to the gods," some of the attackers are reported
   to have also shouted more political slogans, including "Tibet
   is independent." However, at the same time, people in this
   category saw Gyenlo as their partner rather than as part of
   the hated "demons and ghosts" who were ruling Nyemo, even
   though the top Gyenlo leaders were all cadres and mostly Han
   Chinese.

3. those villagers who initially became Gyenlo members because
   of the grain and commune issues but were not deeply involved
   activists. After the nun/Ani Gongmey Gyemo emerged, they
   also came to believe in her powers but saw the nun and Gyenlo
   as different faces of the same campaign. Throwing out the
   old Nyamdre officials, changing economic policy, and restoring Buddhism were all part of the same program for them.
   These "followers" constituted the majority of Gyenlo's Army
   of the Gods.

4. those who had been loyal and dedicated Nyamdre members
   but later felt compelled to join Gyenlo for their own safety.
   They did not really support either Gyenlo or the nun but were
   afraid to do anything else but obey Rangjung and the warrior-
   hero mediums. This category also included the villagers who

had tried to stay neutral and unaffiliated with either Gyenlo or Nyamdre but toward the end similarly felt compelled by fear to declare allegiance to Gyenlo.

Consequently, when the attacks began, important differences existed among the people who made up Gyenlo's Army of the Gods. However, notwithstanding this, the attackers clearly did not revolt to drive the Chinese out and set up an independent country. They fought to empower new officials and make major changes in local rules regarding taxes, communes, economics, and religion. Analysis of seventy-five interviewees from Nyemo, some of whom were Nyamdre, some Gyenlo, and some uninvolved with either faction, supports this. We found that thirty (40 percent) of the interviewees mentioned no reason for the attacks in their interviews, but of the remaining forty-five (60 percent), the overwhelming majority, thirty-eight (84 percent), mentioned eliminating such things as the grain taxes, the power holders, the party, Red Guards, and/or restoring religion as the reason, whereas only 7 (16 percent) name independence as their reason. (And this last group of respondents were all Nyamdre cadres and activists who were anti-Gyenlo.)

If we return to the original question we posed in the Introduction, we think Smith, Shakya, *and* Wang all highlighted relevant aspects of the incident. However, all also oversimplified a complex event and in the process inadvertently distorted the historical reality. Rather than a simple dichotomy, angry Tibetans spontaneously organizing and striking back at hated Chinese or Tibetans rising to fight only for their material interests, there were multiple levels and multiple actors, Tibetan and Chinese, with different motives, using and manipulating one another for different end goals.

This entire episode, moreover, was a kind of shadow play, able to exist only in an artificial world in which the state stood back and refused to use its monopoly of force to maintain order between revolutionary factions. As we saw, once the seriousness of the Nyemo problem was accepted—that is, after the attacks of 13–14 June—the state concluded that this went beyond interfactional fighting and ordered the PLA to move to Nyemo. After a brief round of fighting in Phusum and Bagor, the nun was captured, and most villagers, feeling forsaken by their mediums and gods, took the PLA's offer of leniency and voluntarily surrendered.

However, we should not minimize what clearly fueled this incident: the anger many rural Tibetans felt at the direction party policies had taken, not only in the realms of taxation and economic freedom, but also toward religion and culture. It is also important to note that these villagers were not the elite class enemies of the old society trying to rise up again; rather, they were the rural proletariat who had been "liberated" by the Democratic Reforms in 1959. Gyenlo understood this and worked pragmatically and brilliantly to utilize this anger and fear for its own ends, telling the villagers what they wanted to hear and offering them a powerful, and seemingly safe, way to express their anger and change their society—what we have called the *Gyenlo agenda*. Just as Gyenlo's leaders were angry about Nyamdre, the PLA, and the Regional Party Committee and were willing to do something about their influence, hundreds of Tibetans were also dissatisfied with their present situation and anxious about their immediate future and were willing to fight to do something about conditions. The Gyenlo incident, therefore, was created from two very different matrices of discontent: that of the Gyenlo activists on the one side and that of the Tibetan villagers on the other.

Finally, it should be emphasized that analogous to how Mao, for his own purposes, had allowed the revolutionary factions to contest each other and party elites, Gyenlo in Nyemo had allowed the nun and warrior-hero mediums to operate there for its own purposes. And we believe that just as Beijing eventually intervened and brought the conflict to an end, had Gyenlo's leftist revolutionary leaders been able to seize and hold power in Nyemo, they would have intervened to control the nun and prevent Nyemo from "belonging to the gods," as the nun/Ani Gongmey Gyemo had prophesied. The Tibetan villagers who marched on the county and district seats in June 1969 were, therefore, really pawns in the hands of Gyenlo revolutionaries, who themselves were also pawns in the larger political struggles created by Mao Zedong and the Cultural Revolution.

CHAPTER 8

Epilogue

The Nyemo incident was one of many violent disturbances that occurred in the name of Gyenlo within a period of a few months in the spring, summer, and early fall of 1969. The proximity of these incidents raises the obvious question of whether they were the independent product of parallel social, political, and economic forces or whether they were an artifact of an underlying grand strategy employed by Gyenlo General Headquarters in Lhasa. Unfortunately, very few data are available about these different disturbances, and, in fact, it is not even clear how many occurred. Most Chinese sources refer to incidents occurring in eighteen counties, but some also say over forty individual disturbances occurred. The official Chinese chronology of important events in Tibet mentions only the following five incidents, giving for each just the very briefest of thumbnail sketches:

> 9 March 1969. A counterrevolutionary riot occurred in Dengchen (ch. *dinqing*) County [in Chamdo Prefecture].
>
> A handful of counterrevolutionary elements of Dengchen County estab-lished the so-called general headquarters to defend religion in the area of the Gyamo Ngulchu (ch. *nujiang*) and Dzachu (ch. *liancangjiang*) rivers. They attacked the local offices and troops stationed there and stole more than 300 different types of weapons, together with more than 900 head of livestock from the state's livestock farm, as well as more than 520,000 *jin* of grain from the state's storehouse. They also beat and killed more than twenty people of the masses and cadres.[1]

20 May 1969. A counterrevolutionary riot occurred in Bembar (ch. *bianba*) County [in Chamdo Prefecture].

At the end of January, a handful of counterrevolutionary elements in Bembar County decided on a reactionary guiding principle called the "three no's," which said there will be: "no CCP, no submitting of the public's grain, and no socialism [communes]." Afterward they established the "army to defend Buddhism in the four rivers and six mountains" (tib. *chushigandru*) and the so-called revolutionary Gyenlo Headquarters of liberated serfs. On 20 May, they attacked the offices of the county party committee and injured more than thirty cadres and staff. On 8 June, they assembled more than two thousand people to attack the organizations of the county party committee and grabbed weapons and all the official seals of the county revolutionary committee. Then they launched an attack on the offices and organizations of Bembar County and District as well as the Military Propaganda Team there. They robbed weapons and ammunition from the county's Department of Armed Forces and demolished the residences of the Military Propaganda Team. They carried out beatings, lootings, and smashings for seventeen days and hurt more than a hundred cadres and soldiers. They took savage measures, such as chopping hands, gouging eyes, and cutting open stomachs and slaughtered more than fifty cadres and soldiers.[2]

13 June 1969. A counterrevolutionary riot occurred in Nyemo County [Lhasa Municipality].

One reactionary Buddhist nun in Nyemo County utilized religious superstition and the sorcerer's dance [going into a trance] to instigate the masses to surround and beat a military propaganda team. All twenty-two people in the Military Propaganda Team were killed.[3]

July 1969. Incidents of rioting occurred in various counties in Shigatse Prefecture, such as Namling (ch. *nanmulin*).

Reactionary elements in counties such as Namling, Shey Tongmönling (ch. *xietongmeng*), Lhatse (ch. *lazi*), and Ngamring (ch. *angren*) in Shigatse Prefecture spread rumors that confused the masses and created disturbances. They destroyed many revolutionary committees at the prefecture, county, and *xiang* level.[4]

26 July 1969. A counterrevolutionary riot occurred in Biru County [Nagchuka Prefecture].

In the first half of the year, a handful of bad people sneaked into the mass organizations and used religious superstition to organize a "white holy army." They rampantly carried out smashing, looting, and beatings and mistreated cadres in the counties and *xiang*. Some of them set up obstructions along the roads and destroyed bridges. They disrupted 17 road maintenance squads and grabbed more than 260 horses, 1,800 cows, and

5,920 sheep from the state farm. On 26 July, some evil people plotted and instigated the masses to break into the ammunition supply dump, where they killed and injured quite a number of soldiers. The looting and killing lasted as long as seven days. They seized nineteen guns of various models, two cannons of the number 60 model, two rocket launchers, and about five thousand hand grenades, as well as some bombs and bullets. On 1 August, they instigated the masses from twelve villages and eight districts of the region to wage an attack on the county organizations and local army. They also fired at the county people's government. The organizations and armies had to counterattack.[5]

These published accounts, though interesting, are too truncated to be useful for comparison with one another or with Nyemo, other than to reveal that, in general, each involved armed attacks targeting county offices and cadres ("the authorities in power"), and all but one account indicate that religion was a component.

Comparative data, however, do exist for one of the above-mentioned areas—Shigatse Prefecture—where a nomad community that Goldstein has been studying rose up under the banner of Gyenlo in 1969. Located in Ngamring County, about 325 kilometers west of Lhasa, the Tibetan nomadic pastoralists of Phala provide a useful window into a somewhat different manifestation of the 1969 disturbances.

THE PHALA INCIDENT

Phala traditionally was part of Lagyab Lhojang, a large nomad feudal estate that belonged to the Panchen Lama. The people there were full nomadic pastoralists, living in the traditional black yak-hair tents and subsisting by raising yaks, sheep, goats, and horses. They did not grow crops.

Following the 1959 Tibetan uprising, a new administrative structure was organized there, placing the nomads under Tsatsey District, in Ngamring County.[6] At this time, new local officials were appointed from among the poorest nomads, and old debts were either rescinded or recalculated with reduced interest. The nomads were allowed to keep their livestock with the exception of one family that was classified as an "agent of the lord" whose animals were expropriated and divided among twenty other poor nomad families. Culturally, as in Nyemo, monastic religion was terminated, and monks returned home. Nevertheless, on a day-to-day basis, the essential elements of the nomadic way of life continued. Each nomad family retained control over the timing of both moving its animals and bartering or selling its products. And, as in Nyemo, households were permitted to maintain altars and perform private rites and prayers. No attempt was made to constrain or eliminate nomadic customs and taboos, and the core social unit, the extended family, persevered as the basic unit of production and consumption.

This situation changed markedly in late 1968–69 with the onset of the Cultural Revolution there. At that time, the campaign against the four olds and the ban on private religion began, and the plan to implement communes was announced. Almost overnight, the nomads found themselves poised to lose control of the herds they had worked so hard to develop and maintain. For almost all nomads, the specter of a system of collectively organized pastoralism, in which households no longer owned their animals or controlled their economic and management decisions, was anathema. It was seen as being analogous to the life of servants in the old society, in the sense that they would not own productive resources and would have to work when and at whatever they were ordered to do. Consequently, a climate of fear and anger analogous to that which we saw in Nyemo existed in Phala regarding their economic future. And, as in Nyemo, this was exacerbated by the new prohibitions on all individual religious prayer and ritual.

At this juncture, in the summer of 1969, the Gyenlo-Nyamdre conflict arrived in Phala and Tsatsey. It began when the head of Tsatsey *xiang* heard about Gyenlo starting in Shentsa, a nomad county to the northeast, in Nagchuka Prefecture, and rode there with another nomad to see what was going on. He came back not only carrying the red armband of Gyenlo but also infused with the basic Gyenlo agenda—namely, with the belief that Gyenlo was an organization that, on the one hand, was following the instructions of Chairman Mao to root out the bad "power holders" and, on the other hand, would postpone the start of communes, permit private economic activities, and also allow religious freedom. Moreover, he had been told that the struggle between Gyenlo and Nyamdre was part of a larger struggle going on all over China in which the PLA was committed to neutrality between the factions. He was told that, with the PLA neutral, the Phala nomads could easily overcome their local, district, and county officials, just as those in Shentsa were doing. Given this amazing news, a large number of nomads quickly created a Gyenlo branch in Tsatsey. Those who supported the status quo administration became Nyamdre.

The Gyenlo organization in Tsatsey set up its own administrative structure, which, like the headquarters in Lhasa, they called Gyenlo's General Headquarters (tib.-ch. *gyenlo jigyab bu*). The heads of this were called *gegen* (teacher), and the military commanders were called *donglen* (the vanguard). The members lived at home but, like a militia, were expected to be always ready to saddle up and fight.

Gyenlo in Tsatsey quickly went on the offensive. The first attack there occurred when forty Gyenlo horsemen armed with Tibetan matchlock muskets and swords suddenly arrived at the district headquarters. The district's party secretaries were away that day in another nomad area, but a visiting county head was there. The Gyenlo riders seized and berated him, accusing him of being one of the power holders that Mao had said they must oppose. They also announced that Tsatsey District's absent party secretaries would be seized later, as would any other Nyamdre cadres they caught. This occurred around 3 July 1969. At this point, virtually all Nyamdre cadres working in the district fled for safety to the county seat at Ngamring. Two, however, delayed departing and were surrounded by a group of Gyenlo activists, who beat them to death.

When the fleeing Tsatsey cadres reached Ngamring and explained what was happening, the county leadership sent a group of fifteen unarmed PLA soldiers and about twenty district cadres back to Tsatsey to try to persuade the nomads to stop supporting Gyenlo and end their disturbance. When this group arrived in Tsatsey, they found the district compound (the offices and the surrounding buildings) deserted and wrecked. All the doors had been busted open, and all the glass bottles in the hospital were broken. The grain had also been taken from the district granary, and the district's store had been looted. All of Mao's pictures had been torn up. They did not come face-to-face with any Gyenlo nomads there but verified that the two cadres had been killed and that others had been seized and were being subjected to struggle sessions. They immediately sent two members back to the county leadership to report these developments. The leadership now sent an attack force to Tsatsey to put down the Gyenlo disturbance. It consisted of a hundred armed PLA troops with seven officers, along with about forty local cadres and nomads to guide them. They surrounded the district and attacked just before sunrise. Some Gyenlo nomads surrendered immediately, but most grabbed their horses and were able to flee. Nevertheless, the Tsatsey District was again under the control of the government/Nyamdre. This occurred in mid- to late September.

Meanwhile, in Phala, the first transfer of the Gyenlo agenda came when a poor nomad named Tenzin visited Tshomey, an adjacent nomad district to the east. He recalled,

> When I went to visit a relative of mine in Tshomey, everyone there had already accepted Gyenlo. Then when I returned to Phala, I heard that Gyenlo had also started in [our district of] Tsatsey, so I went there and

said that if the principles of Gyenlo are to reinstate religious freedom, then I also want to join.[7] . . . I joined Gyenlo because of religious freedom. In the old society, if you worked well no one abused you, and even if you were a beggar [as this nomad had been] you could practice religion. If you lied or stole you would get whipped, but then it was over—not like [prison] nowadays.[8]

The leaders of Gyenlo in Tsatsey gave Tenzin a red Gyenlo armband and oral instructions (he was illiterate) on the principles of Gyenlo. They also gave him the rank of *gegen* (because he would be the first member in Phala) and told him to return to Phala to proselytize his people and organize Gyenlo. He returned and enthusiastically told others how all the nomads in Tsatsey and Tshomey had joined Gyenlo and were going to kick out the cadres in power and implement new rules. He emphasized that Gyenlo stood for two main things, the first being religious freedom. He said that if there was no religious freedom, then when one died there would be no religious rites, and that meant their deaths would be just like that of dogs. The second thing Gyenlo stood for is that one's wealth and property would belong to oneself; in other words, there would be no commune to take all of the animals and equipment. Another Phala nomad who became a local Gyenlo leader corroborated this, adding that Tenzin used the term *revolutionary Gyenlo* (tib. *sarje gyenlo*) in his discussions.

As in Tsatsey, the movement spread rapidly, and, with the exception of nine nomads who followed Nyamdre and three or four others who remained neutral, everyone in Phala joined Gyenlo. As one nomad explained, only the "poor class" (tib. *üpung*) (who had received redistributed animals in 1959) and local cadres supported Nyamdre, although for Tenzin the prohibition on practicing religion outweighed the material benefits he had received as a poor nomad. One of the nomads who chose to follow the authorities (i.e., Nyamdre) explained what happened to him:

Then the Gyenlo people had a meeting in Nanag [a subarea of Phala]. The main leader at the meeting . . . told people that they should decide whether they wanted to be Gyenlo or Nyamdre. Going with Nyamdre, he said, meant the continuation of the current policy and the start of communes, but going with Gyenlo meant religious and economic freedom and no communes. I thought about this but decided that since I am from the poor class and have received many benefits from the party, I should continue to support it [so I did not join Gyenlo].

For some days after this meeting no one said anything to me, but Gyenlo was getting stronger and stronger, and it began to send groups of horsemen to neighboring *xiang* to spread the Gyenlo agenda and start organizations there. Then someone told me that the Gyenlo leaders had decided to arrest Shibum [my brother] and me, so we ran away that night and hid on the [nearby] grassland plains. However, after five or six days, we ran out of food and had to return to pick up more supplies, and at that time we were captured. . . . I personally wasn't subjected to any struggle sessions at the hands of the Gyenlo, but my brother Shibum was subjected to three.[9]

As the movement took hold in Phala, the leaders of Gyenlo in Tsatsey called the Phala leaders to attend a meeting. One nomad who went recalled the rhetoric:

At this meeting we were told that we should proselytize for Gyenlo in [the adjacent *xiang*]. They said that we should send someone whom the nomads there will trust, so they decided to send me and two others who were originally from [there], since we were rich [respected] families and the Nyingo people would believe us. The main idea was to tell people there, "Unless Gyenlo takes control, the commune will be established, and, except for a very small amount of land, everything will be managed by the government, and you will have no control over what to eat or wear—you will have control over only your own body's work capacity. And you won't be able to wear any jewelry, gold, et cetera. But if you join Gyenlo, then there will be religious freedom and the freedom to control your property. [In this sense] [i]t will be like it was in the 'old society.'"[10]

For the next three months, from roughly the start of July to mid- to late September, Gyenlo groups were in charge of Phala, as well as Tshomey, Nyingo, Tsatsey, and probably many other areas in Ngamring County. From other sources, we know that Gyenlo movements also occurred in Lhatse and Shey Tongmönling as well as in Nagtsang, in Nagchuka.

Meanwhile, in Phala, one of the two Nyamdre members that Gyenlo had seized recalled how he was finally set free:

First, they tied my hands in front and put me on a horse. Someone held the reins and another whipped the horse from behind. They told me such things as, "You are our enemy and you have to go to a Gyenlo meeting in Tsatsey." They threatened us, saying that if we didn't watch out, we would end up like the two officials in Tsatsey [who were murdered].

Shibum, myself, and eight horsemen went, but at Parong la Pass we met twenty Gyenlo horsemen returning from Tsatsey. The Gyenlo people held a brief meeting, and then they changed plans, saying we have to go to cut grass for fodder in the north, so they went off to Nyingo still holding us prisoner. Along the way, one of the Gyenlo leaders told me that we were very lucky because Tsatsey had fallen to the PLA and Nyamdre [so we had avoided the struggle sessions that were awaiting us].

They took us to Nyingo, where we were still "under arrest" and guarded by two Gyenlo nomads. . . . Then early one morning at dawn I saw two horsemen coming. When I looked carefully, I saw lots of riders. As they came nearer and nearer, I recognized Nyingo's party secretary Nanga Wangchug, an enemy of Gyenlo, so I knew it was a pro-Nyamdre force. I started to leave the tent to get a better look, but Tobjung [my guard] said, "Where are you going?" so I said, "I am sorry," and immediately pretended to go back to sleep. Then I heard five or six shots, and my friends came to release me. Nyamdre had defeated Gyenlo in Nyingo and had come to release me. Shibum was so happy, he started crying. He had been beaten a lot by the Gyenlo people, so he now took his revenge and beat them up.[11]

After Tsatsey District was retaken by the PLA and the accompanying Nyamdre cadres, groups of about twenty to thirty troops, officials, and nomads were sent to retake control of each *xiang*, including Phala.

When word reached Phala of the collapse in Tsatsey, some Gyenlo leaders fled north to Shentsa County to stay with their Gyenlo comrades there, but when the Gyenlo nomads there came under heavy attack, they returned to Phala, where they were captured. They were then taken to Tsatsey District and imprisoned and interrogated. One of these nomads recalled being put in a room with about ten others and ordered to join a "study class" just like those in Nyemo. He was kept in the district headquarters for about forty days, after which he was released. However, he was formally labeled (with the hat of) a reactionary (tib. *logjöba*) for six years, had most of his property confiscated, and was subjected to severe struggle sessions. In the end, the PLA arrested about 160 Gyenlo members in Tsatsey and brought them to the district, where they underwent struggle sessions. Of these, thirty-two of the leaders were sent to prison in the county, nine were executed, three committed suicide, and two died in the district prison. Tenzin, the poor nomad who first brought the Gyenlo message to Phala, was subjected to five days of struggle sessions in Tsatsey and then was taken to the county where he spent two and a half years in prison.

The Phala-Tsatsey incident reveals striking similarities to, as well as differences from, the Nyemo incident. First, as in Nyemo, the underlying matrix of anger and fear was generated not by any particularistic local conditions unique to Phala or Tsatsey but rather by policies that were implemented at that time by "the authorities" all over Tibet. These policies were essentially the same as in Nyemo, except for the obvious differences resulting from the absence of farming in these nomadic areas.

Second, as in Nyemo, the disturbance was not the outcome of disgruntled local nomads getting together on their own to take control of their area and change policies. Rather, the Gyenlo *agenda* provided the nomads with the same ready-made explanation, justification, and mode of action that we saw in Nyemo. As a result of this, these remote nomads talked as Nyemo villagers did about the accord between their actions and Mao's call to bombard the headquarters and about Mao's assurances that rebellion was okay.

Third, although no continuing contact occurred with a higher-level Gyenlo headquarters as it did in Nyemo, the potential for that kind of contact was present in Phala and Tsatsey, since the nomads held a strong belief that all Gyenlo members were comrades and should support one another. In Nyemo, we saw this come into play when Gyenlo members there sought to help comrades in adjacent counties by inviting them to come and see what they were doing to mobilize their villagers. Consequently, by accepting the Gyenlo agenda, the nomads in Phala and Tsatsey became more than a local group fighting to take control of their area; they became part of a Tibet-wide organization sharing the same views and aspirations—what we can think of as "Gyenlo Tibet."

But there is also an obvious significant difference between the two places. In Phala and Tsatsey no charismatic religious leader emerged analogous to the Nyemo *ani,* nor did warrior-hero mediums appear; all the Phala-Tsatsey leaders were laymen. This difference is important because it reinforces our earlier conclusion that while the nun and the warrior-hero mediums were important elements in the Nyemo disturbance, they were not a necessary condition for the incident to occur. Gyenlo in Nyemo had successfully used the Gyenlo agenda to mobilize the villagers well before the nun was involved, and even in the 27 November attacks, only one group of villagers expressed reticence at the last minute about going forward; the others were ready to go without the nun.

All of this raises an obvious question: Was Gyenlo General Headquarters in Lhasa masterminding all of these incidents? Many in Tibet think they were. For example, one Tibetan PLA soldier who was among the troops sent to suppress the disturbances in Shigatse Prefecture said that he and his fellow troops felt these were not isolated attacks but part of a larger plan. "They [Gyenlo] planned to attack and take over [the area] county by county. They said that once they took over the counties, it would be easy to take over the prefecture [Shigatse]."[12] Gyenlo General Headquarters in Lhasa, moreover, was actually organized to facilitate this, because it was divided into a number of subheadquarters that included not only different parts of Lhasa but also other parts of Tibet and even part of Qinghai Province.[13] A top Gyenlo leader discussed this broader structure.

> Nyingtri (in Kongpo) belonged to the Third Headquarters, Golmud (under Qinghai) belonged to the Eighth Headquarters. Both of them were not considered independent areas and were directly connected to Lhasa. In a simple way we numbered our headquarters up to the number eight, but there were no clear boundaries between headquarters.
>
> When the leaders of the Central Committee [in Beijing] interviewed us [in attempts to get Nyamdre and Gyenlo to agree to end their fighting], we were asked how many people we had in Lhasa. I was not prepared for that question and had to say that there might be around two hundred thousand or three hundred thousand. Then the Central Committee leaders criticized me, saying, "The Lhasa Headquarters should be responsible only for Lhasa, *not the whole region.*" I replied that we were not *trying* to be responsible for the whole region; however, other people wanted to depend on us. I said I had explained to those people and organizations that the Central Committee did not encourage us to form alliances, but I couldn't stop them from coming to us.[14]

Gyenlo General Headquarters in Lhasa, consequently, was structurally in a position to influence the course of all the incidents behind the scenes, and it certainly knew what was going on in Nyemo. Recall the comment of a Gyenlo leader in Nyemo who said that Lhasa not only had knowledge of what the faction was doing with the nun but also approved of it. "The cadres from the Lhasa headquarters agreed with the method we took and indicated that we should use the religious dances [trances] to activate the masses to attack."[15] But there is also evidence that Gyenlo General Headquarters played a more active role, for example, when it sent a propaganda dance troupe to Nyemo in 1968 on the anniversary of the Jokhang killings to incite the masses and motivate the activists.

Not surprisingly, many TAR leaders after 1969 blamed the leaders of Gyenlo General Headquarters in Lhasa, such as Tao Changsong, for secretly instigating the disturbances all over Tibet. However, the Gyenlo leaders emphatically denied this, and no evidence has ever been reported in support of that charge, despite thousands of hours of interrogations with captured Gyenlo activists. Thus, it seems unlikely to us that Gyenlo's headquarters in Lhasa was *actively* involved in directing these incidents, but at the same time, we do not find it hard to conclude that Gyenlo Lhasa was playing a crucial *indirect* role by developing, sanctioning, encouraging, and spreading the Gyenlo *agenda*.

The Nun's Manifesto

zongzhi: shen jianglin renshi, jiushi weile zhengfu mogui zhege diren. caipanzhe jiushi mao zhuxi, duiyu tancai de huo tun cai de, duiyu zhe zhong ren de caipanzhe shi meiyou fayan quan de shen, zheng yi qian ge shenwang he zheng yi qian ge nvshen. zhu zai shuyu ziji fangzi li de ren, ruguo you ren lai tiaoxin de hua, jiuyao an zhe jiang qing tongzhi suo shuo de na yang, yao jianjue ziwei fanji. dan zeng jia cuo (yi zai zhu yi) de guojia bei zuie de lama (yi zai zhu er) jiao gei mao zhuxi le, mao zhuxi you ba ta song gei shen jie, guoqu yinwei meiyou fayan quan, du li you huo, zui li bu gan mao yan, qiu shen de ren bi ru (yi zai zhu san) yi dai lai le yi qian duo ren, dui tamen shuo: "buyao tan meng, buyao jidu, dui houen de fumu, buyao dingzui, jiali de ren yao chi hao, yao yu linju qin-jin, yao zuncong dang de hua", zai qiu shen de ren dangzhong, qizhong you sanshi duo ge hao ren, qiyu de ren yihou zai xiang jiu. yong yige zang ga ga bu (yi zai zhu si) keyi zuo yige du mu fo xiang. jiefang jun shushu mingbai yidian hao! ruguo nimen tingxin gebie ren de hua, zhe yang de dong qiang dong dao, name, cong jintian qi, bie zuo chifan de dasuan ba, cong jitian qi jiushi fengzi ye bu zai chifan le. zhengge guo-jia dou bushi mao zhuxi he dan zeng jia cuo de guojia, ershi women shen de guojia. suiran nimen bu leyi, danshi cong shu yang de na nian qi, jiu yi bei shen jieguan le. zai liuyuefen nei you hao xi kan. xiexie nimen su ren shushu men, nimen yi en jiang chou bao le, fo yi xi luo bu he hu fa shen men, keyi manman de baoda" gei nimen, yi qian ge seng zhong pai lai le nigu, kong lin jia mu zhu ji ba la shan shang, guo de hen hao. zai zhege difang you yao mo gui guai, zai huo de renshi shang, dui caichan de caipanzhe shi mao zhuxi, dui xinling shan e de caipanzhe, shi wo zhege nigu. wo shi an zhe weida de mao zhuxi zhishi qianlai de, su ren shushu men, nimen de shouming haoxiang yancong li jiandao de guangxian (yi zhe zhu wu), you de ren xinxiong xiazhai, dui su ren shushu men zaocheng le zaihuo, tian liang le, taiyang chulai de shihou, ma ji de ji la mu nvshen yao qianlai shenpan, su ren shushu men, nimen xiang de dao hao, ni xiang yong yige ga ga bu zuo yige fo xiang, shen meiyou zao guo yaoyan, duiyu su ren shushu men jinxing jiaoyu, feng shanglai de hada, ye gezi tuihuan, nigu kong lin jia mu duiyu heixin de he shisu de ren gandao fennu, zui da e ji de jiushige ren yijing luo dao shou le, hai you dai yu luo dao shou de ren, you zongjiao xinyang de ren, gai xin de difang zai zheli, meiyou xinyang de ren, xiang zaonie de difang zai zheli, yao jianjue di jinxing ziwei fanji.

　　feng nan he feng nv xian . . . . . . yue . . . ri . . . ji xiang cheng
　　yizhe shuoming:
　　zhu yi: zhi dalai lama, dan zeng jia cuo
　　zhu er: da huo fo
　　zhu san: bi ru shi ge difang ming
　　zhu si: xiao yin bi
　　zhu wu: duanzan de yisi
　　jian zonghe cailiao diqi bufen di 298 ye
　　—301 ye

Leaflet Publishing the Text of a Speech Criticizing the Regional Party Committee

Contrast the spirit of the editorial published in the fifteenth issue of the journal *Red Flag* with the behavior of some of the major leaders of the Regional Party Committee of Tibet who stubbornly insisted on following the reactionary bourgeois line.

SPEECH AT A MEETING TO COMPLETELY UNCOVER THE
REACTIONARY BOURGEOIS LINE OF THE REGIONAL COMMITTEE
OF THE CCP IN LHASA ON 26 DECEMBER 1966

One. Hail the editorial in the fifteenth issue of the journal *Red Flag*.

[Skipped praise]

Two. Our several points:

1. During the Great Cultural Revolution in our region, the Regional Party Committee did not have just a few minor shortcomings or errors; it mistakenly carried out the reactionary bourgeois line and lost its direction.

2. We do not agree with the opinion of some comrades that "the Regional Party Committee carried out the reactionary bourgeois line *unconsciously*." We think that the Regional Committee of the CCP *completely and consciously* carried out the reactionary bourgeois line in the Great Cultural Revolution. It attempted to suppress the revolutionary masses and to protect a handful of leaders who held the capitalist line. The Regional Party Committee also tried to suppress the Great Cultural Revolution in our region.

3. Besides Guo Xilan, who has already been proved to oppose Mao

Zedong, other leaders in our Regional Party Committee are still implementing the reactionary capitalist line. *We are determined to uncover these leaders no matter how much they have contributed to the party and no matter how high their current positions are. No one can protect them.*

4. We cannot treat the comrades in the Regional Party Committee alike. We will criticize those who have formulated and are still implementing the reactionary capitalist line in Tibet. We will overthrow those who stubbornly insist on the reactionary capitalist line and oppose the revolutionary line of Mao Zedong.

5. Some major leaders of the Regional Party Committee have not been truly implementing the instructions of Chairman Mao and the Central Committee and have not been working hard with the masses to criticize the reactionary line. On the contrary, they have been playing tricks and taking new measures to trick the masses as well as insisting on the reactionary capitalist line. There are indications that their following the reactionary line has become a more and more serious problem.

Three. Please look at how these major leaders of the Regional Party Committee have stubbornly insisted on the reactionary capitalist line.

1. After Comrade Lin Biao launched the fighting call to completely criticize the reactionary capitalist line on the rostrum of Tiananmen on 1 October 1966, some major leaders of the Regional Party Committee took no notice of it and treated the call casually. The first secretary of the Regional Party Committee, Comrade Zhang Guohua, opposed the spirit of the Central Committee and regarded the incident of attacking the [19 September] big-character poster by the Control Committee of the Great Cultural Revolution [in Lhasa] as a "normal phenomenon." He thought the situation was good when the reactionary line was on the rampage during the Great Cultural Revolution. He completely ignored the problem of confounding right and wrong in criticizing the reactionary line. What was he up to?

   Comrade Wang Qimei, the secretary of the secretariat of the Regional Party Committee and the head of the Leading Team of the Great Cultural Revolution drew the "conclusion" by himself [i.e., without the agreement of the masses] that the problem did not exist at all. He did not mobilize the masses to study the instructions from the Central Committee. Neither did he mobilize the masses to rise up and criticize the reactionary line. What was he up to? All these indicate that Comrade Wang Qimei considered himself guilty and was afraid that the masses would rise up to criticize the reactionary capitalist line he was implementing.

2. With the advancement of the revolutionary line of Chairman Mao, the movement to criticize the reactionary capitalist line has become imperative. Under this situation, some major leaders of the Regional

Party Committee have had to confess to the masses that they have made mistakes of direction. They raised the placards: "Burn the Regional Party Committee" and "Criticize the reactionary capitalist line." However, what actually happened? The editorial in the fifteenth issue of *Red Flag* gave us instructions, including: "We should determine whether they truly or falsely criticized the reactionary capitalist line according to their *actual* behavior." And judging from the actual behavior of the Regional Party Committee, we say that they did not truly oppose the reactionary capitalist line. On the contrary, they just pretended to oppose the reactionary capitalist line. Did the Regional Party Committee implement the five rules of correcting the mistakes that were presented in the editorial of the fifteenth issue of *Red Flag*? No, they didn't. Did they earnestly and sincerely criticize themselves? No, they didn't. Did they sincerely announce the masses' rehabilitation? No, they didn't. Did they use the examples of their own mistakes to help the junior cadres and the masses who had been deceived to improve their understanding of the revolution? No, they didn't. Did they go down to the grassroots units and work with the people there to criticize the reactionary capitalist line? No, they didn't. Did they firmly support the leftists and fight against the handful of leaders who held the reactionary capitalist line? No, they didn't. They did nothing from beginning to end.

It is worth noting that some major leaders of the Regional Party Committee of the CCP delayed solving the problems that had appeared in the movement to criticize the reactionary line. They did not reply to many questions and problems presented by the revolutionary masses. They put off solving the problem of the 19 September big-character poster incident of the Control Committee of the Great Cultural Revolution. They also delayed the rehabilitation of those who wrote the big-character poster. [Omitted five paragraphs of satiric ridicule.]

Four. Several incidents that recently occurred in Lhasa reveal that the problem of the Regional Party Committee insisting on the reactionary capitalist line has become more and more serious.

1. the problem of delaying the announcement of the rehabilitation of those who wrote the [19 September] big-character poster by the Control Committee of the Great Cultural Revolution

    This poster was a great incident that caused a great sensation in Lhasa. It was also a great incident that uncovered the reactionary capitalist line of the Regional Party Committee. After a long period of delay, the Regional Party Committee [only] secretly announced the rehabilitation of the authors at midnight on the 12th. Only three representatives of the masses attended the meeting. After that, only a simple leaflet recording the meeting was released. This was a new form of cheating the masses. This was also a sign of cheating the broad revolutionary masses, because the reactionary group could hardly further delay solving the problem after the editorial of the fifteenth issue *Red Flag* was published.

2.   the problem of the Forestry Company Massacre

It is worth noting that the Forestry Company Massacre happened on 24 August [1966], [well] after the "sixteen-points" document was announced and distributed.[1] However, this company's "group for reforming people through labor," which was its private organization for suppressing the masses, was not dismissed until the end of November. This was the most serious incident resulting from the reactionary capitalist line of the Regional Party Committee. It indicated that the Regional Party Committee's problem of insisting on the reactionary capitalist line had become more and more serious. Among nearly 600 workers in the Forest Company, as many as 120 were denounced as "monsters and demons" [and counterrevolutionaries, etc.]. Those workers were subjected to inhuman persecution from the slaughterers, who were implementing the reactionary line. Many workers shed their blood; some were seriously injured. A few others were even tortured to death. The slaughterers were so ruthless and cruel. Here we express our greatest sympathy to our class brothers, the workers, who suffered tortures, as well as our most intense anger toward the slaughterers, who created the massacre. However, how did the Regional Party Committee treat this incident? They did not tell the masses about the incident, attempting to get by using pretenses. Comrade Wang Qimei even said, "No bloody incident has happened in Tibet." After the incident was uncovered, the Regional Party Committee appointed Ma Guishu as the head of the investigation team, even though he was directly involved in creating the massacre. Many from different units among the revolutionary masses protested this decision and requested that Ma Guishu be dismissed. However, the Regional Party Committee ignored these requests. When some members of the revolutionary masses organized a group to convey sympathy and solicitude, the Regional Party Committee used all means to obstruct them. We want to question our leaders in the Regional Party Committee. Why were you so indifferent to the bloody incident at the Forestry Company, where the slaughterers tortured our revolutionary masses? Why did you obstruct the group conveying sympathy and solicitude? Who are you? What are you up to? When you found out that you could not obstruct the group formed by the masses, you organized your own so-called group of conveying sympathy, in a flurry. What was your goal in doing this?

3.   the problem of treating the Red Guards from Beijing

Some major leaders of the Regional Committee of the CCP were so afraid of the Red Guards from fighting units such as Blazing Prairie that they tried to obstruct them before they came [from Beijing], and they sent people to watch them after they arrived. After the Central Committee issued its notice to stop the great alliance temporarily, they [leaders of the Regional Committee] tried their best to drive the Red Guards out. They held a "send-off meeting," [sending the Red Guards back] in a hurry, long before the time limit, the 21st, which was stipulated by the Central Committee [in Beijing]. Why were you so afraid of the Red Guards? Does that mean that you were ashamed of what you had done? You were afraid because the Red Guards had complete revolutionary spirit and never gave up to the reactionary line. Comrades of our three fighting units of the broadcasting station discussed this problem with Comrade Zhang Zaiwang. But Comrade Zhang Zaiwang would not accept our opinions and insisted on driving the Red Guards out. What is the result now? The team from the Central Great Cultural Revolution Committee [in Beijing] supported them to stay in Tibet and carry on the revolution with the local revolutionary masses. This was the clearest and loudest reply to those who insisted on driving the Red Guards out. We most strongly support this decision and enthusiastically welcome the Red Guards from fighting units such as Blazing Prairie to carry on the revolution together with us. Those who abused Blazing Prairie and tried to drive it out should shut up now. The problem of maltreating the Red Guards was also shown in the serious incident of attacking those from the 80th School of Beijing (ch. *beijing ba shi zhong*) at the Regional Committee of the CCP on 9 December. According to many uncovered facts, this was a well-organized attack on the Red Guards from the 80th School of Beijing. These so-called heroes not only abused the Red Guards but also obstructed their trucks and injured them by throwing sand. We cannot tolerate such behavior. Some people obviously instigated the struggle among the masses in order to protect themselves.

Five. Our several requests:

1. We strongly request that the slaughterers who were involved in the Forest Company Massacre be identified and punished without mercy.
2. We absolutely do not accept the rehabilitation carried out secretly at the Control Committee of the Great Cultural Revolution on the night of the 12th. We request that a mass meeting be held openly to rehabilitate the persons involved. The creators of this incident, such as Chen Wei, Tu Qingyuan, Niu Gengmin, et cetera, should make open self-criticisms. The Regional Party Committee should also assume the corresponding responsibilities and completely liberate the suppressed revolutionary masses. It should also clear up the bad influence of suppressing the masses. It should firmly refute those who chanted, "There is no need to reverse the verdicts," as well as openly opposed the Central Committee.
3. We firmly agree with the request of Comrade Chen Dongfeng from the *Tibet Daily* newspaper office that all the secret information about the Red Guards collected [by the Regional Party Committee] in the past should be openly burned.

4. We strongly support the requests of the Red Guards to uncover those in the Regional Party Committee who plotted to attack the Red Guards on 9 December.

5. Some major leaders of the Regional Party Committee should make a self-criticism to the masses immediately and confess their reactionary line in the Great Cultural Revolution. They should also guide the masses to further criticize the capitalist reactionary line of the Regional Party Committee.

6. We firmly request that some major leaders of the Regional Party Committee should go to the grassroots units and use their own mistakes as examples to help the lower-level cadres and the cheated masses to improve their understanding. We believe they should especially concentrate on cleaning up the bad influence of the capitalist reactionary line in the education department and its subunits. And last, let us call out:

Long live the revolutionary line of Chairman Mao! Long live our almighty leader—Chairman Mao!

Allied headquarters (ch. *lianhe zuozhanbu*) of the broadcast station in Tibet (26 December 1966)[2]

The Truth about the Struggle to Seize the Power of the *Tibet Daily Newspaper* Office

The primary concern of the revolution is political power. All power should belong to the revolutionary left.

The revolutionary left rebel groups of the *Tibet Daily Newspaper* started their fight to rebel and seized power on the night of 10 January. The "Revolutionary Rebels of Red News" were the main force among the leftist groups. However, after the incident, some people said that we had already seized control from Jin Sha, so after that the power was already in the hands of proletarian groups. Consequently, when the struggle to seize power was again carried out, weren't they [Gyenlo] attempting to seize power from the proletariat? Others, however, said that this rebellion was great, because after the struggle, the leading power was returned to the *real* revolutionary rebel groups. What is the truth? Why did a struggle of seizing power happen at the office of a newspaper? What was its process? What were its characteristics? These questions are the concerns of most of the people of Tibet right now. This incident has a direct impact on the Great Cultural Revolution in Lhasa and [elsewhere] in Tibet. Therefore, according to the highest instructions, we, the soldiers of the Blazing Prairie Combat Regiment and the Red Flag (ch. *hong qi*) group from the Beijing Academy of Aviation, carried out investigations and found the truth. We believe this incident was a revolutionary one. The revolutionary leftists did a good job.

Without investigation, it is perfunctory to make conclusions. Only after careful examination can we get the points right.

One. Why did they seize power?

Chairman Mao told us that we should never accept wrong leadership, because it will do harm to the revolution. We should suppress those people who dare to attack Chairman Mao, and we should not hesitate to reject any work that goes against the instructions of Chairman Mao. We should suppress those who dare to oppose Chairman Mao and also suppress all work that opposes the instructions of Chairman Mao. The leaders of some regions who are carrying out the bourgeois reactionary line that runs counter to the thoughts of Chairman Mao should be dismissed from office until they are able to carry out the line of Chairman Mao. Dismissing those leaders is a revolutionary action. Nobody should say no to it.

Someone said that actions like this [taking control of the *Tibet Daily*] do not follow the leadership of the Communist Party. That is total nonsense. The leaders of the Central Committee, Chairman Mao, and the thoughts of Chairman Mao are the real leading powers of the Communist Party. As for Tibet, the leaders of the Regional Party Committee of the TAR are just leaders of the local area. They are not equal to the leaders of the Central Committee of the Chinese Communist Party. Those who believe that "the leaders of the Regional Party Committee of the TAR are as powerful as those of the Central Committee" are definitely wrong, and they will fail if they use this wrong idea to suppress the movement of the masses in Tibet.

Our most respected and beloved leader, Chairman Mao, launched this Great Proletarian Cultural Revolution. The Great Cultural Revolution touched everybody to his very soul. We should rebel against all things that run counter to thoughts of Chairman Mao in order to create a new bright red China and a new bright red world. *However, with the coming of the Great Cultural Revolution, some leaders of the Regional Party Committee of the TAR became very frightened. They started to use the publishing house of the* Tibet Daily Newspaper, *which was controlled by them, to serve the reactionary bourgeois line. They did not allow reports* [to be published] *about the spirit of rebellion of the revolutionary masses in the Great Cultural Revolution and the success of Chairman Mao's Red Guards. On the contrary, they used the paper to spread the dark side of the Red Guards, exaggerating the Red Guards' mistakes, slandering the Red Guards, creating a white terror, and blocking information about the Great Cultural Revolution in order to destroy it.*

Was it just a minor problem? No, it wasn't. It was a matter of principle. The newspapers and periodicals of the Communist Party are tools of publicity for the proletarian class, and they should be used to publicize the ideas of Chairman Mao. Chairman Mao said, "We must always stick to the truth, and the truth must have a clear-cut stand." Members of the Communist Party consider it wrong to conceal one's own opinions. The publicity work of our Communist Party should be active, clear, and sharp. No hemming and hawing. However, the *Tibet Daily* became the propaganda tool of some leaders of the Regional Party Committee of the TAR in order to implement the reactionary line of the bourgeoisie. Was it all right? No, it should not have been done.

To rebel, we should resist the wrong leadership of some leaders of the Regional Party Committee of the TAR and completely refuse their ideas. The soldiers of the Revolutionary Rebels of Red News in the *Tibet Daily* started the rebellion under the instructions of Chairman Mao, who said, "It is justified to rebel." They spread the revolutionary spirit of the *Wenhui Daily* (ch. *wen hui bao*) and the *Liberation Daily* (ch. *jiefang ribao*) [newspapers in Shanghai].

On 10 January, the members of Revolutionary Rebels of Red News started the struggle to seize power. On 11 January, they solemnly declared that they firmly support the leadership of the Central Committee of the Communist Party, which is headed by Chairman Mao, and firmly resist the wrong leadership of some leaders of the Tibet Regional Party Committee. *They also said that from then on, all control of the publicity work would be taken away from some leaders of the Regional Party Committee. The power of control will not be given back to those leaders until the reactionary bourgeois line is completely criticized and those leaders of the Tibet Regional Party Committee who persisted in the reactionary line are completely overthrown. This rebellion represented justice, because it was to protect the revolutionary line of Chairman Mao and the thoughts of Chairman Mao.*

Two. A Simple Description of the Process of "The Struggle of Seizing Power"

The incident proceeded as follows: After about 11 P.M. on the night of 10 January, the members of the Revolutionary Rebels of Red News held a meeting and prepared to rebel. Seventy or eighty people attended the meeting. (We did not calculate accurately, but at that time the whole reference room was full of people, including some from other units.) The door was open, and people came and went. It was not a secret meeting. At that time some comrades did not attend the meeting because they were on the night shift or because they worked in the daytime and had already gone to sleep.

The masses worked out plans for the next day's newspaper and sent several workers to supervise Comrade Zhang Guangzhe, who would temporarily take charge of printing it. (Because some workers lacked the professional knowledge to do this, they asked Zhang Guangzhe to do it.) The masses, however, warned Zhang, telling him, "If you do not follow the opinions of the masses and the workers closely, you will be responsible for the consequences." The content and design of the newspaper were decided by the masses attending the meeting. The title of the newspaper would still be *Tibet Daily Newspaper,* which was inscribed by Chairman Mao. And it was Comrade Shu Xiaomei, the head of the Chinese editorial department, who signed the seal of the paper, instead of Comrade Zhang Guangzhe. It was not as some people have described, "This issue of the newspaper was controlled by Zhang Guangzhe and Fang Kang, who were in authority and persisted in the reactionary bourgeois line." Rather, because time was limited, the masses had to let Zhang Guangzhe take charge of the printing of the newspaper temporarily. The masses also decided that [new] leaders of the newspaper would be selected the next day after they discussed this with people from different quarters. The leading power was still in the hands of the revolutionary Gyenlo workers instead of in Zhang Guangzhe's hands. At the meeting, three general orders were put forward. Those orders clearly claimed that all publicity work should no longer be under the control of leaders of the Regional Party Committee of the TAR until the reactionary bourgeois line was completely eliminated.

At that time, the head of the security department, Cheng Dongfeng, was afraid that the conflicts between the two groups [factions] would lead to a violent fight. Therefore, he was appointed to guard the meeting and the printing work that was being done that night. This was a reasonable decision. The firearms department was also guarded that night, and nobody attempted to use force. It was not like what some people said, "The Revolutionary Rebels of Red News sent people to take charge of the firearms that belonged to the people's militia of the newspaper office."

The above is a simple description of this incident. If you do not believe it, you may do some investigations yourself. The truth should never be covered up under rumors and false claims. If someone dares to take measures to trick the revolutionary masses and suppress the revolutionary movement of the masses, he will never attain his evil goal.

Three. Was it "Very Good" or "Very Bad"?

After the incident of seizing power at the publishing house occurred, different opinions appeared. Some people said it was a very bad way of struggling. Were they correct? Of course not! This struggle to seize power was supported by the workers of the revolutionary rebels at the publishing house. The struggle was against the wrong direction of some leaders of the Regional Party Committee and their reactionary bourgeois line. *Those leaders did not allow us to publicize the spirit of rebellion of the revolutionary rebel masses, but we insisted on doing so. Those leaders wanted to propagate the dark side of Chairman Mao's Red Guards, but we insisted in letting people know how the Red Guards have contributed to the Great Cultural Revolution under the instructions of Chairman Mao. Those leaders wanted to implement the reactionary bourgeois line, but we insisted on criticizing it and guarding the revolutionary line of Chairman Mao. How could someone say it was a very bad struggle? Actually it was extremely good. Someone said this incident was a "counterrevolutionary incident" and it was an "adverse current." These were false rumors.* [Slogans omitted.] *Now just a few people still insist on holding this wrong opinion. They are separating themselves from the masses, and they are opposing the masses and the ideas of Chairman Mao. In the end they will fail.* [Slogans omitted.] *We believe "the struggle to seize power" was good, and it was the right direction. Those comrades who are not clearly aware of the facts will agree with us after they know the truth. We insist on supporting the workers of revolutionary rebel groups running the* Tibet Daily Newspaper *as the mouthpiece for the ideas of Chairman Mao. We welcome the new birth of the* Tibet Daily Newspaper. [Slogans omitted.]

[By] [t]he branch of the Red Flag group of the Beijing Institute of Aeronautics (ch. *bei hang hong qi fuzang chuanlian fen dui*), 13 January 1967[1]

Notes

1. For a discussion of conflict during the Cultural Revolution in rural inland China, see Unger 1998, 2007.

2. Nimu wenti fucha zu 1974, 2; Zhonggong lasa shiwei wenjian, guanyu jiang yuanding 1987, 4.

3. A *xiang* is conventionally translated as "a rural township," but it is actually an administrative unit that consists of a number of adjacent villages.

4. Interview, 2000, OR.0045.01, Nyemo, Tibet Autonomous Region, China. The interview notation is explained later in the Introduction.

5. Interview, 2000, OR.0030.01, Nyemo, Tibet Autonomous Region, China.

6. International Committee of Lawyers for Tibet 1995.

7. Pema Dechen 1995, 1.

8. Havnevik 1994, 265.

9. Dalai Lama 1991, 182.

10. Wei Se 2006, 201.

11. During the Cultural Revolution in Tibet, there were two main revolutionary groups, Gyenlo (the Rebels) and Nyamdre (the Alliance).

12. Nimu wenti fucha zu, Fujian #8, 1974, 18; and Zhonggong nimu xian weiyuanhui 1987, 9. Interestingly, a Tibetan intellectual in China recently tried to assess this incident independent of the government but ended up unable to determine whether or not the Nyemo incident was a second Tibetan revolt, concluding that it is the most confusing incident in the history of the Cultural Revolution in Tibet (Wei Se 2006, 201).

13. Tibetan Women's Association 1995.

14. Smith 1996, 548.

15. For example, in his influential essay on unrest in Tibet, the Tibetan in-

tellectual Jigme Ngagpo characterizes the Nyemo event as a large-scale rebellion that was staged for the purpose of independence (Ngagpo 1988, 24).

16. Barnett 2005, 349.

17. Shakya 2002, 39–40. See also Shakya 1999, 343–47.

18. Diemberger 2005, 163–64.

19. Wang 2002, 88.

20. Shakya 2002, 40.

21. Zhu nimu mao zedong sixiang xuanchuan dui bianyin 1971, 7.

22. That Web site's URL is www.case.edu/affil/tibet.

1. THE CULTURAL REVOLUTION IN TIBET

1. The extensive literature that analyzes Mao's deeper political motives and high-level infighting does not concern us in this history and will not be discussed.

2. Zhonggong xizang zizhiqu dangshi ziliao zhengji weiyuanhui bian 1995, entry for 4–26 May 1966, 173.

3. Goldstein is working on a book-length history of modern Tibet from 1959 to 1969 that will include a detailed examination of the Cultural Revolution, so it is examined here only to the extent needed to understand the events in Nyemo.

4. Zhonggong xizang zizhiqu dangshi ziliao zhengji weiyuanhui bian 1995, entry for the end of May 1966, 174.

5. Other cadres to be singled out were Hui Yiran, He Zhuyin, Huang Mao, and Luo Shisheng (Zhonggong xizang zizhiqu dangshi ziliao zhengji weiyuanhui bian 1995, entries for 15 June to 5 and 8 July 1966, 174–75).

6. Zhonggong xizang zizhiqu dangshi ziliao zhengji weiyuanhui bian 1995, entries for 15 June to 5 July 1966, 174.

7. Dittmer 1998, 54–55. During this two-month period Mao was in temporary "retirement," and Liu had assumed temporary command of the Central Committee of the Chinese Communist Party.

8. Zhonggong xizang zizhiqu dangshi ziliao zhengji weiyuanhui bian 1995, entry for 12 July 1966, 175.

9. "White terror" initially referred to the killing of thousands of communists by the Guomindang but was used during the Cultural Revolution to refer to acts of violence carried out against revolutionary students or the masses.

10. These were a major means of debate, struggle, accusations, and popular communication during the Cultural Revolution. They were handwritten wall posters, generally with large characters.

11. Quoted in www.answers.com/topic/cultural-revolution (emphasis added) (accessed 2006). It is also widely known as "the 16 articles." The same Eleventh Plenum also criticized and demoted Liu Shaoqi (Dittmer 1998, 54).

12. Chao 1993, entry for 18 August 1966, 439.

13. Old ideas, old cultures, old manners, and old customs.

14. Chao 1993, entry for 19 August 1966, 439. The entry mentions the 23 August date.

15. Zhonggong xizang zizhiqu dangshi ziliao zhengji weiyuanhui bian 1995, entry for 12 August 1966, 176.

16. Zhonggong xizang zizhiqu dangshi ziliao zhengji weiyuanhui bian 1995, entry for 18 August 1966, 176.

17. Interview, 2001, H.0109.01, Lhasa, Tibet Autonomous Region, China. For interesting photos of Lhasa during this period, see Wei Se 2006.

18. See Goldstein 2007 for a detailed examination of the history of the 1951–55 period, when the "gradualist" policy was developed and utilized.

19. Interview, 1993, H.0056.02, Phündra, Beijing, People's Republic of China.

20. In Beijing, Zhang's position was supported by Zhou Enlai but not by Jiang Qing and the Central Great Cultural Revolution Group (ch. *zhongyang wenhua da geming weiyuanhui*).

21. Dangdai zhongguo congshu bianjibu 1991, 369.

22. In other words, attacking lots of people without specific evidence.

23. Lasa geming zaofan zongbu, qu hu bao lianhe zuozhanbu 1967.

24. "An Open Letter to the Central Great Cultural Revolution Group" 1967 (emphasis added).

25. "An Open Letter to the Central Great Cultural Revolution Group" 1967.

26. Lhasa Revolutionary Rebel Headquarters 1967.

27. Lhasa Revolutionary Rebel Headquarters 1967. Struggle sessions were public meetings held to attack class enemies and others by accusing them of past misdeeds. Pressuring the targets to admit their errors helped them, in theory, to secure their gradual rehabilitation. Use of this device was common during the onset of socialist reforms in 1959–60 and the Cultural Revolution era. The targets at these sessions had to stand at the front of the assembled masses bent over at the waist, face downward, with their arms pointed backward (this was called the airplane style) while the members of the masses yelled criticisms and accusations at them and often hit, kicked, and beat them. These sessions could take hours and sometimes resulted in serious injury or even death. They were a visible demonstration to the Tibetan masses that the power of the old elite was over and that they had nothing to fear from the elite anymore.

28. Zhonggong xizang zizhiqu dangshi ziliao zhengji weiyuanhui bian 1995, entry for 30 September 1966, 177 (emphasis added).

29. Interview, 2002, H.0268.01, Lhasa, Tibet Autonomous Region, China. Also, Zhonggong xizang zizhiqu dangshi ziliao zhengji weiyuanhui bian 1995, entry for 28 October 1966, 179, reports that Zhang Guohua suggested to Zhou Enlai that he remove Ngabö to Beijing for safety.

30. Zhonggong xizang zizhiqu dangshi ziliao zhengji weiyuanhui bian 1995, entry for 28 October 1966, 179. During Zhang Guohua's visit to Beijing, he had received important support from Premier Zhou Enlai on 19 October, when Zhou met with a group of eleven minority students. In answer to one of the students' questions about whether Zhang Guohua had some problems, Zhou Enlai answered, "Zhang Guohua is a good comrade because he always closely follows Chairman Mao, continually working in Tibet even though his physical condition is poor, and he directed the counterattack in defense of the borderline between China and India while taking oxygen. Zhou said that Zhang Guohua might have made this or that mistake in his work, but he still is a good comrade" (Zhonggong xizang zizhiqu dangshi ziliao zhengji weiyuanhui bian 1995, entry for 19 October 1966, 178).

31. Zhonggong xizang zizhiqu dangshi ziliao zhengji weiyuanhui bian 1995, entries for 19 and 28 October 1966, 178–79. Also Yang 1967, 46.

32. "Guanyu qingshi zhichi zuopai qunzhong zuzhi 'dalianzhi' de baogao" 1967.

33. Zhonggong xizang zizhiqu dangshi ziliao zhengji weiyuanhui bian 1995, entry for November 1966, 179.

34. Lhasa Revolutionary Rebel Headquarters 1967.

35. *Royalists* was a standard Cultural Revolution term for people and factions who supported the party leaders.

36. Interview, 2001, H.0109.01, Lhasa, Tibet Autonomous Region, China.

37. Yang 1967, 46. This is also mentioned in Xizang renmin guangbo diantai lianhe zuozhanbu 1967.

38. Xizang renmin guangbo diantai lianhe zuozhanbu 1967.

39. Interview, 1999, H.0112.01, Chengdu, China.

40. "Guanyu qingshi zhichi zuopai qunzhong zuzhi 'dalianzhi' de baogao" 1967, 8.

41. "Guanyu qingshi zhichi zuopai qunzhong zuzhi 'dalianzhi' de baogao" 1967, 1. Zaofan (Gyenlo) was a common name employed by revolutionary groups throughout China, although there was no central command headquarters for all groups named Gyenlo in China. By 1968, the part of Gyenlo led by Zhuang Yanhe splintered off from Gyenlo Headquarters, creating a third revolutionary faction in Lhasa, which they called the Revolutionary Gyenlo Commune; interview, 2001, OR.0109, Lhasa, Tibet Autonomous Region, China.

42. Liang 1968, 633–34. An abridged version is given in Revolutionary Worker, #752, "The True Story of the Maoist Revolution in Tibet," 17 April 1994, http://rwor.org/a/firstvol/Tibet/tibet3.htm.

43. Xizang renmin guangbo diantai lianhe zuozhanbu 1967 (emphasis added).

44. "Guanyu qingshi zhichi zuopai qunzhong zuzhi 'dalianzhi' de baogao" 1967, 1.

45. Interview, 2001, OR.0118.01, Lhasa, Tibet Autonomous Region, China.

46. Interview, 2001, H.0100.03, Wuhan, China.

47. Zhonggong xizang zizhiqu dangshi ziliao zhengji weiyuanhui bian 1995, entry for 11 January 1967, 180.

48. Interview, 2001, H.0109.01, Lhasa, Tibet Autonomous Region, China.

49. Liaoyuan zhandou dui and Beihang hongqi fuzang chuanlian fen dui, 13 January 1967, 2 (emphasis added).

50. "Guanyu qingshi zhichi zuopai qunzhong zuzhi 'dalianzhi' de baogao" 1967, 1.

51. "Guanyu qingshi zhichi zuopai qunzhong zuzhi 'dalianzhi' de baogao" 1967, 23.

52. "Guanyu qingshi zhichi zuopai qunzhong zuzhi 'dalianzhi' de baogao" 1967, 23.

53. Interview, 1999, H.0112.01, Chengdu, China.

54. Interview, 1999, H.0112.01, Chengdu, China.

55. Interview, 2001, H.0109.01, Lhasa, Tibet Autonomous Region, China.

56. Interview, 2001, OR.0164.01, Lhasa, Tibet Autonomous Region, China.

57. "Guanyu qingshi zhichi zuopai qunzhong zuzhi 'dalianzhi' de baogao" 1967, 24.

58. "Guanyu qingshi zhichi zuopai qunzhong zuzhi 'dalianzhi' de baogao" 1967, 24.

59. Zhonggong xizang zizhiqu dangshi ziliao zhengji weiyuanhui bian 1995, entry for 10 February 1967, 181.

60. Lingren shensi de wenti, 13 February 1967, 1.

61. Interview, 2001, H.0109.01, Lhasa, Tibet Autonomous Region, China.

62. Interview, 2001, H.0109.01, Lhasa, Tibet Autonomous Region, China. The interviewee went to Beijing after his release to present a document about the mistreatment Gyenlo had experienced and to argue for the correctness of his side's actions.

63. Interview, 2001, H.0109.01, Lhasa, Tibet Autonomous Region, China.

64. Zhonggong xizang zizhiqu dangshi ziliao zhengji weiyuanhui bian 1995, entry for 15 February 1967, 182.

65. Xizang junqu dangwei 1967, 4 and 7.

66. Specially Attack was a special group within Gyenlo that was set up in early 1967 to compile negative information on Zhang Guohua. Its full name was "the Liaison Committee for Specially Attacking the Local Emperor" (ch. *zhuan da tuhuangdi lianluo weiyuanhui*).

67. "The First Written 'Self-Examination' Yin Fa-t'ang Delivers to Headquarters of Metropolitan Red Guards Bound for Tibet and Rebel Headquarters" 1967.

68. "What I Saw on 10 February 1967 at 10:10 in the Morning" 1967.

69. Interview, 2006, Li Huo, Massachusetts, USA.

70. Zhonggong xizang zizhiqu dangshi ziliao zhengji weiyuanhui bian 1995, entry for 11 May 1967, 183.

71. The "three-way alliance" referred to one among the military, the revolutionary organizations of the masses, and the veteran party and government cadres. In areas where serious factional violence occurred, forming such an alliance was the preliminary step in creating conditions to set up revolutionary committees (Falkenheim 1969, 581).

72. Interview, 2001, OR.0109, Lhasa, Tibet Autonomous Region, China.

73. Zhonggong xizang zizhiqu dangshi ziliao zhengji weiyuanhui bian 1995, entry for 26 February 1968, 185.

74. Interview, 2001, H.0109.01, Lhasa, Tibet Autonomous Region; "Zhongyang shouzhang jiejian xizang zizhiqu geming weiyuanhui, xizang junqu huibao quan ti renyuan de zhongyao zhishi" 1968.

75. Zhonggong xizang zizhiqu dangshi ziliao zhengji weiyuanhui bian 1995, entry for 5 May 1968, 185.

76. Zhonggong xizang zizhiqu dangshi ziliao zhengji weiyuanhui bian 1995, entry for 6 June 1968, 185–86.

77. "Guanyu liuqi shijian de qingkuang baogao" 1968, 9.

78. "Guanyu liuqi shijian de qingkuang baogao" 1968, 9–10.

79. "Guanyu liuqi shijian de qingkuang baogao" 1968, 10.

80. Interview, 2001, OR.0164.01, Lhasa, Tibet Autonomous Region, China.

81. "Guanyu liuqi shijian de qingkuang baogao" 1968, 16–18.

82. Interview, 2001, OR.0281.01, Lhasa, Tibet Autonomous Region, China.

83. Interview, 2000, OR.0253.01, Lhasa, Tibet Autonomous Region, China.

84. Interview, 2001, OR.0167.01, Lhasa, Tibet Autonomous Region, China.

85. "Guanyu liuqi shijian de qingkuang baogao" 1968, 2.

86. On 18 January 1968, Nyamdre mobilized some peasants and attacked Gyenlo strongholds in the northern suburbs, such as the Heavy Machine Repair Factory and the Science Institute, using weapons they had obtained from the army. Gyenlo sent reinforcements and ended up defeating the attackers, despite having almost no modern weapons.

87. This was the study class in Beijing at which leaders of Gyenlo and Nyamdre had been summoned to study their mistakes and agree to end the factional violence.

88. Interview, 2001, H.0109.01, Lhasa, Tibet Autonomous Region, China.

89. "Guanyu liji tingzhi diqu wudou de xieyi" 1968.

90. On the Beijing side were Zhou Enlai, Chen Boda, Kang Sheng, Jiang Qing, Yao Wenyuan, Xie Fuzhi, Huang Yongshen, Wu Faxian, Ye Qun, Wang Dongxin, and Wen Yuchen.

91. "Zhongyang, zhongyang wenge shouzhang jiejian xizang ban bufen xueyuan shi de zhongyao zhishi (jilu gao)" 1968, 8.

92. "Zhongyang, zhongyang wenge shouzhang jiejian xizang ban bufen xueyuan shi de zhongyao zhishi (jilu gao)" 1968, 6.

93. "Xizang junqu dangwei changwei guanyu zhizuo gongzuo zhong suo fan cuowu de jiantao baogao" 1968 (emphasis added).

94. Zhonggong xizang zizhiqu dangshi ziliao zhengji weiyuanhui bian 1995, entry for 5 September 1968, 186.

95. Interview, 2001, OR.0118.01, Lhasa, Tibet Autonomous Region, China.

96. Other discussions of the Cultural Revolution in Tibet can be found in Shakya 1999; Grunfeld 1996; Smith 1996; Barnett 2005; Avedon 1984; Weiner 2002; and Wei Sei 2006.

2. GYENLO AND NYAMDRE IN NYEMO COUNTY

1. This class was called *ngatsab* in Tibetan (ch. *dailiren*), or "agents of a lord." People labeled politically as such were said in communist jargon to have had a label, or "hat" (tib. *shamo;* ch. *maozi*), placed on them and did not have citizenship, as did other peasants. In addition, they were cut off from interaction with other villagers and were legally under the supervision of the masses (tib. *mangdzo dagül;* ch. *qunzhong jiandu*), which usually meant under the orders of activists and cadres. As such they were called to do whatever difficult work the local government or the revolutionary factions needed, without pay, this being a version of "reform through labor" (tib. *ngedzö gyurgö;* ch. *laodong gaizao*). *Ngedzö gyurgö* can also refer to actual separate labor camps, but in rural areas it referred to the individual class enemies who had to do whatever work they were given.

2. Interview, 2002, OR.0345.01, Nyemo, Tibet Autonomous Region, China.

3. For a discussion of this in rural inland China, see Unger 1984.

4. See Goldstein 2007, 1–16, for an overview of how that system operated traditionally.

5. An interim system called Mutual Aid Teams (tib. *rogre tsogjung;* ch. *hu zhu zu*) was started, in which small groups of households cooperated in farming, but the yields from each household's fields were retained by that household.

6. Tashilhunpo, the Panchen Lama's monastery in Shigatse, was a notable exception to this and remained a functioning monastery for some time.

7. Interview, 2002, OR.0304.01, Nyemo, Tibet Autonomous Region, China.

8. A *khe* is a traditional Tibetan volume measurement equal to about fourteen kilograms (for barley).

9. Liu Shaoqi, then the president of China, was one of the main targets of Mao. He was labeled China's number one capitalist-roader during the Cultural Revolution and was placed under house arrest in 1967. In 1968, he was stripped of all his official positions and expelled from the party.

10. Nimu wenti fucha zu 1974, 3–4.

11. A *jin* (tib. *gyama*) is a Chinese weight measure equal to half a kilogram (1.1 pounds).

12. Zhonggong lasa shiwei wenjian, guanyu jiang yuanding 1987, 8.

13. Interview, 2002, OR.0365.01, Nyemo, Tibet Autonomous Region, China.

14. Interview, 2002, OR.0346.01, Nyemo, Tibet Autonomous Region, China.

15. Interview, 2000, OR.0024.01, Nyemo, Tibet Autonomous Region, China.

16. Interview, 2000, OR.0025.01, Nyemo, Tibet Autonomous Region, China.

17. Interview, 2002, OR.0350.01, Nyemo, Tibet Autonomous Region, China. A few villagers' accounts also mentioned that Gyenlo said the people would also receive one brick of tea a month.

18. Interview, 2002, OR.0300.01, Nyemo, Tibet Autonomous Region, China.

19. Interview, 2002, OR.0333.01, Nyemo, Tibet Autonomous Region, China.

20. Interview, 2002, OR.0288.01, Nyemo, Tibet Autonomous Region, China.

21. Zhang Yongfu at this time was said to be the party secretary of Nyemo County's Sangri District (ch. *qu*) (interview, 2002, OR.0300.01, Nyemo, Tibet Autonomous Region, China).

22. Interview, 2002, OR.0345.01, Nyemo, Tibet Autonomous Region, China; interview, 2002, OR.0350.01, Nyemo, Tibet Autonomous Region, China.

23. Zhonggong lasa shiwei wenjian, guanyu jiang yuanding 1987, 8.

24. Correct Tibetan spelling: *gsar brje byed par nag nyes med; gyen log byed par rgyu mtshan yod.*

25. Lhasa Revolutionary Rebel Headquarters 1967.

26. Interview, 2001, OR.0145.01, Nyemo, Tibet Autonomous Region, China. The pejorative name "blue pigs" derived from the blue clothing cadres wore and from their piglike behavior of not working but just sitting around and eating, in this case, "eating" the wealth of the people. The soldiers of the PLA were referred to pejoratively as "yellow dogs" because of the color of their uniforms.

27. Taxpayer households were a category of bound peasant (serf) who held land from their lord's manorial estate and were mainly responsible for providing corvée labor in their lord's demesne fields. They were usually the best off of the village householders, although many were still poor as a result of land fragmentation, heavy debts, and other personal circumstances. For discussions of Tibetan social organization and serfdom, see Goldstein 1971a,b, 1986, 1987, and 1989a. See also Miller 1987 and 1988.

28. For a discussion of monastic households, see Goldstein, in press.

29. Interview, 2000, OR.0025.01, 2002, Nyemo, Tibet Autonomous Region, China; interview, 2007, OR.0060.05, Tibet Autonomous Region, China.

30. Interview, 2006, OR.0060.03, Nyemo, Tibet Autonomous Region, China.

31. This monk was from Shalu Monastery, near Shigatse.

32. Work teams were and still are a common tool for implementing campaigns and investigating problems. These teams consist of officials pulled together from different offices and sent to a location for a specific campaign. Study classes were meetings held to introduce people to the theory of the Democratic Reforms and the new terminology and metaphors used by the Communist Party. The term *study class* also referred to a kind of detention in which individuals were forced to study their own behavior and through this come to realize and confess to their mistakes.

33. Interview, 2000, OR.0004.01, Panam, Tibet Autonomous Region, China.

34. Interview, 2000, OR.0004.01, Panam, Tibet Autonomous Region, China.

35. This meant the amount of land that could be planted with 2.1 *khe* of seed.

36. Interview, 2000, OR.0004.02, Panam, Tibet Autonomous Region, China.

37. Interview, 2000, OR.0004.02, Panam, Tibet Autonomous Region, China.

38. Interview, 2000, OR.0060.01, Nyemo, Tibet Autonomous Region, China.

39. Interview, 2000, OR.0060.01, Nyemo, Tibet Autonomous Region, China.

40. Interview, 2000, OR.0060.03, Nyemo, Tibet Autonomous Region, China.

41. Interview, 2002, OR.0351.01, Nyemo, Tibet Autonomous Region, China.

42. Interview, 2002, OR.0351.01, Nyemo, Tibet Autonomous Region, China.

43. These reports appear similar to the classic symptoms of schizophrenia, which often begins in late adolescence or early adulthood as the result of some trauma or a situation in which a person is overwhelmed by problems and can no longer fulfill his or her ascribed role (Rogler and Hollingshead 1965). Not enough is known about the nun's behavior at this time for us to pursue this line of interpretation further.

44. Sometimes the term *oracle* is used interchangeably.

45. For a detailed discussion of female mediums, see Diemberger 2005.

46. The three lamas living in the area, Chamba Tenzin, Gachen, and one from Chöling *xiang*, were not performing any religious activities at this time because of the Cultural Revolution.

47. Interview, 2000, OR.0060.01, Nyemo, Tibet Autonomous Region, China.

48. Interview, 2000, OR.0060.01, Nyemo, Tibet Autonomous Region, China; and Nimu wenti fucha zu, Fujian #2, 1974, 1.

49. Interview, 2006, OR.0060.02, Nyemo, Tibet Autonomous Region, China; and Nimu wenti fucha zu, Fujian #2, 1974, 1.

50. Interview, 2000, OR.0060.01, Nyemo, Tibet Autonomous Region, China.

51. Interview, 2000, OR.0060.01, Nyemo, Tibet Autonomous Region, China.

52. Nimu wenti fucha zu 1974, 4–5.

53. Nimu wenti fucha zu 1974, 5; and Nimu wenti fucha zu, Fujian #2, 1974, 2.

54. Trinley later became one of the top village leaders of Gyenlo under Rangjung.

55. Nimu wenti fucha zu, Fujian #2, 1974, 2.

56. Nimu wenti fucha zu 1974, 5; and Nimu wenti fucha zu, Fujian #2, 1974, 2–3. Several other Gyenlo leaders also referred to the incident mentioned in these documents.

57. Interview, OR. 0346.01, 2002, Nyemo, Tibet Autonomous Region, China.

58. During the Cultural Revolution, Red Guards and other revolutionary factions wore different identifying armbands.

59. Nimu wenti fucha zu, Fujian #2, 1974, 2.

60. The idea that monks could also be revolutionary activists existed at least in Lhasa, where a group of monks in Drepung named themselves the Red Lamas (tib. and ch. *hongse lama*) and were recognized by Zhou Renshan, a top party official in Tibet who was supported by Gyenlo. Although there is no specific mention of revolutionary monks with regard to the nun, the Gyenlo leaders in Nyemo certainly would have known about the *hongse lama* group.

61. The statue of Jowo Rimpoche was housed in the Jokhang Chapel, so the name Jokhang is often used to denote the entire Tsuglagang Temple.

62. Diemberger 2005, 130.

63. Tathagata refers to the historical Buddha Gautama.

64. Interview, 2002, OR.0345.01, Nyemo, Tibet Autonomous Region, China.

65. Interview, 2000, OR.0025.01, Nyemo, Tibet Autonomous Region, China; interview, 2006, OR.0060.03, Nyemo, Tibet Autonomous Region, China.

66. Interview, 2000, OR.0060.01, Nyemo, Tibet Autonomous Region, China.

67. Interview, 2002, OR.0346.01, Nyemo, Tibet Autonomous Region, China.

68. Interview, 2000, OR.0025.01, Nyemo, Tibet Autonomous Region, China.

69. Interview, 2002, OR.0346.01, Nyemo, Tibet Autonomous Region, China.

70. For more on Gesar, see Samuel 1992 and 1994; and David-Neel and Yongden 1959.

71. Interview, 2000, OR.0060.04, Nyemo, Tibet Autonomous Region, China.

72. Interview, 2000, OR.0029.01, Nyemo, Tibet Autonomous Region, China.

73. Chamba Lodrü's comment in Nimu wenti fucha zu 1974, 5; and Nimu wenti fucha zu, Fujian #2, 1974, 5.

74. Interview, 2007, OR.0060.05, Tibet Autonomous Region, China.

75. Interview, 2002, OR.0346.01, Nyemo, Tibet Autonomouos Region, China.

76. Nimu wenti fucha zu 1974, 5.

77. Interview, 2002, OR.0346.01, Nyemo, Tibet Autonomous Region, China.

3. GYENLO ON THE ATTACK

1. Each village with a significant number of Gyenlo members elected some of its more activist members as representatives.

2. Nimu wenti fucha zu, Fujian #1, 1974, 8.

3. Nimu wenti fucha zu, Fujian #1, 1974, 5.

4. Nimu wenti fucha zu, Fujian #2, 1974, 10.

5. Nimu wenti fucha zu, Fujian #2, 1974, 7.

6. Nimu wenti fucha zu, Fujian #2, 1974, 8.

7. A *chuba* is the traditional robelike dress commonly made in villages from woven wool fabric. It is worn by men and women in Tibet, although men's and women's styles differ.

8. Zhu nimu mao zedong sixiang xuanhuan dui bianyin 1971, 4–5 (emphasis added).

9. Nyemo *xian* and *xiang* were adjacent.

10. Interview, 2002, OR.380.01, Nyemo, Tibet Autonomous Region, China.

11. Interview, 2002, OR.0295.01, Nyemo, Tibet Autonomous Region, China.

12. Interview, 2002, OR.0302.01, Nyemo, Tibet Autonomous Region, China.

13. Actually this was focused mainly in the districts of Nyemo, Phusum, Bagor, and Angang.

14. Nimu wenti fucha zu, Fujian #1, 1974, 9.

15. Interview, 2002, OR.0346.01, Nyemo, Tibet Autonomous Region, China.

16. Technically, the Chinese government makes a distinction between religion and what it calls "superstition," which includes things like divination, spirit worship, mediums, and so forth, but at this time during the Cultural Revolution, all forms of religious practice in Tibet were referred to as superstition.

17. The *wuzhuang bu* was the part of the county government organization and was responsible for organizing and training the people's militia. Usually only a few military officials worked in this department, but it played an important role during the chaos of the Cultural Revolution. The *zhongdui,* by contrast, was a unit of the regular army based in the county. Its officials and soldiers were under the direct administration of the TAR Military Headquarters (i.e., not under the county government). After the November attacks on the Nyamdre cadres and their flight to Lhasa, the county government became defunct, and the *wuzhuang bu* became the de facto government in Nyemo.

18. Nimu wenti fucha zu, Fujian #2, 1974, 6–7 (emphasis added).

19. Nimu wenti fucha zu, Fujian #2, 1974, 12.

20. Nimu wenti fucha zu, Fujian #2, 1974, 12.

21. Nimu wenti fucha zu, Fujian #2, 1974, 27.

22. The term *commune* here refers to communes in the sense of the Paris Commune of 1871, that is, as a local revolutionary council. At least one of the heads of Gyenlo in Lhasa (Tao Changsong) had been very influenced by the history of the Paris Commune, which was widely known in Gyenlo leadership circles.

23. Nimu wenti fucha zu, Fujian #2, 1974, 28.

24. Nimu wenti fucha zu 1974, 5–6.

25. Nimu wenti fucha zu, Fujian #2, 1974, 7.

26. Nimu wenti fucha zu 1974, 6 (emphasis added).

27. This is one of the only indications in our data that Gyenlo General Headquarters in Lhasa knew what was going on in Nyemo.

28. Zhu nimu mao zedong sixiang xuanchuan dui bianyin 1971, 7.

29. Interview, 2002, OR.0346.01, Nyemo, Tibet Autonomous Region, China. Anger over the Jokhang killings also played a role in the disturbances in Biru and Bembar counties.

30. Interview, 2002, OR.0367.01, Nyemo, Tibet Autonomous Region, China.

31. Interview, 2002, OR.0346.01, Nyemo, Tibet Autonomous Region, China.

32. Interview, 2002, OR.0289.01, Nyemo, Tibet Autonomous Region, China.

33. Interview, 2002, OR.0374.01, Nyemo, Tibet Autonomous Region, China.

34. Interview, 2007, OR.0673.01, Nyemo, Tibet Autonomous Region, China.

35. Interview, 2000, OR.0027.02, Nyemo, Tibet Autonomous Region, China.

36. Interview, 2002, OR.0346.01, Nyemo, Tibet Autonomous Region, China.

37. Interview, 2002, OR.0029.01, Nyemo, Tibet Autonomous Region, China.

38. Nimu wenti fucha zu, Fujian #3, 1974, 5.

39. Nimu wenti fucha zu, Fujian #3, 1974, 5.

40. *Ashang* was an informal term of friendship frequently used in regard to a PLA soldier, that is, *ashang jingdrü mami* ("uncle, PLA soldier").

41. This seems to be referring to the 27 November attacks, not the coming mutilations and murders that began at the end of May 1969.

42. Nimu wenti fucha zu, Fujian #3, 1974, 6–7. The notes were part of the document.

43. tib. *digchen nyelwei ma drong, maotrushi phüsong, maotrushi ma drong, lhasin degye püsong.*

44. Interview, 2003, OR.0308.01, Nyemo, Tibet Autonomous Region, China.

45. Potentially important sources of her thinking, her postarrest interrogation transcripts, were not available. However, we interviewed someone who had read the Chinese translation of these, and he reported that they were not laid out in a question-answer format and were very hard to understand. They read, he said, more like a long dream monologue than a focused explication of what had transpired. They talked a lot about religion, visions, and gods and how she had been shocked by the attacks against religion and monasticism at the time of the Democratic Reforms. She repeatedly said that she did not understand why these institutions had to be destroyed and so forth. She also talked about things she had seen, such as a bird landing, which she took as a sign from the Dalai Lama in India, and clouds in which she saw the face of the Dalai Lama. However, there was *no* mention at all of seeking independence for Tibet or driving the Chinese out of Tibet or, for that matter, of Gyenlo or Gyenlo's Army of the Gods (interview, 2003, anonymous, Lhasa, Tibet Autonomous Region).

46. Nimu wenti fucha zu, Fujian #3, 1974, 5.

4. DESTROYING THE DEMONS AND GHOSTS

1. Correct Tibetan spelling: *phyi sgra bzhag nas nang sgra stor.* Interview, 2002, OR.0307.01, Nyemo, Tibet Autonomous Region, China.

2. Correct Tibetan spelling: *phyi char pa'i char thag byas gyang, nang thig pa'i thig thag ma byas.*

3. This is mentioned in Diemberger 2005, 151. Goldstein also recalls that when Surkhang Sawangchemmo, one of the Kashag ministers in the traditional government, was living with him in Seattle, fake mediums and tantric practitioners who were preying on the naïveté of simple villagers in the old society were discussed on several occasions during casual conversations after dinner. Surkhang referred to the kinds of government tests mentioned in Diemberger's article as well as several of his own. One particularly amusing "test" was given to a kind of tantric shamanic practitioner called a "sucker" (tib. *jib rgyabnyen*). These practitioners claimed they were able to suck the illness out of sick people through a rope attached to the patient, visually demonstrating the success of their "operation" by spitting a bloody mass out of their mouth at the end of the ritual. Surkhang did not believe such claims so once invited a practitioner to his house and placed one end of the rope not on the patient but on a wooden banister that was out of sight. He then gave the other end of the rope to the tantric practitioner, who went through the motions of his routine, sucking and sucking on the rope until finally he succeeded in curing the "patient"

by spitting out the bloody diseased mass that was causing its illness. The banister recovered!

4. Another version states that he had killed a lama in the 1959 uprising and had gone to the deity to confess his act and give the deity some of the possessions he had taken from the lama. Possibly both versions are correct.

5. Interview, 2000, OR.0027.02, Nyemo, Tibet Autonomous Region, China.

6. Nimu wenti fucha zu, Fujian #4, 1974, 1.

7. Nimu wenti fucha zu, Fujian #4, 1974, 1.

8. Nimu wenti fucha zu, Fujian #4, 1974, 1. That is one of Mao's famous slogans.

9. Interview, 2002, OR.0350.01, Nyemo, Tibet Autonomous Region, China.

10. Interview, 2002, OR.0060.01, Nyemo, Tibet Autonomous Region, China.

11. Interview, 2002, OR.0351.01, Nyemo, Tibet Autonomous Region, China.

12. Interview, 2000, OR.0028.01, Nyemo, Tibet Autonomous Region, China.

13. Interview, 2002, OR.0384.02, Nyemo, Tibet Autonomous Region, China.

14. Interview, 2002, OR.0335.01, Nyemo, Tibet Autonomous Region, China.

15. Interview, 2002, OR.0292.01, Nyemo, Tibet Autonomous Region, China.

16. Interview, 2002, OR.0304.01, Nyemo, Tibet Autonomous Region, China.

17. Interview, 2002, OR.0289.01, Nyemo, Tibet Autonomous Region, China.

18. Interview, 2002, OR.0316.01, Nyemo, Tibet Autonomous Region, China.

19. Interview, 2002, OR.0305.01, Nyemo, Tibet Autonomous Region, China.

20. Nimu wenti fucha zu, Fujian #4, 1974, 6.

21. Nimu wenti fucha zu Fujian #4, 1974, 7.

22. Nimu wenti fucha zu, Fujian #4, 1974, 7–8.

23. Nimu wenti fucha zu, Fujian #4, 1974, 8.

24. Although the nun did not commit any of the killings or amputations herself, she clearly ordered them done. For a somewhat different example of mass killings during the Cultural Revolution in inland China, see Yang 2006.

25. Nimu wenti fucha zu, Fujian #4, 1974, 3.

5. THE ATTACKS ON BAGOR DISTRICT AND NYEMO COUNTY

1. Interview, 2002, OR.0025.01, Nyemo, Tibet Autonomous Region, China.

2. Interview, 2007, OR.0673.01, Nyemo, Tibet Autonomous Region, China.

3. Interview, 2002, OR.0060.01, Nyemo, Tibet Autonomous Region, China; and interview, 2007, OR.0673.01, Nyemo, Tibet Autonomous Region, China.

4. Interview, 2002, OR.0346.01, Nyemo, Tibet Autonomous Region, China.

5. Nimu wenti fucha zu 1974, 8.

6. Nimu wenti fucha zu, Fujian #5, 1974, 3.

7. Nimu wenti fucha zu, Fujian #5, 1974, 13.

8. Interview, 2002, OR.0353.01, Nyemo, Tibet Autonomous Region, China.

9. Interview, 2002, OR.0300.01, Nyemo, Tibet Autonomous Region, China.

10. Nimu wenti fucha zu, Fujian #5, 1974, 5.

11. Nimu wenti fucha zu, 1974, 9. The nun never left Phusum so did not lead these forces in person.

12. Interview, 2002, OR.310.01, Nyemo, Tibet Autonomous Region, China. This was thought to be part of the Gesar costume.

13. A Nyamdre activist said that he had heard they were carrying a Tibetan flag, but this seems unlikely, since there was no Tibetan government (national) flag in the old society. For example, no flags were hoisted on government buildings and flown on holidays and so forth. The only Western-style flag in Tibet before 1959 was the flag of the Tibetan army. Private individuals, however, did not own or use this flag, nor did county headquarters in the old society, so it is hard to see how anyone in Nyemo would have had one. A Voice of America Tibet service interview with a villager from Nyemo who later fled to India also mentioned a flag, but this individual said that since no one knew what the national flag of Tibet looked like, they had just made a flag with two crossed swords in imitation of the one carried by the Chushigandru fighters in 1959 (cited in Wei Se's blog on tibetcul.net/2005). However, we think that neither kind of flag is likely, since the PLA never found any evidence of such a flag, despite its lengthy and intense interrogations of the participants. On the other hand, given the supercharged atmosphere and Gesar hysteria, nothing can be absolutely ruled out.

14. Interview, 2000, OR.0053.01, Nyemo, Tibet Autonomous Region, China.

15. Nimu wenti fucha zu 1974, 10; Nimu wenti fucha zu, Fujian #5, 1974, 18.

16. Interview, 2002, OR.0380.01, Nyemo, Tibet Autonomous Region, China.

17. Interview, 2002, OR.0304.01, Nyemo, Tibet Autonomous Region, China.

18. Interview, 2002, OR.312.01, Nyemo, Tibet Autonomous Region, China.

19. Nimu wenti fucha zu, Fujian #5, 1974, 19.

20. At this time the county government compound was completely empty because the party committee officials had fled from there to Lhasa after the November 1968 attacks (interview, 2007, OR.0673.01, Tibet Autonomous Region, China).

21. Interview, 2007, OR.0673.01, Tibet Autonomous Region, China.

22. Interview, 2007, OR.0673.01, Tibet Autonomous Region, China.

23. Interview, 2000, OR.0033.01, Nyemo, Tibet Autonomous Region, China. The order of his comments has been slightly rearranged to eliminate repetition.

24. Another attacker, however, said, "Gyenlo surrounded the Military Squadron and took oil from the store and was planning to set fire to the Military Squadron of the Public Security Bureau. I had to go with them." We could not verify this version (interview, 2003, OR.0322, Nyemo, Tibet Autonomous Region, China).

25. Interview, 2002, OR.0294.01, Nyemo, Tibet Autonomous Region, China.

26. Interview, 2002, OR.0313.01, Nyemo, Tibet Autonomous Region, China.

27. Interview, 2002, OR.0374.01, Nyemo, Tibet Autonomous Region, China.

28. It should be noted, however, that one activist follower of the nun said when he fled that he had hoped the PLA would immediately follow them, because then he and the other villagers would be on higher ground and could have attacked the soldiers out in the open and stolen some of their weapons. He said, "At that time, nobody was worried about being killed, and everybody hoped to get some weapons" (interview, OR.0673.01, Tibet Autonomous Region, China).

6. THE CAPTURE OF THE NUN

1. Interview, 2007, OR.0060.04, Nyemo, Tibet Autonomous Region, China.

2. Interview, 2007, OR.0673.02, Nyemo, Tibet Autonomous Region, China.

3. Interview, 2007, OR.0673.02, Nyemo, Tibet Autonomous Region, China.

4. Interview, 2002, OR.0294.01, Nyemo, Tibet Autonomous Region, China. The nun/Ani Gongmey Gyemo had previously prophesied that she would send a crow to drive away the PLA.

5. Interview, 2002, OR.0304.01, Nyemo, Tibet Autonomous Region, China.

6. Interview, 2002, OR.0313.01, Nyemo, Tibet Autonomous Region, China.

7. Interview, 2002, OR.0304.01, Nyemo, Tibet Autonomous Region, China.

8. Interview, 2002, OR.0350.01, Nyemo, Tibet Autonomous Region, China.

9. This fits with the theory of cognitive dissonance, which has shown that several disconfirming incidents are often required for believers to lose their faith in charismatic leaders. See Festinger 1956 for a detailed discussion of cognitive dissonance.

10. Nimu wenti fucha zu, Fujian #6, 1974, 3–4.

11. Interview, 2002, OR.0309.01, Nyemo, Tibet Autonomous Region, China.

12. Nimu wenti fucha zu, Fujian #6, 1974, 1.

13. Nimu wenti fucha zu, Fujian #6, 1974, 1–2.

14. Nimu wenti fucha zu, Fujian #6, 1974, 2–3.

15. Nimu wenti fucha zu, Fujian #6, 1974, 2–3.

16. These damaging letters were later seized and sent to the Armed Force Department in Nyemo, but a Chinese report claims that the army political commissar, Zhang Diantong, destroyed them, saying that they were not powerful enough to be used as evidence (Nimu wenti fucha zu 1974, 11).

17. The troops appeared to leave, but actually they circled behind the mountain in order to position themselves to attack downward from above the monastery, catching the Tibetans in a pincerlike cross fire.

18. Interview, 2002, OR.0060.01, Nyemo, Tibet Autonomous Region, China.

19. Interview, 2007, OR.0673.01, Nyemo, Tibet Autonomous Region, China.

20. Interview, 2002, OR.0316.01, Nyemo, Tibet Autonomous Region, China.

21. Interview, 2002, OR.0060.01, Nyemo, Tibet Autonomous Region, China.

22. Interview, 2007, OR.0060.04, Nyemo, Tibet Autonomous Region, China.

23. Several pistols were said to have been captured in the attack on the county.

24. Interview, 2002, OR.0145.01, Nyemo, Tibet Autonomous Region, China.

25. Interview, 2002, OR.0328.01, Nyemo, Tibet Autonomous Region, China.

26. Interview, 2002, OR.0346.01, Nyemo, Tibet Autonomous Region, China.

27. Interview, 2002, OR.0333.01, Nyemo, Tibet Autonomous Region, China.

28. Interview, 2003, OR.0310.01, Nyemo, Tibet Autonomous Region, China.

29. Interview, 2002, OR.0294.01, Nyemo, Tibet Autonomous Region, China.

30. Interview, 2000, OR.0029.01, Nyemo, Tibet Autonomous Region, China.

31. Interview, 2002, OR.0316.01, Nyemo, Tibet Autonomous Region, China.

32. Interview, 2002, OR.0367.01, Nyemo, Tibet Autonomous Region, China.

33. Zhonggong lasa shiwei wenjian, guanyu jiang yuanding 1987, 4.

34. Nimu wenti fucha zu 1974, 2; and Zhonggong nimu xian weiyuanhui 1987, 4.

35. Zhonggong nimu xian weiyuanhui 1987, 5.

36. Interview, 2001, H.0109.01, Lhasa, Tibet Autonomous Region, China.

37. Interestingly, some parents in Lhasa used the name of the nun to scare

their children. For example, one Lhasan recalled that his mother frequently tried to scare him by saying, "If you are not obedient, Nyemo ani will get you."

38. Interview, 2002, OR.0322.01, Nyemo, Tibet Autonomous Region, China.

39. Nimu wenti fucha zu, Fujian #8, 1974, 16.

40. Ren Rong was officially appointed first secretary in 1971.

41. Interview, 2001, H.0109.01, Lhasa, Tibet Autonomous Region, China. One U.S. dollar in 2007 was worth 7.8 yuan.

42. Interview, 2001, H.0109.02, Lhasa, Tibet Autonomous Region, China.

43. Nimu wenti fucha zu, Fujian #8, 1974, 15.

44. Nimu wenti fucha zu, Fujian #8, 1974, 15.

45. Nimu wenti fucha zu, Fujian #8, 1974, 15.

46. Zhonggong nimu xian weiyuanhui 1987, 6.

47. Nimu wenti fucha zu, Fujian #8, 1974, 19.

48. Zhonggong nimu xian weiyuanhui 1987, 5.

49. Nimu wenti fucha zu, Fujian #8, 1974, 18; and Zhonggong nimu xian weiyuanhui 1987, 9.

50. Nimu wenti fucha zu, Fujian #7, 1974, 19.

51. Interview, 2002, OR.0289.01, Nyemo, Tibet Autonomous Region, China.

7. CONCLUSIONS

1. Nimu wenti fucha zu, Fujian #3, 1974, 7.

2. Nimu wenti fucha zu, Fujian #2, 1974, 7.

8. EPILOGUE

1. Zhonggong xizang zizhiqu dangshi ziliao zhengji weiyuanhui bian 1995, entry for 9 March 1969, 187.

2. Zhonggong xizang zizhiqu dangshi ziliao zhengji weiyuanhui bian 1995, entry for 20 May 1969, 187.

3. Zhonggong xizang zizhiqu dangshi ziliao zhengji weiyuanhui bian 1995, entry for 13 June 1969, 188. It is not clear what the reference to 21 June refers to.

4. Zhonggong xizang zizhiqu dangshi ziliao zhengji weiyuanhui bian 1995, entry for 26 July 1969, 188.

5. Zhonggong xizang zizhiqu dangshi ziliao zhengji weiyuanhui bian 1995, entry for 26 July 1969, 188.

6. In 1988, the system of having a district administrative level (ch. *qu*) between *xiang* and counties was eliminated in favor of creating larger *xiang*, so Phala *xiang* ceased to exist, its territory and nomads being divided between two adjacent enlarged *xiang*: Nyingo and Khunglung. Each of these parts, however, retained a separate administrative sub-*xiang* identity.

7. Phala is separated from Tsatsey by Parong la, a 17,500-foot mountain pass to the north of Tsatsey. It is roughly a one- to two-day trip on horseback.

8. Tenzin, fieldnotes, 1988.

9. Amchila, fieldnotes, 1988.

10. Tsewang, fieldnotes, 1987.

11. Amchila, fieldnotes, 1988.

12. Interview, 2001, OR.0145.01, Nyemo, Tibet Autonomous Region, China.

13. Gyenlo Headquarters' "First Headquarters" was centered in the northern suburbs of Lhasa and included the Machine Repair Factory. Their Second Headquarters was in the western suburbs and included the Road Maintenance and the Motor Vehicles Teams. The delimitation of the Third Headquarters is not clear, but it included Nyingtri (tib. *Kongpo*). The fourth was for local residents in Lhasa. The fifth, sixth, and seventh are not known, but the Eighth Headquarters included Golmud, in Qinghai.

14. Interview, 2001, H.0109.01, Lhasa, Tibet Autonomous Region, China (emphasis added).

15. Zhu nimu mao zedong sixiang xuanchuan dui bianyin 1971, 7.

POSTSCRIPT

1. See Goldstein 2007 for a detailed examination of the history of the period 1951–55.

2. During the early 1950s, one Tibetan faction, led by Fan Ming, had advocated this approach but was unsuccessful because Mao insisted on pursuing his gradualist strategy (see Goldstein 2007).

3. Interview, H.0056.02, Phündra, 1993, Beijing, People's Republic of China. It is interesting to contrast Mao's behavior in inland China and in Tibet with regard to communes. In inland China in 1955, Mao launched a major campaign called the Socialist Transformation campaign, which pushed party leaders all over China to collectivize the countryside rapidly.

4. Ironically, the 1959 decision of Mao to allow private farming in Tibet created the conditions in the Tibetan countryside that made it possible in 1968 for Gyenlo to mobilize the farmers to its side. If communes had been started immediately, there would have been no need to collect sales grain taxes from individual households, and there would have been no anxiety over the impending creation of communes.

APPENDIX 2

1. The massacre came to light only in November, because the Regional Party Committee kept a lid on it.

2. Xizang renmin guangbo diantai lianhe zuozhanbu 1967 (emphasis added).

APPENDIX 3

1. Liaoyuan zhandou dui and Beihang hongqi fuzang chuanlian fen dui 1967 (emphasis added).

Selected Glossary of Correct Tibetan Spellings

ane	a ne
Angang	ang sgang
ani (nene)	a ne (ne ne)
ani chösung	a ne chos srung
Ani Gongmey Gyemo	a ne gong ma'i rgyal mo
ashang	a zhang
ashang jingdrü mami	a zhang bcing sgrol dmag mi
badü	dpa' brtul
Bagor	brag sgo
Bala	dpa' lha
Basang	pa sangs
beja gegen	dpe cha dge rgan
Bejang	spel byang
Bembar	dpal 'bar
Biru	'bri ru
bo serbo	spo bo ser po
Botön Rimpoche	bus ton rin po che
chabdrü	byabs khrus
chala	bya glag

cham	'cham
Chamba	byams pa
Chamba Tenzin	byams pa bstan 'dzin
Chamdo	chab mdo
chandzö	phyag mdzod
chang	chang
chawang	phyag dbang
Chime Gyaltshan	'chi med rgyal mtshan
Chöling	chos gling
Chompelchos	'phel
chönje	chos mjal
chösung	chos srung
Chöying	(spelling unknown)
chuba	phyu pa
chu nyog dzab nyog	chu rnyog rdzab rnyog
Chushigandru	chu bzhi sgang drug
Chushul	chu shur
dag dag	tag tag
Damshung	'dam gzhung
Danden Dorje	(spelling unknown) rdo rje
da yagpo chung	da yag po byung
deja	bde 'jags
deja trurin	bde 'jags zhu ren
Demön	sde smon
denba	bstan pa
Dengchen	steng chen
Denma	ldan ma
digchen nyelwei ma drong,	sdig chen dmyal bas ma 'drongs
maotrushi phüsong,	ma'o kru shis phud song
maotrushi ma drong,	ma'o kru shis ma 'drongs
lhasin degye püsong	lha srin sde brgyad phud song
dongdre	gdong 'dre
donglen	gdong len
Dongpa khangsar	gdong pa khang gsar

dongre dong	gtong res gtong
Dorje Jöpa	rdo rje spyod pa
dotse	rdo tshad
dre	bre
dregpa	dregpa
Drigung Kagyu	'bri gung bka' rgyud
drolma lhagang	sgrol ma lha khang
Drongme	'brog smad
Düjung	'dus byung
dümo	bdud mo
dzabdong	rdzab dong
Dzachu	rdza chu
dzo	mdzo
dzong	rdzong
Gachen	bka' chen
Gampa la	gam pa la
Ganden	dga' ldan
Gargang	(spelling unknown)
Garkhang	bkar khang
garma	skar ma
gegen	dge rgan
Getob	dge stobs
Gombo	mgon po
Gongmai Gyemo	gong ma'i rgyal mo
go thom	mgo 'thoms
Gyagpa	rgyags pa
gyama	rgya ma
Gyamo Ngulchu	rgya mo rngul chu
gyang gyab	gyang rgyag
Gyangön	(spelling unknown)
Gyaram	rgya ram
Gyatso	rgya mtsho
gyeje shungdru	rgyal gces gzhung 'bru
Gyenlo	gyen log

gyenlo jigyab bu	gyen log spyi khyab pu'u
gyenlo lhamag	gyen log lha dmag
gyeshey gyeleng	rgyas bshad rgyas gleng
hako diko meba	ha go 'di go med pa
höntor	hon 'thor
Jagra Bembar	lcags ra dpal 'bar
Jambeyang	'jam dpal dbyang
Jangra	lcang ra
Jangdru Yülha (Thogyur)	'jang phrug g.yu lha (thog gyur)
jib rgyabnyen	'jib rgyag mkhan
Ji lhamo	(spelling unknown) lha mo
Jowo	jo bo
Jowo Rimpoche	jo bo rin po che
Kagyüpa	bka' rgyud pa
Karma Wangdü	karma dbang 'dus
Kejö la	skal chos lags
Kham	khams
Khamba	khams pa
Khangsar	khang gsar
khase shüna guying	kha gsal zhu na gu yangs
tregsung chena tragnön	mkhregs srung byas na drag snon
khata	kha btags
khe	khal
Khunglung	khung lung
khunglung dilung mepa	khungs lung 'di lung med pa
khyamra	'khyam ra
Khyungbo dengchen	khyung po steng chen
Kongpo	kong po
kungre	kung hre
labrang	bla brang
Lagyab Lhojang	la rgyab lho byang
Lay	sle
leydön ruga	las don ru khag
lha	lha

lhaba	lha pa
Lhagong Wangtob	lha mgon dbang stobs
Lhajung	lha chung
Lhalu	lha klu
lha phenyen	lha phebs mkhan
lhapsö	lha gsol
lhasin degye	lha srin sde brgyad
Lhatse	lha rtse
Lhawang	lha dbang
Lhawang Yeshe	lha dbang ye shes
lhayü	lha yul
Lhundrup	lhun grub
Lhundrup Wanggye	lhun grub dbang rgyal
lobjong dzindra	slob sbyong 'dzin grwa
logjöba	log spyod pa
lungden	lung bstan
magdön gagdom uyön lhengang	dmag don bkag 'doms u yon lhan khang
maggur mangje	dmag bkur dmangs gces
magpa	mag pa
mangdzo dagül	mang tshogs lta skul
mangdzö jügyur	dmangs gtso'i bcos sgyur
marbo gyenlo shoga	dmar po gyen log shog kha
marbö yigja	dmar po'i yig cha
Margyang	mar rkyang
Medrogungar	mal gro gung dkar
mongde	rmongs dad
mönlam	smon lam
mönlam chemmo	smon lam chen mo
Nagtsang	nag tshang
Namgang	gnam gang
Namling	rnam gling
namshe	rnam shes
Nanag	na nag
Nanga Wangchug	nam mkha' dbang phyug

nangsa	nang sa
Nangwog	nang 'og
Nechung	gnas chung
Ngabö	nga phod
ngadag	mnga' bdag
ngagba	sngags pa
Ngamring	ngam ring
ngatsab	mnga' tshab
Ngawang Tsering	ngag dbang tshe ring
ngeydzö gyurgö	ngal rtsol sgyur bkod
ngogö sum dang chayan nyi	ngo rgol gsum dang cha yangs gnyis
ngolen yigja	ngo len yig cha
ngologba	ngo log pa
ngönshe	mngon shes
ngöthog dentsö	dngos thog bden 'tshol
Ngudrub	dngos grub
Ngulchu	rngul chu
ngüsang	dngul srang
Norbu Samdrub	nor bu bsam grub
Nyamdre (Tshogpa)	mnyam 'brel (tshogs pa)
Nyemo	snye mo
Nyima Tsering	nyi ma tshe ring
nying	snying
Nyingo	nyi 'go
nyönma	myon ma
Pagbu	phag phu
Parong la	bar rong la
Pehar Gyebo	pe har rgyal po
Phala	bar la
Phongkhang	bong khang
Phug	phug
Phugsa	phug gsar
Phugsu	phug zur
Phujung	bu chung

Phüntso	phun tshogs
Phüntsoling Gyatso	phun tshogs gling rgya mtsho
Phurba	phur bu
Phusum	phu gsum
Rangjung	rang byung
Rangkyim Rangda	rang khyim rang bdag
rimpoche	rin po che
Rimpung	rin spungs
Rinzin	rig 'dzin
Risur Rimpoche	ri zur rin po che
Ritsho	ri mtsho
rogre	rogs re
rogre tsogjung	rogs re tshogs chung
Samling	bsam gling
samlö dütren bande	bsam blo rdul phran 'bar mdel
Sangang	zangs sgang
Sangmu	zangs mu
Sangri	zangs ri
sarje gyenlo	gsar rje gyen log
sarje uyön lhengang	gsar rje u yon lhan khang
Se	sras
semjen	sems can
sem mathangwa	sems ma thang ba
sen	gzan
senril	zan ril
sha	shag
shag	shag
shagtsang	shag tshang
Shalu	zhwa lu
shamo (yaw)	zhwa mo (g.yogs)
Sharam	shar ram
Shechen Riwo Pangyong	shed chen ri bo pang 'gyongs
Shenba	shan pa
Shentsa	shan rtsa

sheyra	bshas ra
Shey Tongmönling	bzhad mthong smon gling
Shibum	shi 'bum
shigla gyabgyang gongwei chilo	shig la brgyab kyang gong ba'i phyi logs
shigmen	shig sman
shigö tragsung	zhi rgol drag srung
Shilok	shi log
Shilok Tsering	shi log tshe ring
shingdring	zhing 'bring
shingdring gongma	zhing 'bring gong ma
shingdrog gyenlo silingbu	zhing 'brog gyen log si ling pu
Shingra	shing ra
shinje	gshin rje
Shu	gzhu
Shuben	(spelling unknown)
Shugbula	shog bu la
Sogang	gso khang
Sonam	bsod nams
sönkhe	son khal
sungdü	srung mdud
Taktse	stag rtse
Tashi Rabden	bkris rab brtan
Tashi Wangchuk	bkris dbang phyug
tawa	lta ba
tensungmag	bstan srung dmag
Tharong	dar rong
Thaser	thar ser
Theshin shegba	de bzhin gshegs pa
Thondrub Ling	don grub gling
thragbö thabdzö	drag po'i 'thab rtsod
thrödru	gros 'bru
thugdrüü	thugs 'phrul
Tobgye	stobs rgyas
Tobjen	stobs chen

Tobjung	stobs chung
Tölung	stod lung
Tongbeb gya	thog 'bab rgyag
tragbö thabdzö	drag po'i 'thab rtsod
tranga garpo	tram ka dkar po
treba	khral pa
tregang	khral rkang
trenyog	bran g.yog
trerim	gral rim
Trinley	'phrin las
Trinley Chödrön	'phrin las chos sgron
Trinley Drolkar	'phrin las sgrol dkar
trongtso	grong tsho
trugba shor	'khrugs pa shor
tsago che	rtsa sgo phye
tsamba	rtsam pa
Tsatsey	rtswa rtse
Tseden Benjor	tshe brtan dpal 'byor
Tseden Wangchuk	tshe brtan dbang phyug
Tsering Chösang	tshe ring chos bzang
tshakang	tsha khang
Tshamla	mtshams lags
Tshampa Yangphel	mtshams pa yar 'phel
tsheyog	tshe g.yog
Tshomey	tsho smad
tshongdru	tshong 'bru
Tsiju	tshe 'gyur
tsöba chembo	rtsod pa chen po
tsogjen umdze	tshogs chen dbu mdzad
Tsuglagang	gtsug lha khang
Tsurpu	mtshur phu
Tülung (Dechen)	stod lung (bde chen)
Uchung	dbu chung
üpung	dbul phongs

uyön	u yon
uyön lhangang	u yon lhan khang
Wangchuk Rabden	dbang phyug rab brtan
Wangtob	dbang stobs
Wujinlaqing	(spelling unknown)
Yangbachen	yangs pa can
Yishi norbu	yid bzhin nor bu
Yönden	yon tan
Yulung	g.yu lung
Zingzing	(spelling unknown)

References

Avedon, John. 1984. *In Exile from the Land of the Snows: The Dalai Lama and Tibet since the Chinese Occupation*. New York: Alfred A. Knopf.

Barnett, Robert. 2005. "Women and Politics in Contemporary Tibet." In Janet Gyatso and Hanna Havnevik, eds., *Women in Tibet*, 285–366. New York: Columbia University Press.

Chao Feng, ed. 1993. *Wenhua da geming cidian* (Chronology of the Cultural Revolution). Hong Kong: Hong Kong Publishing House.

Chen, Anita, ed. 1988. *Liu Guokai: A Brief Analysis of the Cultural Revolution*. Canberra: Australian National University Press.

Dalai Lama. 1991. *Freedom in Exile: The Autobiography of the Dalai Lama*. New York: HarperCollins Publications.

Dangdai zhongguo congshu bianjibu (Contemporary China's Editorial Department), ed. 1991. *Dangdai zhongguo de Xizang* (Contemporary China's Tibet), vol. 1. Beijing: Contemporary China Publishing House.

Dauber, Jean. 1974. *A History of the Chinese Cultural Revolution*. New York: Vintage Books.

David-Neel, Alexandra, and Lama Yongden. 1959. *The Superhuman Life of Gesar of Ling*. London: Rider and Co.

Diemberger, Hildegard. 2005. "Female Oracles in Modern Tibet." In Janet Gyatso and Hanna Havnevik, eds., *Women in Tibet*, 113–68. New York: Columbia University Press.

Dittmer, Lowell. 1998. *Liu Shaoqi and the Chinese Cultural Revolution*. Armonk, NY: M. E. Sharpe.

Esherick, Joseph W., Paul G. Pickowicz, and Andrew G. Walder, eds. 2006. *The Chinese Cultural Revolution as History*. Stanford, CA: Stanford University Press.

Falkenheim, Victor. 1969. "The Cultural Revolution in Kwangsi, Yunnan and Fukien." *Asian Survey* 9, no. 8: 580–97.

Festinger, Leon. 1956. *When Prophecy Fails.* New York: HarperCollins.

"The First Written 'Self-Examination' Yin Fa-t'ang Delivers to Headquarters of Metropolitan Red Guards Bound for Tibet and Rebel Headquarters." 1967. *Hongse zaofan bao* (Red Rebel newspaper), 9 September. Translated in *Survey of China Mainland Press Supplement*, no. 219, 29 February 1968, 26.

French, Patrick. 2003. *Tibet, Tibet: A Personal History of a Lost Land.* New York: Alfred A. Knopf.

Goldstein, Melvyn C. 1971a. "Serfdom and Mobility: An Examination of the Institution of 'Human Lease' in Traditional Tibetan Society." *Journal of Asian Studies* 30, no. 3: 521–34.

———. 1971b. "Taxation and the Structure of a Tibetan Village." *Central Asiatic Journal* 15, no. 1: 1–27.

———. 1986. "Reexamining Choice, Dependency and Command in the Tibetan Social System: 'Tax Appendages' and Other Landless Serfs." *Tibet Journal* 9, no. 4: 79–113.

———. 1987. "On the Nature of the Tibetan Peasantry: A Rejoinder." *Tibet Journal* 8: 61–65.

———. 1989a. "Freedom, Servitude and the 'Servant-Serf' Nyima: A Re-rejoinder to Miller." *Tibet Journal* 16, no. 2: 56–60.

———. 1989b. *A History of Modern Tibet, 1913–1951: The Demise of the Lamaist State.* Berkeley: University of California Press.

———. 1997. *The Snow Lion and the Dragon: China, Tibet and the Dalai Lama.* Berkeley: University of California Press.

———. 2003. "On Modern Tibetan History: Moving beyond Stereotypes." In Alex McKay, ed., *Tibet and Her Neighbours: A History*, 219–26. London: Edition Hans-joerg Mayer.

———. 2007. *A History of Modern Tibet*, vol. 2: *The Calm before the Storm, 1951–1955.* Berkeley: University of California Press.

———. In press. "Tibetan Buddhism and Mass Monasticism." In Adeline Herrou and Gisèle Krauskopff, eds., *Des moines et des moniales dans le monde: La vie monastique dans le miroir de la parenté.* Presses Universitaires de Toulouse le Mirail.

Goldstein, Melvyn C., and Cynthia M. Beall. 1990. *Nomads of Western Tibet: The Survival of a Way of Life.* Berkeley: University of California Press.

Grunfeld, A. Tom. 1996. *The Making of Modern Tibet.* Armonk, NY: M. E. Sharpe.

"Guanyu liji tingzhi diqu wudou de xieyi" (Agreement on immediately stopping the violence in Tibet). 1968. In "Zhongyang, zhongyang wenge shouzhang jiejian xizang ban bufen xueyuan shi de zhongyao zhishi (jilu gao)" (Leaders of the Central Committee and the Central Cultural Revolution Group meet students from Tibet [recorded draft]). Ms., no author, 26 August, 14, in Goldstein's possession.

"Guanyu liuqi shijian de qingkuang baogao." 1968. (Report on the 7 June [1968] incident). Draft ms., no author, in Goldstein's possession.

"Guanyu qingshi zhichi zuopai qunzhong zuzhi 'dalianzhi' de baogao (taolun gao)." 1967. (Report on asking instructions to support the masses' organization of the leftist faction "Great Alliance" [draft for discussion]). Ms., no author, 14–15 May, in Goldstein's possession.

Gyatso, Janet, and Hanna Havnevik, eds. 2005. *Women in Tibet*. New York: Columbia University Press.

Havnevik, Hanna. 1994. "The Role of Nuns in Contemporary Tibet." In Robbie Barnett and S. Akiner, eds., *Resistance and Reform in Tibet*, 259–66. London: Hurst.

Hopkirk, Peter. 1982. *Trespasser on the Roof of the World: The Race for Lhasa*. London: John Murray.

International Committee of Lawyers for Tibet. 1995. "Violence against Tibetan Women." Tibet Justice Center Report, 10 March. www.tibetjustice.org/reports/violence/html.

Lasa geming zaofan zongbu, qu hu bao lianhe zuozhanbu, xizang youdian xuexiao xin yu zhandou dui (the Lhasa Revolutionary Rebel Headquarters, The "Driving Out Tigers" United Operational Headquarters, The "New Universe" Combat Team of the Tibet Post and Telecommunications School). 1967. "Qu dangwei gongkai duikang zhongyang zhishi" (The Regional Party Committee openly opposed instructions from the Central Committee). Ms. poster, 23 January, in Goldstein's possession.

Lhasa Revolutionary Rebel Headquarters, Lhasa Revolutionary Rebel Commune, Tibet Red Guard Revolutionary Headquarters, Tibetan Nationalities Institute Red Rebel Regiment. 1967. "Chronology of the Great Proletarian Revolution in the Tibet Region." *Hongse zaofan bao* (Red Rebel newspaper), 6 August, 30. Translated in *Survey of China Mainland Press Supplement*, no. 216, 26 January 1968.

Liang Nai-min. 1968. *Tibet 1950–67*. Hong Kong: Union Research Institute.

Liaoyuan zhandou dui (Blazing Prairie Combat Regiment) and Beihang hongqi fuzang chuanlian fen dui (Branch of the Red Flag group of the Beijing Academy of Aviation who entered Tibet for liaison). 1967. "Yetan xizang ribao she 'duoguan douzheng de zhenxiang'" (Called "The Truth about the Struggle to Seize Power of the *Tibet Daily Newspaper* Office"). Ms., 13 January, in Goldstein's possession.

"Lingren shensi de wenti" (A problem worth pondering). 1967. Ms., no author, 13 February, in Goldstein's possession.

Miller, Beatrice. 1987. A Response to Goldstein's "Reexamining Choice, Dependency and Command in the Tibetan Social System." *Tibet Journal* 7, no. 2: 65–67.

———. 1988. "Last Rejoinder to Goldstein on Tibetan Social System." *Tibet Journal* 8, no. 3: 64–67.

Ngagpo, Jigme. 1988. "Behind the Unrest in Tibet." *China Spring Digest* (January–February): 22–32.

Nimu wenti fucha zu (Nyemo Investigation Team). 1974. "Guanyu 1969 nian nimu fangeming panluan wenti de fucha baogao (xiugai gao)" (Report on reexamination of the counterrevolutionary rebellion in Nyemo in 1969). Ms., in Goldstein's possession.

Nimu wenti fucha zu, Fujian #1 (Nyemo Investigation Team, Appendix #1). 1974. "Liyong liangshi wenti, gongji dang de liangyou zhenggou zhengce, wei fangeming panluan qile shandong zuoyong" (Using food to attack party policy and requisition purchases of grain and butter and to incite a counterrevolutionary rebellion). Ms., in Goldstein's possession.

Nimu wenti fucha zu, Fujian #2 (Nyemo Investigation Team, Appendix #2). 1974. "Liyong zongjiao mixin, kending nigu tiaoshen zuoyong chengli (zaofan shen-jun)" (Using religious superstition to affirm the sorcerer's dance in a trance and establish "Gyenlo's Army of the Gods"). Ms., in Goldstein's possession.

Nimu wenti fucha zu, Fujian #3 (Nyemo Investigation Team, Appendix #3). 1974. "Fandong wengao de paozhi he chulong" (The fabrication and appearance of a reactionary statement). Ms., in Goldstein's possession.

Nimu wenti fucha zu, Fujian #4 (Nyemo Investigation Team, Appendix #4). 1974. "Jie zhaokai jinian '6.7' dazhaosi shijian yizhou nian huiyi, shandong pan-luan" (Inciting rebellion in the name of holding the anniversary commem-oration meeting of the "7 June" Jokhang Temple incident). Ms., in Goldstein's possession.

Nimu wenti fucha zu, Fujian #5 (Nyemo Investigation Team, Appendix #5). 1974. "6.13 fangeming wuzhuang panluan)" (13 June armed counterrevolutionary rebellion). Ms., in Goldstein's possession.

Nimu wenti fucha zu, Fujian #6 (Nyemo Investigation Team, Appendix #6). 1974. "Li Jianhua, Huang Guojie, Xu Dean dengren xiang panfei mibao junqing, duikang pingpan" (Li Jianhua, Huang Guojie, Xu Dean and some other peo-ple secretly sent military information to the rebels to oppose the suppression of the rebellion). Ms., in Goldstein's possession.

Nimu wenti fucha zu, Fujian #7 (Nyemo Investigation Team, Appendix #7). 1974. "Zhanzai panfei lichang shang, gongji pingpan" (Taking the rebel bandit's position and attacking the suppression of the rebellion). Ms., in Goldstein's possession.

Nimu wenti fucha zu, Fujian #8 (Nyemo Investigation Team, Appendix #8). 1974. "Li Jianhua, Zhou Longquan deng shi yu ren jianchi cuowu lichang, chuan-lian fan'an" (More than ten people, including Li Jianhua and Zhou Longquan, hold on to the wrong standpoint and try to reverse the verdict). Ms., in Gold-stein's possession.

"An Open Letter to the Central Great Cultural Revolution Group." 1967. Lhasa leaflet, 6 January. Translated in *Survey of China Mainland Press Supplement* 223, 22 April 1968, 25.

Pema Dechen. 1995. *The Role of Tibetan Women in the Independence Struggle of Tibet*. Berkeley, CA: Tibetan Justice Center.

Rogler, Lloyd, and August B. Hollingshead. 1965. *Trapped: Families and Schiz-ophrenia*. New York: John Wiley and Sons.

Samuel, Geoffrey. 1992. "Gesar of Ling: the Origins and Meaning of the East Tibetan Epic." In S. Ihara and Z. Yamaguchi, eds., *Tibetan Studies: Proceed-ings of the 5th Seminar of the International Association for Tibetan Studies, Narita, 1989*, 711–22. Narita: Naritasan Shinshoji.

———. 1994. "Gesar of Ling: Shamanic Power and Popular Religion." In G. Samuel, H. Gregory, and E. Stutchbury, eds., *Tantra and Popular Religion in Tibet*, 53–78. Sata-Pitaka Series, 376. New Delhi: International Academy of Indian Culture and Aditya Prakashan.

Shakya, Tsering. 1999. *The Dragon in the Land of the Snows*. New York: Co-lumbia University Press.

———. 2002. "Blood in the Snows." *New Left Review* 15 (May–June): 39–60.

Smith, Warren. 1996. *Tibetan Nation: A History of Tibetan Nationalism and Sino-Tibetan Relations*. Boulder, CO: Westview Press.

Survey of China Mainland Press Supplement. 1966–68. Hong Kong: United States Consulate General.

Tibetan Women's Association. 1995. "Roof of the World: A Celebration of Culture, Peace and Protest." Bombay, India. www.tibet.ca/en/wtnarchive/1995/3/15-2_1.html.

Unger, Jonathan. 1984. "The Class System in Rural China: A Case Study." In J. Watson, ed., *Class and Social Stratification in Post-revolutionary China*, 121–41. Cambridge: Cambridge University Press.

———. 1998. Cultural Revolution Conflict in the Villages. *China Quarterly* 153: 82–106.

———. 2007. "The Cultural Revolution at the Grass Roots." *China Journal* 57: 109–37.

Wang Lixiong. 2002. "Reflections on Tibet." Translated by Liu Xiaohong and A. Tom Grunfeld. *New Left Review* 14 (March–April): 79–111.

Weiner, Benno. 2002. "When the Sky Fell to Earth: The Great Proletarian Cultural Revolution in the Tibet Autonomous Region, 1966–1971." MA thesis, Columbia University.

———. N.d. " 'Has the Party Committee Turned Putrid?' The Development and Composition of Cultural Revolution-Era Factionalism in the Tibet Autonomous Region." Unpublished ms.

Wei se (Öser). 2005. "Nyemo Incident." www.tibetcul.net/blog/blog.asp?name = oser.

——— 2006. *Sha jie: Sishi nian de jiyi jinqu jingtou xia de xizang wenge, di yici gongkai* (Forbidden Memory: Tibet during the Cultural Revolution). Taipei: Lotus Publishers.

"What I Saw on 10 February 1967 at 10:10 in the Morning." 1967. Lhasa handbill. Translated in *Survey of China Mainland Press Supplement*, no. 179, 26 April, 1967, 13.

Wylie, Turrell V. 1959. "A Standard System of Tibetan Transcription." *Journal of Asiatic Studies* 22: 261–67.

Xizang junqu dangwei (Tibet Military Headquarters Party Committee). 1967. "Guanyu lasa liangge geming qunzhong zuzhi de qingkuang he women de yijian" (On the situation of the two organizations of revolutionary masses in Lhasa and our opinions about it, a draft from late July 1967). Doc. 6265–69, 14 August, 7, in Goldstein's possession.

"Xizang junqu dangwei changwei guanyu zhizuo gongzuo zhong suo fan cuowu de jiantao baogao." 1968. (The written self-criticism on the mistakes made by the Standing Committee of the Party Committee of Tibet Military Region in the work of supporting the Left). Doc. 51, ms., 27 August, in Goldstein's possession.

Xizang renmin guangbo diantai lianhe zuozhanbu (Allied headquarters of the broadcast station in Tibet). 1967. "Yong hongqi zazhi shiwu qi shelun de jingshen zhao yi zhao qu dang wei mouxie zhuyao lingdaoren shi zenyang wangu de jianchi zichanjieji fandong luxian de" (Contrast the spirit of the editorial in the fifteenth issue of *Red Flag* with the behavior of some major leaders of the Regional Party Committee who stubbornly insist on following the reactionary bourgeois line). Leaflet publication of a speech at a meeting on 26 December, in Goldstein's possession.

Yang Su. 2006. "Mass Killings in the Cultural Revolution: A Study of Three Provinces." In Joseph W. Esherick et al., eds., *The Chinese Cultural Revolution as History*, 96–124. Stanford, CA: Stanford University Press.

Yang Tsang-hao. 1967. "The Reality of the Power Seizure in Tibet." *Chinese Communist Affairs* 4, no. 3 (June): 45–52.

Zhonggong lasa shiwei wenjian, guanyu jiang yuanding, no. 40 (Document 40 of the Lhasa Municipal Party Committee of the CCP, Distributed by the Municipal Party Committee). 1987. " 'Nimu xian wuzhang panluan' gaiding wei fangeming 'sharen shijian' qingshi" (About the request to change the previously named "armed rebellion in Nimi County" to the "counterrevolutionary killing incident"). Ms., in Goldstein's possession.

Zhonggong nimu xian weiyuanhui (Nyemo County Party Committee of the CCP). 1987. " 'Nimu xian wuzhuang panluan' gaiding wei fangeming 'sharen shijian' qingshi" (About the request to change the previously named "armed rebellion in Nyemo County" to the "counterrevolutionary killing incident). Ms., 23 March, in Goldstein's possession.

Zhonggong xizang zizhiqu dangshi ziliao zhengji weiyuanhui bian (Committee for Collecting Materials on the Party History of the Chinese Communist Party of the Tibet Autonomous Region), ed. 1990. *Zhonggong xizang dangshi dashiji (1949–1966)* (Chronicle of major events of the Chinese Communist Party in Tibet, [1949–66]). Lhasa: Xizang renmin chubanshe (Tibet People's Publishing House).

———, ed. 1995. *Zhonggong xizang dangshi dashiji (1949–1994).* (Chinese Communist Party's chronicle of major events in Tibet [1949–1994]). Beijing: Xizang renmin chubanshe (Tibet People's Publishing House).

"Zhongyang shouzhang jiejian xizang zizhiqu geming weiyuanhui, xizang junqu huibao quan ti renyuan de zhongyao zhishi." 1968. (Important instructions from the leaders of the Central Committee when they interviewed all the personnel of the group reporting from the TAR Revolutionary Committee and the Tibet Military Region). Ms., no author, 8 September, in Goldstein's possession.

"Zhongyang, zhongyang wenge shouzhang jiejian xizang ban bufen xueyuan shi de zhongyao zhishi (jilu gao)." 1968. (Leaders of the Central Committee and the Central Cultural Revolution Group meet students from Tibet [recorded draft]). Ms., no author, 26 August, in Goldstein's possession.

Zhu nimu mao zedong sixiang xuanchuan dui bianyin, xizang zizhiqu xizang junqu (Composed and published by the propaganda group called Mao Zedong's Thoughts Living in Nyemo). 1971. "Gongzuo jianbao, #18" (Brief report on work [for examining the Nimu County 27 November counterrevolutionary affair], #18). Ms., no author, 30 November, in Goldstein's possession.

Index

Academy of Aviation, Beijing, 28, 195
Allied Combat Team, PLA, 35, 36
Ani Gongmey Gyemo, 82–85, 91–93, 97–109, 163, 166; Gesar and, 82–85, 91, 97–106, 166–67; god of Gyenlo, 88–89, 165–66; after Gyenlo's defeat at Nyemo, 137; and November 1968 attacks, 88–89, 92, 97, 164–65, 169; nun's identity blurred with, 168; "Nyemo belongs to the gods," 105, 123, 169, 171; Tsesum killing, 119; weapons blessed by, 123
aristocracy, Tibetan, 6, 19, 60–61, 73, 163, 183
armbands, 209n58; Gyenlo, 80, 88, 92, 163, 165, 175, 177
armies. See Gyenlo's Army of the Gods; military; People's Liberation Army (PLA); weapons

Bagor: PLA departure, 137–39; PLA vs. Gyenlo/nun, 121–36, 138, 144, 146
Barnett, Robert, 5, 6
Beijing: Central Great Cultural Revolution Group, 22, 52, 185, 203n20; Central Military Committee, 35–40; Ngabö, 20, 203n29; Red Guards from, 20–23, 28, 35, 185, 192–95; school chaos, 13; "study class" for top leaders of Gyenlo and Nyamdre (1968), 44, 45, 51–52; Zhang Guohua visit, 44, 203n30

Bembar County, disturbances, 173, 210n29
"big-character posters," 13, 202n10; by Gyenlo, 32, 33, 86; by Red Guards in Beijing, 14; vs. Regional Party Committee, 17–21, 190–92; violent, 33
"big debates," 33
Biru, 103, 104, 173, 210n29
Biru County, counterrevolutionary riot in, 173, 210n29
Blazing Prairie Combat Regiment, Beijing, 20–23, 28, 192–95
"blue pigs," cadres as, 67–68, 89, 133, 207n26
broadcast stations, 40, 49–50
Buddhism: and deities possessing mediums, 81, 82–83; Gyenlo position on, 84–85; nun linked to restoration of, 167, 168, 169; prohibited, 60–61, 66, 68, 74, 81, 161, 174, 175, 177; revolutionaries founded to defend, 94, 172–74. See also monasticism; warrior-hero mediums

Case Western Reserve University, Center for Research on Tibet, 8, 9
Central Great Cultural Revolution Group, Beijing, 22, 52, 185, 203n20
Central Military Committee, Beijing, 35–40
Chamba Tenzin, 155, 208n46; captured and executed, 148, 150fig, 154; nun and, 78, 82–83, 88, 104

Chen Boda, 44–45
Chen Dongfeng, 193
Chen Mingyi, 26, 43, 44–45
Chen Yin, 156
Cheng Dongfeng, 198
China: Cultural Revolution in, 1, 11, 13–
    14, 27, 182, 184, 207n9; *People's
    Daily*, 14; State Council, 21–22, 37–
    38, 40; strategies for incorporating
    Tibet into, 15–19, 25, 182–85, 216n2.
    See also Beijing; Chinese Communist
    Party (CCP); Red Guards
Chinese Communist Party (CCP), 202n7;
    Eleventh Plenum of the Eighth Central
    Committee, 13, 19; gradualist policy
    in Tibet, 15–19, 25, 182–85, 216n2;
    May 16th Notice, 11–12, 17, 196;
    Nyemo incident interpretations, 4,
    5; purges, 11; Tibetan interfactional
    conflicts affecting, 163; Tibetans
    favoring Mao over, 83. *See also* Mao
    Zedong; Regional Party Committee,
    TAR; Zhou Enlai
Chinese documents, source material, 8,
    9–10
chuba, 88, 209n7
Chushigandru (Khamba)-led uprising.
    See 1959 uprising
cognitive dissonance, 214n9
collectivization. *See* communes
communes, 6, 8, 67, 161; farming, 15,
    60, 64, 159–60, 183–84; gradualist
    policy, 15–16, 183–84; "Gyenlo
    communes," 94, 210n22; Gyenlo
    members' interests, 169; Gyenlo vs.
    PLA and, 133, 134; Mao and, 15–
    16, 184, 216nn3,4; Tsatsey, 175
Communist Party. *See* Chinese Commu-
    nist Party (CCP)
Cultural Revolution, 1, 11–26, 57, 182,
    184, 202n3; in China, 1, 11, 13–14,
    27, 182, 184, 207n9; Chinese docu-
    ments, 9–10; "Decision concerning
    the Great Proletarian Cultural Revo-
    lution," 13; vs. "four olds," 14–16,
    25, 59, 66, 75–76; Gyenlo attempt-
    ing takeover, 27–31, 180–81; Janu-
    ary Storm, 27; and Liu Shaoqi, 207n9;
    Nyemo incident in context of, 4,
    10, 162–63, 185; Phala, 175; PLA
    suspending practice of, 35–36, 184–
    85; radical phase, 22; revolutionary
    factions as pawns of, 171; spearhead
    of, 13–14; TAR Regional Party Com-
    mittee criticized for handling of, 20–
    25, 27–30, 31–32, 35, 185, 189–94;
    Tibetan era of collectivization and

(1966 on), 8. *See also* Democratic
    Reforms; revolutionary mass
    organizations

Dalai Lama (Tenzin Gyatso), 87; flight,
    69, 183, 184; in gradualist policy,
    183; Mao said to be replacing, 78,
    103; mediums consulted by, 77;
    nun on gods replacing, 103, 105;
    in nun's visions, 6, 76, 211n45;
    and Nyemo incident, 3–4, 6
Danden Dorje, 127
Defenders of the Thoughts of Mao
    Zedong, 21, 25, 27, 30–32, 42
Democratic Reforms, 15, 65–66, 163,
    171; historic era, 8; monks and
    nuns, 60–61, 68, 73; officials, 128
Dengchen County, 172
Deng Xiaoping, 140, 159, 161
Department of Armed Forces, Nyemo
    County, 129; Gyenlo vs., 92, 95–96,
    122, 131–33, 139–40, 214n16;
    wuzhuang bu, 92, 210n17
Diemberger, Hildegard, 5–6, 81
Ding Yongtai, 46, 48
Dong Xue'an, 95, 142
Drepung monks, 9, 209n60

80th School of Beijing, Red Guards, 193

Fang Kang, 198
farming: collective, 15, 60, 64, 159–60,
    183–84; by former monks, 74–75;
    private, 15, 60, 61, 184, 216n4.
    See also grain policies
Financial Compound, PLA attacking
    Gyenlo, 45–47, 50–51, 55
flags: army, 43–44, 213n13; Tibetan,
    125, 213n13
food shortages, 61–64, 66, 159–60
Forestry Company massacre, 17–18, 192,
    216n1
"four olds": Cultural Revolution vs.,
    14–16, 25, 59, 66, 75–76; openly
    practiced, 168. *See also* religion
"free airing of views," 33

Ganden, 126, 146
Gao Zemin, 141–42
Gesar: Ani Gongmey Gyemo and, 82–
    85, 91, 97–106, 166–67; nun and,
    5, 82–85, 91, 97–106, 166–67, 169;
    warrior-hero mediums and, 98–99,
    100, 105, 166–67, 169
Goldstein, Melvyn, 8, 9, 174, 202n3, 211n3
    gradualist policy, 15–19, 25, 182–85,
    216n2

grain policies, 216n4; food shortages
from, 61–64, 66; Gyenlo members
and, 62–64, 66–67, 86–89, 169;
Nyemo County, 61–68, 84–91, 159–
65, 170–71; "patriotic government
grain," 61, 91; "sales grain," 61,
91, 162
Guo Xilan, 25, 189–90
Gyenlo agenda, 139, 161, 165, 175–81;
defined, 171
"Gyenlo communes," 94, 210n22
Gyenlo faction, 4–8, 15, 86–141, 201n11;
allegiances among members, 26;
Allied Combat Team in PLA, 35,
36; armbands, 80, 88, 92, 163, 165,
175, 177; cadres targeted, 67–68,
89, 107–8, 133; Cultural Revolution
takeover attempted, 27–31, 180–81;
after defeat by PLA, 137–41, 154–
61; Dictatorship Committee, 31;
execution of leaders, 160; founding,
20, 23–25; and grain policies, 62–
64, 66–67, 169; Gyenlo agenda, 139,
161, 165, 171, 175–81; interfactional conflict, 7, 10, 21, 33–35, 40,
42–51, 57–86, 89–91, 96–97, 122,
155, 162–64, 175–81, 185; name,
204n41; negotiations to end interfactional violence, 43–44, 51–52,
57, 185; number of members, 40,
58, 86; nun with, 7, 65, 78–96, 100–
109, 113, 119–27, 131, 135–37,
144–45, 158–59, 163–69, 180–81;
Nyemo County, 45, 58–97, 100,
121–44, 164–65, 180; oral histories,
8; as "organized crime group," 159;
Phala, 177–78, 180; PLA and, 35–
56, 93–96, 102, 121–61, 210n29;
recognition as revolutionary organization, 37, 38, 163; Red Rebels
part of, 19; Regional Party Committee attacked by, 20–25, 27–30, 31–
32, 35, 185; religion/nun used by, 7,
79–80, 84–89, 91–96, 110, 119–21,
158, 159, 164–69, 171, 177, 181;
Revolutionary Rebels of Red News,
27–29, 195–99; Specially Attack,
40–41, 205n66; "struggle sessions"
forced by, 86, 89–90, 129; "study
class" for cadres (1971), 9–10, 158–
59; Tao Changsong, 44, 156, 181,
210n22; *Tibet Daily Newspaper*
takeover, 27–30, 38–40, 195–99;
Tibet Military Region Headquarters
invaded by, 35–38, 40; Tibet Post
and Telecommunications School
headquarters, 17; Tsatsey, 175–76,
178–80; violence by, 31–32, 89–90,
99, 107–35, 140–41, 172–74, 176,
178; weapons, 43, 123–24, 130–
37, 140–41, 146, 206n86, 213n28.
See also Rangjung; Zhang Yongfu
Gyenlo General Headquarters: Lhasa, 41,
45, 55, 96, 172, 180–81, 204n1,
210n27, 216n13; Nyemo County,
78; Tsatsey, 175–76
Gyenlo Headquarters of Farmers and
Herdsmen, 93–95
Gyenlo's Army of the Gods, 110; after
defeat by PLA, 137–41; four different types of Tibetans in, 168–
70; naming, 94–95, 165; nun and
warrior-hero mediums as part of,
167; PLA attacked by, 121–42;
Rangjung as field commander, 65,
94–95, 100–101, 106, 119–31, 137,
148, 167; weapons, 123–24, 130–
37, 140–41, 146, 213n28; Zhang
Yongfu arrested for organizing, 158

Havnevik, Hanna, 3
Headquarters of Defending Mao
Zedong's Thoughts, 21, 25, 27,
30–32, 42
historical eras, 8
Huang Guojie, 96, 106, 143

incense, prohibition on, 81
insecticides, as weapons, 49–50
interviews, Tibet, 8–9

January Storm, Shanghai, 27
Jiang Qing, 14, 44–45, 140; and Chinese
Red Guards in Tibet, 22, 185, 203n20;
on self-defense and counterattack,
103, 105
Jin Sha, 12, 27, 28, 195
Jokhang Temple, 209n61; PLA attacking
Gyenlo, 45, 48–51, 55, 96, 121–22,
210n29

Kang Sheng, 44–45
killings. *See* violence

Lagyab Lhojang, 174
land allocations, 6, 16, 60–61, 67, 73, 74
Leading Team of the Great Proletarian
Cultural Revolution, Lhasa, 12
Lhasa: Gyenlo General Headquarters,
41, 45, 55, 96, 172, 180–81, 204n1,
210n27, 216n13; interfactional conflict, 10, 42–51, 57–58, 185; Leading
Team of the Great Proletarian Cultural Revolution, 12; Municipal

Lhasa (continued)
    Party Committee, 62; Revolutionary
    Rebels of Red News, 27–29, 195–
    99; schools, 15, 16–17, 21, 156;
    "study class" for Gyenlo cadres
    (1971), 9–10, 158–59; Temporary
    Lhasa City Committee, 27
Lhasa Middle School, 15, 21, 156
Lhawang Yeshe, 109–10
Li Jianhua, 106, 142–43
Li Yongchang, 78
Liao Buyun, 44–45
Lin Biao, 14, 52, 56, 190
Liu Shaoming, 23, 31–32, 44
Liu Shaoming's wife, 31–32
Liu Shaoqi, 13, 140, 202n7, 207n9
Lu Yishan, 44–45

Ma Guishu, 192
maimings, 167, 212n24; Bembar County,
    173; after Gyenlo's defeat in Nyemo,
    140–41; Nyemo incident (June 1969),
    1–3, 2fig, 111–21, 115fig, 126, 128–
    29; rationale behind, 116
Mao Zedong, 25, 28, 91, 171, 202n1;
    "April" directive, 41, 54; and com-
    munes, 15–16, 184, 216nn3,4;
    Cultural Revolution started by, 11–
    17, 196; Dalai Lama said to be
    replaced by, 78, 103; Defenders of
    the Thoughts of, 21, 25, 27, 30–32,
    42; gradualist policy in Tibet, 15–
    16, 182–84, 216n2; Gyenlo follow-
    ing, 94, 162–63, 175, 176, 180; vs.
    Liu Shaoqi, 207n9; nun and, 78,
    80–83, 91, 102–5, 122, 154, 163,
    165; and Red Guards from China
    in Tibet, 16, 185; religion's power
    compared with, 87, 103, 105; revo-
    lutionary groups' interfactional
    disputes about adherence to, 7, 33,
    67; TAR Regional Party Committee
    and directives of, 16–30, 189–90;
    temporary "retirement," 202n7;
    Tiananmen Square meetings, 13–
    14; Tibet Daily and, 27, 29–30,
    196–99; Tibet Military Region
    Headquarters mistakes admitted
    to, 52–57; work team to publicize
    thoughts of, 158
Mao Zedong's wife. See Jiang Qing
marriage, former monks and nuns, 75
martial law, PLA in Tibet, 36, 55
Martyr's Park, 4
May 16th Notice, 11–12, 17, 196
mediums, 76–78, 166; fraudulent, 108,
    112, 211n3; gods possessing, 81,

82–83. See also Trinley Chödrön
    (nun)—possession; warrior-hero
    mediums
Metropolitan Red Guards, Beijing, 20–
    22, 35
military: Central Military Committee
    in Beijing, 35–40; military control
    commissions in China, 1; military
    control offices in TAR, 40, 43. See
    also Military Squadron, Nyemo
    County; People's Liberation Army
    (PLA); Tibet Military Region Head-
    quarters; weapons
Military Squadron, Nyemo County, 120,
    121; Gyenlo vs., 92, 95–96, 122,
    131–35, 213n24; weapons denied
    to, 124; zhongdui, 92, 210n17
monasticism: discontinued (after 1959),
    60–61, 68–73, 174, 183; Drepung
    monks, 9, 209n60; Panchen Lama,
    15–16, 174, 207n6; Red Lamas,
    209n60; "struggle sessions" for
    monks and nuns, 68, 70–72; "study
    classes" for monks and nuns (after
    1959), 68–70, 73, 74, 75. See also
    Dalai Lama (Tenzin Gyatso); Trinley
    Chödrön (nun)
Mutual Aid Teams, 206n5

nationalism, Tibet, 170; and Nyemo
    incident, 4–6, 125, 162
Nationalities Institute, Xianyang, 16, 21,
    25, 64
Nechung, official state medium, 77
Ngabö, 15–16, 19–20, 203n29
Ngudrub, 128–30
1959 uprising, 4–6, 164; Army for
    Defending Buddhism, 94; gradualist
    policy until, 15, 182, 183; historical
    period, 8; monasticism discontinued
    after, 60–61, 68–73, 174, 183; new
    socialist political system after, 15,
    60, 183; Phala after, 174
nomadism, Phala, 174–75
nuns. See monasticism; Trinley Chödrön
    (nun)
Nyamdre faction, 4, 10, 201n11; alle-
    giances among members, 26; core,
    25; formed, 21, 33; and Gyenlo-PLA
    conflict, 45–51, 122–23, 127–30;
    independence from Chinese sought
    by some, 170; interfactional conflict,
    7, 10, 21, 33–35, 40, 42–51, 57–86,
    89–92, 96–97, 122, 155, 162–64,
    175–81, 185; Liu Shaoming, 23, 31–
    32, 44; members feeling compelled
    to join Gyenlo for their own safety,

169–70; negotiations to end interfactional violence, 43–44, 51–52,
57, 185; number of members, 40;
nun and followers' violence toward,
108–21; Nyemo County, 58–86,
89–92, 96–97, 109, 160–61, 166;
officials in Nyemo, 59–60, 62, 64,
66–67, 109, 166; oral histories, 8;
Phala, 177, 178, 179; Tsatsey, 175–
76, 178–79; weapons, 43, 206n86
Nyemo Ani. *See* Trinley Chödrön (nun)
Nyemo County, 1; "belonging to the
gods" (Ani Gongmey Gyemo), 105,
123, 169, 171; and collectivation,
60, 64, 159–60; families persecuted
by both factions, 59, 66; and food
shortages, 61–64, 66, 159–60; grain
policies, 61–68, 84–91, 159–65,
170–71; Gyenlo faction, 45, 58–97,
100, 121–44, 164–65, 180; Gyenlo
vs. PLA, 121–44; interfactional conflict, 58–86, 89–91, 96–97, 155,
162–64; Nyamdre faction, 58–86,
89–92, 96–97, 109, 160–61, 166;
oral history interviews, 8–9; PLA, 1,
2, 5, 64, 67, 121–44, 160–61, 170.
See also Department of Armed
Forces; Military Squadron; Nyemo
incident
Nyemo incident (June 1969), 1–4, 80,
106–36, 158–61, 170–73; casualties, 1, 4, 153–54, 156; counterrevolutionary rebellion or counterrevolutionary incident, 141–43, 159;
Cultural Revolution context, 4, 10,
162–63, 185; grain policies and, 62–
63, 162, 164; Gyenlo vs. PLA, 42,
126–36, 155, 157–58; interpretations, 3–7, 10, 141–42, 155, 157–
58, 170, 201–2nn12,15; interviewees' names changed, 9; maimings,
1–3, 2*fig*, 111–21, 115*fig*, 126, 128–
29; Martyr's Park commemorating,
4; nationalism and, 4–6, 125, 162;
nun and, 1–3, 2*fig*, 106–21, 115*fig*,
155; Phala-Tsatsey incident com-
pared, 179–80; reinvestigations of,
158–59; Second Tibetan Revolt, 5,
6; "struggle sessions" after, 159*fig*;
TAR government report on (1974),
62; Tibet Justice Center report, 3;
warrior-hero mediums, 107–29, 155,
160–61, 180

old society (up to 1959), 8, 60. *See also*
"four olds"
One Thousand Serf Fighters, 21, 25

oral histories, Tibet, 8–9
organizations. *See* revolutionary mass
organizations

Panchen Lama, 15–16, 174, 207n6
"peaceful liberation," 183
People's Assembly of the TAR, 12
People's Daily, China, 14
People's Hospital, Gyenlo-held, 42
People's Liberation Army (PLA):
admitting mistakes fighting Gyenlo,
52–57; Allied Combat Team, 35, 36;
"cherish the masses and support the
army," 122; commanders in Tibet,
12; Cultural Revolution suspended
in, 35–36, 184–85; Eighteenth Army
Corps, 12; Gyenlo faction and, 35–
56, 93–96, 102, 121–61, 210n29;
after Gyenlo's defeat, 137–41; and
interfactional conflict, 33–35, 43–
44, 45–51, 175, 185; nun's capture
and execution, 6, 137, 144–49, 154,
170; nun's followers arrested, 149–
51; Nyamdre and Gyenlo-PLA conflict, 45–51, 122–23, 127–28; Nyemo
County, 1, 2, 5, 64, 67, 121–44,
160–61, 170; Potala Palace, 33–
35; Public Security Bureau, 30, 40,
93, 110, 130, 152, 213n24; after
Seventeen-Point Agreement (1951),
183; Shigatse Prefecture, 180;
Tsatsey, 176, 178–79; weapons,
43, 47, 124, 144–45, 147–48, 158,
206n86, 213n28; "yellow dogs,"
133, 207n26. *See also* Department
of Armed Forces, Nyemo County;
Military Squadron, Nyemo County;
Tibet Military Region Headquarters;
Zhang Guohua
Phala, 215nn6,7; Phala-Tsatsey incident,
174–81
Phündra, 15–16
Phusum, 80, 98; Angang villagers in, 88–
89, 92; and Army for Defending
Buddhism, 94; Chamba Tenzin, 78;
nun (Trinley Chödrön), 68, 79, 83–
87, 92–102, 109–13, 119–23, 127,
131, 135–36, 144–49; PLA cap-
turing nun and followers, 144–49;
PLA vs. Gyenlo/nun, 122–23, 130–
61; Trinley from, 92–93, 96, 101–
2; violence, 109–11, 119–21, 130;
warrior-hero mediums staying with
nun in, 99
PLA. *See* People's Liberation Army (PLA)
political killings, 109–21
possession. *See* mediums

posters. *See* "big-character posters"
Potala, Nyamdre-held, 42
Potala Palace, PLA, 33–35
Procuratorial Bureau, military control, 40
Propaganda Department, Regional Party Committee, 12, 18–19
Public Security Bureau, 110, 152; Gyenlo vs., 30, 40, 93, 130, 213n24

Qinghai Daily, 40

Rangjung, 65, 89, 129, 168; fleeing and vanished, 145–46, 148–49, 161; grain collectors attacked by, 86–89; Gyenlo's Army of the Gods field commander, 65, 94–95, 100–101, 106, 119–31, 137, 148, 167; and nun and warrior-hero mediums, 65, 87–88, 93–96, 100–104, 108–9, 119, 120, 123, 125, 136–37, 144–45, 164–69; vs. PLA, 93, 122–31, 134, 136, 137; and Trinley, 93, 208n54; and Tsesum, 95, 119–20; violent reputation, 65–66; wife, 148
Red Documents, 100
Red Flag, Beijing, 28, 195
Red Flag journal, 189–94
Red Guards, 11–16, 32; from Beijing, 20–23, 28, 35, 185, 192–95; conflict over Chinese Red guards in Tibet, 20, 21–22, 185, 192–93, 203n20; and Gyenlo-Military Region Headquarters meeting, 43–44; Red Guard Combat Team, 19; vs. Regional Party Committee, 20–25, 192–93, 194; religious paraphernalia collected and destroyed by, 66; *Tibet Daily Newspaper* coverage of, 27, 193; and Tibet's gradualist policy, 18; warrior-hero mediums as Buddhist Red Guards, 100
Red Lamas, 209n60
Red Rebels, 19–20
Regional Party Committee, TAR, 12–32, 196; "big-character posters" vs., 17–21, 190–92; Forestry Company massacre, 17–18, 192, 216n1; gradualist policy, 15–19, 184–85; mass organizations criticizing, 16–32, 35, 185, 189–94; mass organizations supporting, 25, 30–32; Propaganda Department, 12, 18–19; Revolutionary Committee government replacing, 43, 44–45; split between Zhang Guohua and Zhou Renshan, 26. *See also* Zhang Guohua

religion: Gyenlo using, 7, 84–89, 92–96, 100, 119, 158, 164–69, 171, 177; power of, 87, 96, 100; private, 81, 175; "superstition," 210n16. *See also* Ani Gongmey Gyemo; Buddhism; mediums
Ren Rong, 26, 43, 44–45, 155, 158
revolutionary committees: in China, 1; in Tibet, 43–45, 52, 55, 57, 158
revolutionary mass organizations, 4, 7, 19–23, 47, 163, 201n11; Gyenlo faction recognized as, 37, 38, 163; Regional Party Committee criticized by, 20–25, 27–30, 31–32, 35, 185, 189–94; Regional Party Committee supported by, 25, 30–32. *See also* Gyenlo faction; Nyamdre faction; Red Guards
Revolutionary Rebels of Red News, Lhasa, 27–29, 195–99
revolutionary workers, Cultural Revolution, 11, 13, 17–18

schools: Beijing chaos, 13; Lhasa, 15, 16–17, 21, 156
Second Tibetan Revolt, 5, 6
Serf Fighters, Nationalities Institute, 21, 25
Seventeen-Point Agreement (1951), 182, 183
Shakya, Tsering, 5, 6–7, 170
Shigatse Prefecture, rioting, 173, 174, 180
Shilok Tsering, 109–10, 111–12
sixteen-points document, 192
Smith, Warren, 4–5, 6, 170
socialist economic system, 61–62
socialist political system, new, 15, 60, 183
sources: Chinese documents, 8, 9–10; interviews in Tibet, 8–9
State Council, China, 21–22, 37–38, 40
"struggle sessions," 163, 203n27; airplane style, 203n27; Gyenlo forcing, 86, 89–90, 129; against Gyenlo leaders, 160; for monks and nuns, 68, 70–72; after Nyemo incident, 159*fig*; Tsatsey, 179
"study classes," 208n32; for arrested followers of nun, 148–54; for Gyenlo and Nyamdre leaders (Beijing 1968), 44, 45, 51–52; for Gyenlo cadres (1971), 9–10, 158–59; for monks and nuns (after 1959), 68–70, 73, 74, 75; Tsatsey, 179
Surkhang Sawangchemmo, 211n3

Survey of China Mainland Press Supplement, 9

Tao Changsong, 44, 156, 181, 210n22
TAR (Tibet Autonomous Region), 1.
    See also Tibet
Tashi Rabden, 126, 127, 133–34
taxes: Nyemo County, 61–68, 84–91,
    159–60, 162. *See also* grain policies
taxpayer households, 73, 74, 207n27
Temporary Lhasa City Committee, 27
Tenzin, 176–77
Tenzin Gyatso. *See* Dalai Lama
"three no's," 173
"three-way alliance," 43–44, 205n71
Tiananmen Square, massive meetings,
    13–14
Tibet: China's strategies for incorporat-
    ing, 15–19, 182–83; Tibet Autono-
    mous Region (TAR), 1; war readi-
    ness (against India), 44. *See also*
    Cultural Revolution; Lhasa; Nyemo
    County
Tibet Academy of Social Sciences, 8
Tibetan Nation (Smith), 4
Tibetan Teacher's College, 15
Tibet Autonomous Region (TAR), 1.
    See also Tibet
Tibet Daily Newspaper, 12, 13; Chen
    Dongfeng, 193; editor Jin Sha, 12,
    27, 28, 195; Gyenlo takeover, 27–
    30, 38–40, 195–99; PLA trying
    peacefully to regain control of, 37–
    40
Tibet Justice Center, 3
Tibet Military Region Headquarters, 12;
    captured nun, 147–48; and Gyenlo
    faction, 35–44, 52–57, 140. *See also*
    People's Liberation Army (PLA)
Tibet Oral History Collection and
    Archive, common-folk subcollection,
    8–9
Tibet People's Broadcasting Station,
    military control, 40
Tibet Post and Telecommunications
    School, 16–17
traditional society. *See* old society
Trinley, 79, 92–93, 96, 101–2, 208n54
Trinley Chödrön (nun), 1, 68–69, 75–
    96, 211n45; captured and executed
    by PLA, 6, 137, 144–49, 154, 170;
    Chamba Tenzin and, 78, 82–83,
    88, 104; Dalai Lama visions, 6, 76,
    211n45; with Gyenlo, 7, 65, 78–96,
    100–109, 113, 119–27, 131, 135–
    37, 144–45, 158–59, 163–69, 180–
    81; Gyenlo plan to arrest, 95, 167–

68; after Gyenlo's defeat at Nyemo,
    137–41; manifesto, 101–6, 187–88;
    and Mao, 78, 80–83, 91, 102–5,
    122, 154, 163, 165; mental insta-
    bility, 75–76, 79, 81–82, 208n43;
    as Nyemo Ani, 5, 180, 214–15n37;
    Nyemo incident, 1–3, 2*fig*, 106–21,
    115*fig*, 155, 160–61; in Tibet Justice
    Center report, 3; violence ordered
    by, 1–3, 2*fig*, 106–21, 115*fig*, 123–
    25, 140–41, 212n24; warrior-hero
    mediums with, 99, 105, 107–21,
    125, 145
Trinley Chödrön (nun)—possession, 1,
    76–78, 80–85, 97–111, 168; and
    Gesar, 5, 82–85, 91, 97–106, 166–
    67, 169; Gyenlo using, 7, 84–85, 88,
    91–93, 110, 119, 166–67; weapons
    blessed by, 123. *See also* Ani
    Gongmey Gyemo
Trinley Drolkar, 114–15
"The Truth about the Struggle to Seize
    the Power of the Tibet Daily
    Newspaper Office," 28
Tsatsey, 174–81, 215n7
Tsering Chösang, 146
Tsesum, 95, 118–20
Two Nine Revolts, 4. *See also* 1959
    uprising; Nyemo incident (June
    1969)

violence: arrests and executions of nun
    and followers, 145, 148, 150*fig*,
    151, 154, 155*fig*, 156*fig*; casualty
    figures from 1959 uprising, 4;
    casualty figures from Nyemo inci-
    dent (June 1969), 1, 4, 153–54, 157;
    execution of Gyenlo leaders, 160;
    Forestry Company massacre, 17–18,
    192, 216n1; by Gyenlo faction, 31–
    32, 89–90, 99, 107–35, 140–41,
    172–74, 176, 178; Gyenlo-PLA con-
    flicts, 40, 41–42, 45–56, 125–35,
    140–41, 145; interfactional, 33–35,
    42–51, 57–58, 89–90, 176, 178,
    185; 1968 agreement by factions to
    end, 51–52, 57; nun ordering, 1–3,
    2*fig*, 106–21, 115*fig*, 123–25, 140–
    41, 212n24; as payments for those
    who died, 157; political killings,
    109–21; Rangjung known for, 65–
    66; "struggle sessions," 203n27;
    suicide of lama, 72; "three-way
    alliances" and, 205n71; by warrior-
    hero mediums, 99, 108–21, 124–29,
    167; "white terror," 13, 31, 202n9.
    See also maimings; weapons

Wang Chenghan, 44–45
Wang Lixiong, 6, 170
Wang Qimei, 12, 140, 190, 192
Wangchuk Rabden, 127
warrior-hero mediums: arrested servant
    of, 152; captured and executed, 148,
    154; Gesar and, 98–99, 100, 105,
    166–67, 169; after Gyenlo's defeat
    at Nyemo, 137; Nyemo incident,
    107–29, 155, 160–61, 180; PLA vs.,
    124–29, 133–35, 145; violence by,
    99, 108–21, 124–29, 167
weapons: Gyenlo's Army of the Gods,
    123–24, 130–37, 140–41, 146,
    213n28; insecticides as, 49–50;
    interfactional conflict, 43, 49–50,
    185, 206n86; nun as, 167–68; nun's,
    147; PLA, 43, 47, 124, 144–45,
    147–48, 158, 206n86, 213n28
"white terror," 13, 31, 202n9
women in Tibetan politics, 3, 5. See also
    Trinley Chödrön (nun)
workers. See revolutionary workers
work teams, 208n32; for chaos in Beijing
    schools, 13; on grain policies linked
    with disturbances, 62; Mao disap-
    proving of, 13; for monks' "study
    classes," 69–70; to publicize thoughts
    of Mao and reinvestigate Nyemo
    incident, 158; Zhang Guohua's
    stability policy, 16
Wu Lide, 87, 106
wuzhuang bu, 92, 210n17

xiang, defined, 201n3
Xianyang Nationalities Institute, 16, 21,
    25, 64
Xiao Dorje, 140
Xiao Yong, 79, 96, 139–40, 142
Xinhua News Agency Office, 27
Xu De'an, 142–43

"yellow dogs," 133, 207n26
Yin Fatang, 40–41, 44–45, 140
Yu Zhiquan, 43–44
Yue Zongming, 18–19

Zeng Yongya, 44–45, 155, 156, 158
Zhang Diantong, 111, 124, 214n16
Zhang Guangzhe, 198
Zhang Guohua, 12–26, 185, 190;
    Beijing, 44, 203n30; director of TAR
    Military Control Commission, 43;
    "indigenous emperor," 23; Ngabö
    removed to Beijing, 20, 203n29;
    opponents of, 20–24, 38, 50; Spe-
    cially Attack and, 205n66; stability
    policy, 12, 15–16, 18–19, 25, 26,
    184; supporters of, 26, 27, 31
Zhang Yongfu, 65, 79, 162; arrested,
    158; and grain policies, 62, 66–
    67, 86–89; and Gyenlo's Army of
    the Gods, 95, 106, 110, 119; after
    Gyenlo's defeat at Nyemo, 139;
    and PLA, 121, 122, 123, 142, 155,
    158; reason for victory, 92–93; and
    religion/nun in Gyenlo, 84, 95, 96,
    100, 106, 141, 165; sentenced and
    rehabilitated politically, 159; and
    Tsesum, 95, 120; and violence
    initiated by nun, 108, 110, 167
Zhang Zaiwang, 12, 193
Zhao Yongfu, 40
zhongdui, 92, 210n17
Zhou Enlai: and Chinese Red Guards
    in Tibet, 20, 185, 203n20; and
    gradualist policy, 15–16, 184; and
    new revolutionary committee, 44–
    45; Ngabö removed to Beijing, 20,
    203n29; and PLA vs. Gyenlo, 52;
    on Zhang Yongfu, 203n30
Zhou Longquan, 83, 142
Zhou Renshan, 26, 140, 209n60

              Text: 10/13 Sabon
           Display: Sabon
           Indexer: Barbara Roos
      Cartographer: Bill Nelson
        Compositor: Integrated Composition Systems
 Printer and binder: Sheridan Books, Inc.